CHINA'S MILITARY AND INDIA

中国军事与印度

CHINA'S MILITARY AND INDIA

中国军事与印度

Srikanth Kondapalli (Editor)

PENTAGON PRESS

***China's Military and India* / Srikanth Kondapalli** (Editor)

ISBN 978-81-8274-689-3

First Published in 2012

Published by
PENTAGON PRESS
206, Peacock Lane, Shahpur Jat,
New Delhi-110049
Phones: 011-64706243, 26491568
Telefax: 011-26490600
email: rajan@pentagonpress.in
website: www.pentagonpress.in

Printed at Aegean Offset Printers, Greater Noida

Dedicated to

Giri Deshingkar

CONTENTS

ACKNOWLEDGEMENTS

This collection of articles were presented at a workshop at India International Centre on August 30, 2010 , organized by the Institute of Chinese Studies, Delhi. The editor and the contributors to this volume would like to thank Honorary Director Sreemati Chakraborti, colleagues and staff for all the help and the Ministry of External Affairs for the grant. However, none of the institutions or individuals cited in the volume is responsible for the errors or opinions expressed here.

CONTRIBUTORS

Gurmeet Kanwal is Brigadier (Retired) in the Indian Army and Director of Centre for Land Warfare Studies, New Delhi.

Srikanth Kondapalli, Ph.D. is Professor in Chinese Studies and Chairman at Centre for East Asian Studies, School of International Studies, Jawaharlal Nehru University, New Delhi

Navneet Kumar is Brigadier in the Indian Army and currently on a study leave at Institute of Chinese Studies, Delhi as a Visiting Fellow

M.V. Rappai, retired from the Government of India and currently Visiting Fellow at Institute of Chinese Studies, Delhi

Vijay Sakhuja, Ph.D. is Commander (Retired), Indian Navy and currently Director, (Research) at Indian Council for World Affairs, New Delhi

Vishal Nigam is Wing Commander, Indian Air Force and currently on a study leave at Centre for Air Power Studies, New Delhi

Ajey Lele, Ph.D. is Wing Commander, Indian Air Force and currently on study leave as Research Fellow at Institute of Defence Studies & Analyses, New Delhi

ABBREVIATIONS

APC	Armoured Personnel Carrier
ASBMs	Anti-Ship Ballistic Missiles
C4ISR	Command, Control, Communications, Computers, Intelligence, Surveillance & Reconnaissance
CAR	Central Asian Republic
CASC	China Aerospace Corporation
CNO	Computer Network Operations
CNSA	China National Space Administration
DF	Dong Feng [East Wind] missile
ECM	Electronic Counter Measures
ESM	Electronic Support Measures
EW	Electronic Warfare
FMCT	Fissile Material Cut-off Treaty
GAD	General Armaments Department
GLD	General Logistics Department
GPD	General Political Department
GSD	General Staff Department
ICBM	Inter-Continental Ballistic Missile
IMO	International Maritime Organisation
IRBM	Intermediate Range Ballistic Missile
IW	Information Warfare
LAC	Line of Actual Control
MBT	Main Battle Tank

MIRV	multiple independently targetable re-entry vehicles
MTCR	Missile Technology Control Regime
OVL	Oil and Natural Gas Commission Videsh Limited
PAP	People's Armed Police
SAM	Surface to Air Missile
SCO	Shanghai Cooperation Organisation
SIGINT	Signals Intelligence
SLBM	Submarine Launched Ballistic Missile
SRBM	Short Range Ballistic Missile
START	Strategic Arms Reduction Talks
UAV	Unmanned Aerial Vehicle
WTO	World Trade Organisation

LIST OF TABLES/GRAPHS/MAPS

INTRODUCTION

Several significant developments—internal and external—are affecting China's military (cumulatively, the People's Liberation Army, PLA) today, which is the third largest such forces in the world after the United States and Russia. The transition in the PLA are clearly visible: on January 11, 2007, China conducted an anti-satellite test with a ground-based missile destroying one of its retired Fengyun satellite located at about 860 km in orbit. Later, on the same day in 2010, China successfully conducted an interceptor missile test for beefing up its ballistic missile defence (BMD) networks. The PLA Air Force (PLAAF) had unveiled newer versions of multirole aircraft (J-10), while acquiring others from Russia (Su-27 and Su-30), even as it commander in chief Xu Qilian proposed plans for furthering the offensive capabilities of not only the air force but also in the space arena. In October 2006, a Chinese conventional submarine trailed *USS Kittyhawk* near Okinawa—reflecting to the new-found confidence in the country's naval forces. Further, the Chinese navy sent ships for Somalia counter-piracy operations in the Indian Ocean from December 2008 and its naval officers argued for "permanent supply bases" abroad, including in Oman, Yemen and Pakistan. China in April 2009 also organised an international fleet review—underlining the global tasks of its naval forces. In December 2006, the PLA has also indicated in its white paper on national defence that China would increasingly deter regional conflicts from breaking out and would manage conflicts in the short to medium term. Further instructions for Revolution in Military Affairs' (RMA) applications were issued through the January 2009 white paper on national defence. In the Beijing parade on October 1, 2009, China unveiled 52 new weapon systems, including newer inter-continental and intermediate range ballistic missiles. In 2011, China reported that it will operationalise the refurbished Varyag aircraft carrier, even as it unveiled two more aircraft carrier programmes.

The above points indicate that the PLA is no longer a traditional armed force and that it had indicated to transiting towards RMA scenarios and out of area operations. These developments were seen either as providing an opportunity for those who are close to China or as a challenge to some of the neighbours, affected as it were, with sovereignty and territorial integrity issues or to larger international or regional power issues. Specifically, as Taiwan front receded for the PLA in the last couple of years, that of South China Sea and border areas with India has been activated further. Although, India and China had initiated defence ministry level annual dialogue process and confidence-building measures and joint operations between the Armies, Navies (and possibly in near future between Air Forces), [See Annexure 4] tensions between the two on the border issue and other larger regional/global issues have threatened to derail the bilateral relations. In this background, former Army Chief Deepak Kapoor's observation in October 2009 (and reiterated by his successor Gen V.K. Singh in October 2010) that India is preparing for a two-front (Pakistan and China) war under nuclear conditions and later followed by the Indian defence minister's observations to the standing committee of defence of the parliament that the strategic assets (possibly nuclear or ballistic missiles) of the country would be shifted to northeast India, are relevant in this context. Also, the report of the Standing Committee on Defence of the Indian Parliament, which was released in September 2010, suggested that India should prepare to counter the Chinese military logistics build up in Tibet by initiating infrastructure projects across the Indian-side of the Line of Actual Control. The two above—China's military preparations and Indian responses – are attracting global and regional attention from policy planners, defence officials, academics and journalists. Indeed, the above developments have triggered many a speech and publication in the recent period in India and abroad. This is broadly the subject matter of the current volume.

The reasons for the renewed interests of scholars working on the PLA are obvious. The massive modernisation programme launched in 1978 also encompassed the military sphere as the fourth modernisation in which the PRC has made considerable progress. One fallout of this effort, in addition to a relative proliferation of research material, is the unambiguous statements emanating from the Chinese leadership itself about several issues which were either dormant or were altogether neglected by the leadership in the earlier period.[1] The PLA as a pressure group in the decision-making and stake-holder of the People's Republic of China (PRC), apart from the Chinese Communist Party (CCP)'s small leading groups and institutions, Ministry of Foreign Affairs, think-tanks, emerging business lobbies and civil society groups, etc. is well known. In relation to India, the PLA has a special role as it effectively controls vast tracts of territories (in the name of national security) in and around areas adjoining India.

Today the PLA studies in the world have been blossoming and various authors published several refreshing works, Chinese included. It was estimated that there are about 50 PLA specialists, some of them with proficiency in utilising Chinese language primary sources, currently engaged in a re-evaluation of the PLA legacy of its eight decades of existence and practice. Studies on the PLA, however, have had a chequered history. In contrast to the previous scholarship, recent scholarship has thrown open new methodologies, inquiries on unexplored areas of PLA and have been relatively more open ended, if at times polemical. Gone are the days of limited scholarship on certain facets of the Chinese armed forces of the yore when scholars were handicapped with only a few translated versions of the official handouts on the state of the PLA, mainly, if not exclusively, routed through the British and American intelligence outposts in Hong Kong and Taiwan. These earlier efforts focused on studies related to the importance of certain statements of leaders like Mao Zedong, Zhou Enlai, Peng Dehuai, Lin Biao, Nie Rongzhen, Xu Xiangqian, Ye Jianying, Liu Bocheng, Deng Xiaoping and others, limited information and analyses of "bean-count" of the hardware, the civil-military relations and the like. Clearly, the dominant school of thought during the cold war, as exemplified in Samuel Huntington's thesis on gauging the praetorian features of the armed forces in the developing countries, the influence of the Soviet Red Army in the internal and external decision-making processes of the erstwhile USSR, have shaped the scholarship on the PLA.[2] In this context, the then continental focus of the PLA drew the attention of the doyen of Chinese studies at the Harvard University, John King Fairbank, who dubbed the Chinese as "land lubbers".[3] The assertions of Peng Dehui during the foundation of the PRC in 1949 that the PLA would march to support the anti-colonial movements in the third world, and Lin Biao's efforts to make the PRC a regional power in the 1960s were brushed aside as lacking any credibility, given the absence of a major thrust in the development of power projection forces at that time.[4] However, several of the recent publications delved deeper into the Chinese reality with rich archival Chinese material released recently thanks to the relative transparency on some subjects, though the factor of settling political scores of the current regime against the previous one may also be an important element in this aspect.[5] The net effect is that we are able to throw light on various facets of the PLA hitherto shrouded in "mystery". While consulting primary sources became the norm in the social sciences research over two decades ago, insisting on the same rules for the PLA studies has expanded our knowledge about the "mysterious" armed forces of the world. In a way these "rules" of research are expected to pay rich dividends in the coming years. Chinese themselves started reflecting on these aspects, though boasting of their country's military capabilities need to be critically evaluated. Large-scale sale of weapons to other countries could also be one of the motivations in such publicity for the Chinese military in the recent phase.

Several recent Chinese publications have graphically described the developments made by the PRC for the past six decades in the field of the development of the armed forces. Among these, several are written by authoritative military leaders and scholars themselves, including those from the Academy of Military Science, National Defence University, and various concerned departments of the PLA.[6] These have considerably broadened our scope of inquiry on the nature and content of the armed forces of the country. Relative lack of material in the early period have created several problems in comprehensively explaining the earlier history of the PLA, even though the monolithic nature of Communist systems have been broken by the criticism/counter-criticism/self-criticism campaigns and the mass movements that were unleashed in the PRC. Specifically, the Red Guard publications, with their intention to rip through certain leaders' political ideas, inadvertently touched upon military issues. Certain methodological precautions need to be observed while dealing with the information revolution that has been pervading the country under observation. In an effort to criticize everything that the "capitalist roaders" [*zouzi pai*] did, the accounts of the Red Guards in the 1960s contain sweeping remarks which need to be carefully analysed and avoided. On the other hand, the powers-that-be in the current scheme of things in the PRC has gone to the other extreme position. That is, in several publications in the recent period, there is a certain irredentist approach to the subject matter.[7] On the development of the armed forces in the country, the stereotypical approaches of the writers serving the current regime have the following major departures:

1. That the growth of the country's armed forces has been stultified by the imperialist aggression on the country in the 19th Century.
2. That the development programme of the armed forces suffered largely due to the activities of the Red Guards (here the role of the factional struggles and work teams unleashed by the "capitalist roaders" was neatly ignored or suppressed).
3. That there is a need for further modernisation and revamping of the armed forces even by adopting several military features of the "hegemonic" powers' as models for such a programme of development.

Several recent accounts written by the serving Chinese PLA officers subscribe to such a paradigm. Such an analysis, while criticizing the commissions and omissions of imperialist schemes, ironically vies for a similar scheme of development. The "contest" for such a discourse is clearly visible in most of the official Chinese writings in the recent period. One can understand the tradition of anti-imperialist historiography in the PRC; however, to try to fit into such shoes of imperialism would be detrimental to the interests of the developing countries, especially the neighbours. In the recent Chinese writings, one gets precisely that impression. The discourse on the control of resources and territories, sovereignty rights, marine rights and so on of a "great nation" in the making with the goal of becoming a global power and the efforts to achieve these is clearly a recurring theme in the Chinese writings. In a way, then, the discourse clearly has all elements of a "contest" for hegemony.

Chinese writers on the PLA also reflected on several of these positions. Here, generally speaking, the internal documents of the party [*neibu faxing*] and that of the military [*junnei faxing*] are generally critical of the military capabilities of the PLA, even though the effort clearly is to garner more support and budgetary allocations for the modernisation efforts.[8] On the other hand, open source materials [*gongkai ziliao*], which have been flooding the open market, thanks to the growing demand and the relative transparency, have elements of exaggeration or overlooking the combat and organisational weaknesses of the PLA.Broadly, while the earlier Chinese methodology stressed the importance of balancing the three major features of the PLA's guidelines, viz., modernisation [*xiandaihua*], regularisation [*zhengguihua*], and revolutionisation [*geminghua*], one could detect a change in the order of preference towards that of the modernisation aspect. Even when the other aspects were mentioned, more often these are revised to serve the reorganisation of the PLA for a possible future warfare.

In a study of the PLA one comes across two approaches based on threat perceptions and military capabilities. Threat reduction or threat enhancement, forms a crucial variable in analyzing any military's capabilities. Based on either of these two approaches, several writers have analyzed the development of the PLA. Among the western scholars on the PLA, there exist an inveterate hostility between the so-called "panda-huggers" and the emerging "blue team". While the former has been identified broadly with the "engagement" school of thought, the latter is for evolving measures to "contain" China. Perhaps such cleavages in the American Sinology can be traced to as far as the animated discussions between the "One Million" against China campaign of Karl Witfogel in the 1950s and "sinicisation" school of thought of John King Fairbank, Benjamin Schwarz, Conrad Brandt and others. While the context has changed drastically from the previous period of "encirclement" of the 1950s and 1960s to the relative triumph of Kissinger's "engagement" policy from the 1970s but more sharply the recent "co-evolution" suggestions in the recent period, these clashes in the American Sinology have been a constant phenomenon. The result, however, is a partisan review of how China impacts on the global issues.

The main difference between these two approaches is what Mark Stokes calls as the "hedging school of thought" of the panda huggers. In other words, these scholars deny the possibility of China emerging as a major challenge to the US or even to China's neighbours in the near future. To buttress their argument, they suggest to the widening military technological gap between the US and that of the Chinese inventory or combat capabilities. Many of the panda-huggers enlist several indicators like the comparative military strengths of the US or its allies with that of the PLA, or status of the defence industries and the relative lack of sophistication among the Chinese for military technology absorption, effective power projection forces [like long-range bombers, aircraft carriers, cruise missiles, etc], or foreign military visits, defence budgets, and the like to prove that the PRC may not pose a security problem for the US. On the other hand, the "blue team" mainly points to the "aspirational" aspects of the Chinese leadership to that of a global power. Main elements in this scholarship are the broad outlines drawn by the PLA to modernize its arsenal and organisational apparatus based on the current western models of military development. They note the change in the defence strategy of the PRC towards that of waging "local wars under high tech conditions" or as the latest discourse suggests "under informationised conditions", with first and punitive strikes, and hence of *offensive* orientation and power projection elements like the rapid reaction forces, blue navy, long-range aircraft development aided by air-refuelling and early warning efforts, and R&D on miniaturisation of the nuclear weapons, development of solid-propellant long-range missiles for quick launch, changes in the training programme towards high-tech combined military manoeuvres.

Several aspects of the Western historiography on the Chinese armed forces development, nevertheless, has its drawbacks, though it must be admitted that it has been diverse and intellectually stimulating. After the Sino-US rapprochement of 1971 and the subsequent policy of Western "engagement" with China, trade became the main aspect that influenced a majority of the Western writings. Basic to the burgeoning symbiosis of the Western countries is the neglect, or rather ignoring of the defence capabilities of the China. Nevertheless, this is not to belittle the influence within the Western establishments of a different opinion. Indeed, as mentioned above, the "China Threat" theorists do exist in the West. However, that pertains to the conservative elements among the Western groups. In the process, however, a comprehensive and objective analysis of China or the PLA becomes a casualty. This is compounded by a general neglect in the scholarship of what China's neighbours perceive the goals of PLA modernisation could be.

In this context it would be instructive to analyze a few works published in China—mostly by the PLA officers—for their different flavour and revisionist approach. The first one is by Qiao Liang and Wang Xiangsui wrote the *Unrestricted Warfare*.[9] In the wake of the Kosovo bombings in which part of the Chinese Embassy was razed to ground by the NATO air strikes, two serving PLA senior colonels published this book in February 1999. The fact that this was published by the PLA Literature and Arts Publishing House in Beijing and it was publicized extensively at home and abroad, as can be seen in the CCP's Youth League official daily newspaper *Zhongguo Qingnian Bao* on June 28, 1999, gives credence to the view that the views expressed in this volume are at least a strand of thought within the PLA leadership.[10] The work, according to the two authors emerged out of the hectic preparations carried out in Fujian Province in mid-1990s in what was called as "missile crisis" across the Taiwan Straits, though other major influences that affected in the making of the book include a re-reading of the experience of the Gulf War and the changes that occurred in military technology and thinking ever since in the world.[11]

The basic ideas of this book are as follows. Though China has initiated a review of its national defence strategy of People's War [*renmin zhanzheng*] and modified that into a "Local War under high-tech conditions" [*jubu zhanzheng zai gao jishu tiaojian xia*] in the early 1990s in the wake of the Allied forces attacks on Iraq in 1991, and has made several amendments to its force structures, arms procurement policy and training programme and the like, the PLA still lagged behind in terms of waging a high-tech war. That is, to elaborate, despite a decade of reforms following the mid-1985 "strategic transformation" [*zhanlue zhuanbian*], the Chinese discovered that they are still not in a position, technologically, to counter a potential enemy with similar weapons used by the NATO forces in Yugoslavia. This fundamental dilemma in the PLA leadership led to some of them to contemplate development of different tactics to counter a superior enemy. Several new features of warfare are proposed to weaken the enemy in "another" sphere of "borderless" [p.221] warfare, including hacking into websites [like those on defence establishments, Babha Atomic Research Centre in the aftermath of Pokhran II tests, on Microsoft networks, etc.], targeting financial institutions, stock exchanges [Bombay stock exchange?], terrorism [Osama bin Laden], manipulating the media [CNN, etc], urban guerrilla warfare and others. For, according to the authors, the need is to "transcend" various aspects of traditionally fought battles. [p.221]. To elaborate,

> ... warfare is no longer an activity confined only to the military sphere, and that the course of any war could be changed, or its outcome decided, by political factors, economic factors, diplomatic factors, cultural factors, technological factors, or other non-military factors. Faced with the far-reaching influence of military and non-military conflicts in every corner of the world, only if we break through the various kinds of boundaries in the models of our line of thought, take the various domains which are so completely affected by warfare and turn them into playing cards deftly shuffled in our skilled hands, and thus use beyond-limits strategy and tactics to combine all the resources of war, can there be the possibility that we will be confident of victory. [p.191]

While some western scholars have argued that such works remind one of the Maoist paradigms, several statements, like the following one, clearly indicate the determined nature of the current thinking in the PLA. According to these two writers,

> "Even a *quasi-world power* like China already has the power to jolt the world economy just by changing its own economic policies. If China were a selfish country, and had gone back on its word in 1998 and let the Renminbi lose value, no doubt this would have added to the misfortunes of the economies of Asia [during the recent financial crises]. It would also induced a cataclysm in the world's capital markets, with the result that even the world's number one debtor nation, a country which relies on the inflow of foreign capital to support its economic prosperity, the United States, would definitely have suffered heavy economic losses. Such an outcome would certainly be better than a military strike." [emphasis added] [p.195]

Other works by the PLA officers worth noting here for the vast change in the perceptions of the PLA from its founding leaders include Lt Gen Xiong Guangkai, Maj Gen. Zhu Chenghu, Senior Colonel (Brigadier rank) Dai Xu (reportedly also writes in the pen name of Long Tao), Maj Gen Luo Yuan (son of Marshal Luo Ruiqing)[12] and Rear Adm. Ying Zuo. Xiong retired as the deputy chief of General Staff of the PLA which is a joint command post in China. In the late 1970s and 1980s when the Soviet Union occupied Afghanistan, Xiong as the then Senior Colonel in the PLA military intelligence reportedly trained, along with other instructors, Uighurs and the Mujahideen to counter the Soviets. Later, he had extensively written about the impact of the 1991 and 2003 Gulf Wars, 1999 Kosovo campaign and the Afghanistan war. Xiong had highlighted the Revolution in Military Affairs and the need for the PLA to learn from these campaigns and transform to become an "informationised" force.[13] In a July 2005 statement, Gen Zhu had indirectly remarked, like Xiong earlier to Ambassador Chas Freeman,[14] that China could possibly use nuclear weapons against the US to overcome China's conventional capability. Senior Col Dai Xu, of the National Defence University, had argued that conflict between China and the United States is inevitable, possibly occurring in a time frame of 10-20 years.[15] Dai had been a frequent contributor to the popular media in China and hence his views have wide publicity.[16] According to Admiral Ying Zuo, a senior researcher at the Chinese navy's Equipment Research centre, permanent base in the region would help supply Chinese ships. Yin said: "We are saying to fulfill our international commitments, we need to strengthen our [naval] supply capacity."[17] Possible spots across the globe include bases in Pakistan, Yemen, Oman, Somalia's eastern coast, and some of the harbours in northern Sudan.[18]

The above writings, in conjunction with the rising nationalism across China, indicates to the emergence of a new breed of PLA officers and writers who are mounting pressures on the Chinese leadership to transform the country's policy into what the above authors have suggested to a stiff response towards the United States and the neighbouring countries, Also, in conjunction with the "peaceful rise" of China (*zhongguo jueqi*), these writers also emphasised on the "military rise" (*junguo jueqi*) with wider consequences to the stability and security of the region.[19]

In this context, the Indian scholarship on the PLA is an emerging field. Giri Deshingkar (1932-2000), to whom this collection is dedicated, was a pioneer of the PLA studies in India. His work was compiled in *Security and Science in China and India* and published in 2005.[20] According to him, China never posed threat to India (pp. 24-33). He did, however, acknowledged that "truth was distorted on both sides" (p.23) in India-China relations. He was also critical of the Chinese "crude negative ideological statements about India" (p.13). While raising the question "should we play the game [of realpolitik] at all" (p.35) in relation to China, Deshingkar argued that India and China should "steer away from international superpower politics in Asia" (p.24). The costs of such entanglements are high while dividends few or even negative to the participants.

In several essays, Deshingkar has elaborated succinctly his critique of the "cult of the nation state" of Asian elites. For him, the inequality that existed between tributary state systems of the Middle Kingdom is less lethal than the "subordination of 'equal' modern nation-states to the world market and the global arms culture" (p.429). As one after the other Asian state joined the nation-state category after the decolonisation process over five decades ago, with the attendant paraphernalia of defining and securing borders, standing armies and centralisation, according to Deshingkar, these states have lost their moorings. He was critical of the late 1970s four modernisations programme of China as that firmly sets the course for making the country into a modern nation state (p.413).

Deshingkar had a distinct definition to offer on security matters. He stated: "The security system of a country is far more than a sum of its discrete parts: weaponry is only one part of the entire system" (p.140). In other words, unlike a major trend in scholarship till the 1980s, he saw little of importance in a "bean count" approach to gauge military capabilities of a country. More significant was his discussion on the military strategy of China.

Deshingkar's analysis of the People's War strategy of China is unique among the military specialists. He considered that the "strategic doctrine of a country is invariably a part of that country's social system and is tailored to meet the goals of that system vis-à-vis the external military environment" (p.79). He raised several "peculiar incongruencies" (p.75) between the theory of People's War and its practice after 1949, specifically in the Korean War and India-China war. Deshingkar was one of the first who foresaw the possibility of the Chinese military doctrine changing from Mao Zedong to Deng Xiaoping in future as a result of the "two line struggles" in China and towards its offensive orientation (pp. 97-98). He also foresaw the current debate on anti-ballistic missile defence system (ABM) emerging in future (p. 177), as with European countries exploring possibilities of exporting arms to China (p. 372). Likewise, several civil-military scholars miss out his keen observation that the Chinese military is under transformation from being a defender of socialism to a defender of the Chinese revolution "often against the military threats posed by other socialist regimes" (pp. 126-27).

Apart from Deshingkar, several Indians have reflected on the PLA. The 1962 border clashes, China's military logistics build-up in Tibet and areas contiguous to Indian borders, nuclear and ballistic missile technology or platforms assistance to Pakistan, conventional arms supplies to Pakistan, Bangladesh, Nepal, Sri Lanka, Burma/Myanmar and China's role in the Indian Ocean Region—all could be said to be part of the triggers for several Indians to focus their research on the PLA. Several Indian scholars—some trained in China and in Chinese studies—found it worthy to conduct research on the PLA. A number of think-tanks also contributed to this process and the field is fortunately getting diversified with professionals, academics, journalists, policy-makers joining this effort of late.

This book is a collection of articles from Indian perspectives on various aspects of the PLA and its implications for India. The contributors to this volume have been engaged in operations/research/policy in the Indian establishment or think-tanks or academia on the Chinese military developments. While a number of new developments such as integrated joint operations, revolution in military affairs, "informationisation", joint logistics, full-spectrum dominance, and the like have been currently in vogue in the Chinese military and indeed are being studied and implemented across the board, the collection of articles below follows the traditional outline of the armed forces. That is, the contributors to this volume evaluate China's military modernisation, strategy, different armed services (viz., ground, air, naval and strategic), in addition to the impact of the robust space programme. Secondly, although several contributors to this volume have worked/participated in discussions with several agencies and institutions, the views expressed in this collection do not represent the views of any agency or institution and that these are the respective contributors' personal views.

Gurmeet Kanwal, in the first article in this volume, noted the "revisionist" shifts in China's strategy from territorial defence to that of maritime and space domains. After outlining major changes in China's threat perceptions, doctrinal changes in the armed forces, troop composition across the services, Kanwal suggests that the PLA is geared towards waging asymmetric warfare with hi-tech adversaries. He argued that "...China's military buildup is broadening the reach of its forces in Asia and poses a long-term challenge not only to Taiwan but also to other military forces operating in the Pacific and to regional powers such as India and Japan". Given the increases in the PLA capabilities in Tibet—from "sustaining 20 to 25 divisions in Tibet over two summer seasons" to currently "up to 30 to 35 divisions", Kanwal argued that India needs to enhance its military capabilities. As the territorial dispute had not been resolved between these two countries, despite more than three decades of talks, India needs to be on guard.

Srikanth Kondapalli's article traces the main drivers in China's grand strategic formulations by highlighting the renewed effort of China in enhancing its comprehensive national power, protecting its perceived "core interests" and gearing up for the global power transition. After a brief discussion on China's debates in this regard, he identified three main strands in China's policy vis-à-vis India. As two rising countries in Asia, whose CNP is being constantly increased, China could follow a balancing, mutually beneficial interdependency or a constructivist policy towards India.

The focus of Navneet Kumar's article is on the evolution, process, concepts and highlights of China's national military strategy, specifically after former president Jiang Zemin issued the military strategic guidelines in 1993 and modified by his successor Hu Jintao in 2002. He argued that there has been a perceptible shift in national military strategy towards non-war missions, even as the national military strategy of China became well ensconced with the civilian leadership's aspirations and agenda. On the impact of the military strategy of China on India, Kumar obliquely mentions the Chinese critique of Indian acquisitions of advanced technology platforms.

The next set of articles in this volume is on the PLA forces—strategic and conventional forces, in addition to China's space assets. Exercise of the nuclear option as a political weapon is vital to China's policy, according to MV Rappai. He traces to the preparations and policies of China in acquiring nuclear weapons and observes "[a]fter it acquired the position of a 'status quo nuclear weapon power' it [China] conveniently forgot some of its good intentions". In the light of China's nuclear stockpile, modernisation and ballistic missile deployments, he argues that India should enhance its nuclear deterrence capabilities vis-à-vis China.

Vijay Sakhuja's article focuses on China's naval modernisation programme including the aircraft carrier programme, submarines, large replenishment ships, anti-ship ballistic missile programme and argues that India could face problems in the Indian Ocean Region with China's dispatch of contingents to the Indian Ocean Region for counter-piracy operations, naval visits and cooperation with the other South Asian navies, etc or get marginalized in the Arctic. In the light of the recent crisis in the South China Sea, Sakhuja also suggests that "India is an important stakeholder in the evolving security dynamics in South China Sea and any insecurity in the region could adversely impact on India's trade and economy."

Vishal Nigam's reflections on improvements in China's air force—since its inception—including its aviation platforms, command structure, modernisation, jointness, etc lead him to the conclusion that it could pose a challenge to India in quantitative superiority and strategic surprise domains. However, according to him, the main challenge from China will be from "ballistic and cruise missile attack on command and control centers, use of MiG 19 drones or UAVs to bring down early warning and GCI network and jamming the AWACS radar."

Last, but not the least, the significant strides China made in the space domain are covered extensively by Ajey Lele. Outlining the main space faring efforts of China in satellite launches, manned spacecraft, lunar probe efforts and modernisation of launch vehicle technology and precision systems, Lele suggests that the two key components of China's efforts include striving for space supremacy and information warfare. Although India need not panic at this moment, Lele argues that the impact of China's space programme on India could range from geopolitics to technology. These include China's plans to "dictate [to India or others] from a position of strength" in the proposed new space disarmament treaties despite conducting anti-satellite test. China could also enhance precision guidance and control of Pakistani missiles through space cooperation or even target Indian Remote Sensing satellites or jam the GPS.

The annexures at the end of the volume, compiled by the editor, provide for a comparative military profile of the Indian and Chinese military forces, budgetary allocations, China's arms transfers to the neighbours of India and contacts between the establishments of the PLA forces and Indian armed forces. This collection is being offered to both the specialist as well as the lay person on the developments in the PLA and their possible impact on India.

END NOTES

1. For an assessment of the research methods on the PLA see David Shambaugh, "A Bibliographical Essay on New Sources for the Study of China's Foreign Relations and National Security" in Thomas W Robinson and David Shambaugh eds. *Chinese Foreign Policy: Theory and Practice* (Oxford: Clarendon Paperbacks, 1998) first published 1994 pp. 603-18; David Shambaugh, "PLA Studies: A Maturing Field" in James Mulvenon and Richard Yang eds. *The PLA and the Information Age* (Santa Monica: RAND Corporation, 2000); Evan Medeiros, "Undressing the Dragon: Research the PLA Through Open Source Exploitation" Paper submitted at the 2001 CAPS-RAND PLA Conference at Washington DC 21-24 June 2001 and Taylor Fravel, "The Revolution in Research Affairs: Online Sources and the Study of the PLA" paper submitted at the above conference. Broadly on the China programme, see Robert Ash, David Shambaugh and Seiichiro Takagi, eds. *China Watching: Perspectives from Europe, Japan and the United States* (London: Routledge, 2007).
2. See for the trend setting work of this period, Samuel P. Huntington, *Political Order in Changing Societies* (Yale University Press, New Haven, 1977); Huntington, *The Soldier and the State: The Theory and Politics of Civil-Military relations* (Cambridge: MA, Harvard University Press, 1957); and Amos Perlmutter and Bannet, *The Political Influence of the Military: A Comparative Reader* (Yale University Press, New Haven, 1980). The influence such an approach is clearly visible in the writings and debates of Ellis Joffe, *The Chinese Army after Mao* (George Weidenfeld and Nicholson, London, 1987); Ellis Joffe, *Party and Army: Professional and Political control of the Chinese Officer Corps 1949-1964* (Cambridge: Harvard University Press, 1965); William Whitson (ed.), *The Military and Political Power in China in the 1970s* (New York: Praeger, 1972); William R Heaton, "Professional military education in the PRC" in Paul H B Godwin (ed) *The Chinese Defence Establishment: Continuity and Change in the 1980s* (Westview, Boulder, Colorado, 1983) pp 121-38; Monte R Bullard, *China's Political-Military Evolution: The Party and Military in the People's*

Republic of China 1960-1984 (Westview, Boulder, 1985); Gerald Segal "The Military as a Group in Chinese Politics" in David S Goodman (ed) *Groups and Politics in the PRC* (Cardiff University Press, 1984) pp. 94-97 David Shambaugh, "The building of the civil-military state in China, 1949-1965: bringing the soldier back in" in Timothy Cheek and Tony Saich eds. *The Construction of State Socialism in China, 1949-1965* (Armonk, NY: ME Sharpe, 1996) and James C. Mulvenon and Andrew ND Yang eds. *Seeking Truth From Facts: A Retrospective on Chinese Military Studies in the Post-Mao Era* (Santa Monica: RAND Corp, 2001).

3. JK Fairbank cited in "China-A Maritime Nation" *The Naval Review* vol. 64 no. 1 January 1976 pp. 33-44 (cited on p. 34).
4. Limited progress in the development of such power projection forces as strategic missilery is seen as *defensive* in nature rather than having any *offensive* capabilities, if not intentions.
5. The following Chinese works considerably reflect the archival material on the PLA. Several leaders' works and their biographical sketches have been useful in this context. See, for instance, *Mao Zedong Junshi Wenji* [Collected Military Writings of Mao Zedong] 6 vols. (Beijing: Jiefangjun Chubanshe, 1994); Gu Shuohang et.al eds. *Mao Zedong junshi sixiang jiaocheng* [Educational Regulations of Mao Zedong's Military Thought (Nanjing: Southeast University Publications, 1992); General Logistics Department' commanding department ed. *Mao Zedong junshi houqin lilun yanjiu* [Research on the theory of Mao Zedong's military logistics] (Beijing: Jindun Chubanshe, 1993); National Defence University Science Research Bureau ed. *Mao Zedong junshi sixiang zai zhongguo de xingli yu fazhan* (Beijing: NDU Publications, 1994); Lin Jiangong et al (eds.) *Mao Zedong junshi zhexue sixiang chutan* [Preliminary explorations in the military philosophical thinking of Mao Zedong] (Beijing: National Defense University [NDU] Publications, 1991); *Mao Zedong Junshi nianpu* [Chronological Military Life of Mao Zedong] (Nanning: Guangxi Renmin Chubanshe, 1994); Zhang Jiagu and Yuan Deqin eds. *Mao Zedong junshi sixiang yanjiu* [Research of the military thought of Mao Zedong] (Beijing: Renmin Zhongguo Chubanshe, 1993). On Zhou Enlai, see *Zhou Enlai junshi wenxuan* [Selected Military Works of Zhou Enlai] Vol.4. On Deng Xiaoping, *Deng Xiaoping xinshiqi jundui jianshe sixiang gailun* [An Introduction to the Thought of Deng Xiaoping' Army Building in the New Era] (Beijing: Liberation Army Daily, 1994); Wang Chengbin et.al eds. *Deng Xiaoping xiandai junshi lilun yu shijian* [Theory and Practice of Deng Xiaoping's Modern Military Affairs] (Nanchang: Jiangxi People's Publications, 1993). Other leader's writings have also been published. See *Zhu De Junshi Wenxuan* [Selected Military Works of Zhu De] (Liberation Army Press, Beijing, 1996); Peng Dehuai, Memoirs of a Chinese Marshal – The autobiographical notes of Peng Dehuai (1898-1974) (tr. Zheng Longpu) (English text edited by Sara Grimes) (Beijing, Foreign Languages Press, 1984); Nie Rongzhen, Inside the Red Star: The Memoirs of Marshal Nie Rongzhen (New World Press, Beijing, 1988) (first published in Chinese in 1984); *Chen Yi Junshi Wenxuan* [Selected Military Writings of Chen Yi] (Liberation Army Publications, Beijing, 1996); Ye *Jianying Junshi Wenxuan* [Selected Military Works of Ye Jianying](Jiefangjun Chubanshe, Beijing, 1996); *Liu Bocheng Junshi wenxuan* [Selected Military Writings of Liu Bocheng] (Liberation Army Press, Beijing, 1992); *He Long Junshi Wenxuan* [Selected Military Works of He Long] (Liberation Army Publications, Beijing, 1989);

Xu Xiangqian Junshi wenxuan [Selected Military Works of Xu Xiangqian (Liberation Army Publications, Beijing, 1993); *Li Da Junshi Wenxuan* [Selected Military Writings of Li Da] (Liberation Army Publications, Beijing, 1993) and *Yang Chengwu Junshi Wenxuan* [Selected Military Writings of Yang Chengwu] (Liberation Army Publications, Beijing, 1997). Two lacunae, however, can be noticed in the above expositions. One it is still a taboo to publish works of similar nature on Lin Biao, Gang of Four or others, although they were associated with the PLA. Second, except for a few passages, the above works are relatively silent on views, postures and motivations of the PLA on India.

Other than the leaders perceptions about the military affairs, there is also a rich resource base in various aspects of the development of the armed forces including, to mention a few, in Xin Ming ed. *Zhongguo renmin jiefangjun junguan shouce: Hangkong fence* [Chinese PLA Officers Manual: Air Force Part (Qingdao: Qingdao Publications, 1991); Zhu Yide ed. *Zhongguo renmin jiefangjun junguan shouce: Haijun fence* [Chinese PLA Officers Manual: Navy Part (Qingdao: Qingdao Publications, 1991); Liu Shunyao [chief ed.] *Kongjun Da Cidian* [Air Force Dictionary] (Shanghai: Cishu Publications, 1996); *Dangdai Zhongguo Kongjun shi* [Contemporary Chinese Air Force History] (Beijing: Chinese Academy of Social Sciences, 1989); *Haijun shi* [Naval History] (Beijing: Liberation Army Press, 1989); Yang Guoyu et.al Eds. *Dangdai Zhongguo haijun* [Contemporary Chinese Navy] (Beijing, Chinese Academy of Social Sciences, 1987). Relatively speaking the coverage on India (specifically policies and programmes on protecting sovereignty issues and deployments in Tibet, 1962 border clashes, logistics, etc) are considerable, if not extensive. Two works that need to be mentioned on China's perspectives on the 1962 border clashes include *Zhongyin bianjiang ziwei fanji zuozhanshi* [History of the Sino-India border self defensive war] (Beijing: Junshi kexue chubanshe, 1994) and Xu Yan, *Zhongyin bianjie zhizhan lishi zhenxiang* [True history of the Sino-Indian border war] (Hong Kong: Cosmos Books Ltd, 1993]. See also John W. Garver, "China's Decision for War With India in 1962," in Robert S. Ross and Alastair Iain Johnston, *New Directions in the Study of Chinese Foreign Policy* (Stanford, California: Stanford University Press, 2006) accessed at <http://chinaindiaborderdispute.files.wordpress.com/2010/07/garver.pdf>; Cheng Feng and Larry M. Wortzel. "PLA Operational Principles and Limited War: The Sino-Indian War of 1962," in Mark A. Ryan, David Michael Finkelstein, and Michael A. McDevitt, Ed. *Chinese Warfighting: The PLA Experience Since 1949* (Watertown, Massachusettes: East Gate Books, 2003)

Besides these we are also fortunate to have at least 20 journals and magazines on or related to the PLA. These include *Junshi Kexue* [Military Science Journal of the Academy of Military Science] (Beijing) [considered to be "authentic" in the profession]; *Zhanlue yu Guanli* [Strategy & Management] (Beijing); *Junshi Xueshu*; *Guofang* [National Defense] (Beijing); *Jiefangjun Bao* [Liberation Army Daily] (Beijing); *Junshi Shijie* [Military World] (Beijing); *Xiandai Junshi* [Contemporary Military] (Beijing & Hong Kong); *Zhuangjiacheliang* [Tank and Armoured Vehicles] (Beijing); Jianchuan Zhishi [Naval and Merchant Ships] (Beijing); *Hangkong Zhishi* [Aerospace Knowledge] (Beijing); *Guoji Hang Kong* [International Aviation] (Beijing); *Bingqi Zhishi* [Ordnance Knowledge] (Beijing); *Junshi lishi* [History of Military Affairs] (Beijing); *Zhongguo Junshi Kexue* [China Military Science] (Beijing) ; *Xiandai*

Jianchuan [Modern Ships] (Beijing); *Shijie Junshi* [World Military Affairs] (Beijing); *Junshi Shilin* ; *Xiandai Bingqi* [Modern Weaponry] (Beijing), etc. Besides these military journals, several other journals like *Shijie Zhishi* [World Affairs] (Beijing) reflect on the strategic environment. In addition, annual assessments of the global strategic events are available at *Guoji Xingshi nianqian* [Survey of International Affairs] (Shanghai: Jiaoyu Chubanshe, various) and other works. Unlike the other sources mentioned above, the articles published in these journals are extensive in nature with almost every issue carrying at least one article on developments in the Indian military modernisation and other related topics. However, the coverage on other forces, rather than on the PLA, is noticeable. When indeed issues of the PLA are discussed, it is mostly on historical aspects rather than an extensive coverage on the contemporary dynamics. As Lora Saalman's research indicated, these military journals focus on India had substantially increased. See Lora Saalman, "Divergence, Similarity and Symmetry in Sino-Indian Threat Perceptions" *Journal of International Affairs* (Spring/Summer 2011) Vol. 64, No. 2. pp. 169-94.

A few academic websites from China are quite useful in their collections of Ph.D. theses, MA Dissertations, conference reports, journal or newspaper articles on the PLA, viz., <http://search.cnki.net/>; <http://www.ilib.cn/>; <http://www.wanfangdata.com.cn/>; and <http://ipub.zlzx.org/>. In addition, the George Washington University's collections of declassified documents or those of the Woodrow Wilson Institute's project on the Cold War materials in the Russian archives have considerably expanded our knowledge on the PLA. See entries at <http://www.gwu.edu>; <http://cwihp.si.edu >.

6. To mention a few, Han Huaizhi ed. *Dangdai Zhongguo jundui de junshi gongzuo* [China Today: The Military Affairs of the Chinese Army] 2 vols (Beijing: Chinese Academy of Social Sciences, 1989); *Zhongguo renmin jiefangjun* [Chinese PLA] (Beijing: Dangdai Zhongguo Chubanshe, 1994) 2 vols; *Zhongguo Da baike Quanshu: Junshi* [Chinese Encyclopedia: Military Affairs] (Beijing: Chinese Encyclopaedia Publications, 1989) 2 vols; Military Science Academy History Research Bureau (ed.) *Zhongguo renmin jiefangjun liushiniandai shiji* [Main Events of the sixty years of the Chinese People's Liberation Army] (Military Science Academy, Beijing, 1988); Military Science Academy Military Research Department (ed.),*Zhongguo renmin Jiefangjun de Qishi nian* [Seventy Years of the Chinese People's Liberation Army] (Beijing: Junshi Kexue Chubanshe,1997); the Chinese National Defence University (NDU) Military Training Department and the Scientific Research Bureau commissioned and edited by Liu Gongji and Luo Haixi, *Guofang Lilun* [Theory of National Defence] (Beijing, NDU Publications, 1996).
7. Such irredentist approaches were fuelled by the February 1992 National People's Congress resolution on expanding the country's security perimeters to include not only the traditional topics like Taiwan and Senkaku [Diaoyutai] Islands but also far-flung areas like the Paracels and Spratly's Islands in the South China Seas. Reported extensions of "core interests" from Tibet and Taiwan to the South China Sea further has aggravated regional security environment.
8. While the US Department of Commerce publication of translations from the Chinese press in the Foreign Broadcast Information Service bulletins and the British Broadcasting Corporation's Selected World Broadcasts have been some of the invaluable collections on different aspects of China, including PLA, more often

these are selections of the Chinese materials. Consulting and cross-checking with other Chinese publications, which are increasingly being uploaded on the Internet, could rectify over-emphasis on any subject, any mistakes or inconsistencies in these materials.

9. *Unrestricted Warfare* (Beijing: PLA Literature and Arts Publishing House, February 1999) translated by Foreign Broadcast Information Service: China Daily Report [FBIS-CHI (Internet edition)] in 254 pages including Preface [228 pp. in print of the FBIS- all references are to this translated version] available from 1996 at available at <http://wnc.fedworld.gov>
10. For a critique of these work see Kao Chieh-chien, "What Limits Has 'Unrestricted Warfare' Exceeded—Also Discussing the Phenomenon Where 'Readers and Experts Stick to Their Own Views" *Ta Kung Pao* June 21, 2000 in FBIS-CHI-2000-0621 July 5, 2000. See also Michael Pillsbury ed. *Chinese Views of Future Warfare* (New Delhi: Lancer Publications, 1997) and for the views of these two authors on the September 11 events, see <http://www.sinopolis.com/archivesindex/topstory/ts%5F010912%5F01.htm>.
11. In the backdrop of the current spat between China on the one hand and Vietnam and the Philippines on the South China Sea dispute, Qiao Liang suggested that China should learn from the US exercise of smart power to garner more support for its policies. See "China needs to think more like the US: general" *Want China Times* May 8, 2012.
12. Luo Yuan recently argued, in the backdrop of the China- Philippines spat on the South China Sea islands dispute at Scarborough Shoal in April 2012 that the PLA Navy should attack the Philippines. See *Global Times* April 26, 2012 accessed at <http://opinion.huanqiu.com/1152/2012-04/2667720.html>
13. See Xiong Guangkai, *International Strategy and Revolution in Military Affairs* (Beijing: Qinghua University Press,2003) and International Situation and Security Strategy (Beijing: Qinghua University Press, 2006).
14. This is cited in Greg May, "China's Opposition to TMD Is More About Politics Than Missiles" *Foresight* magazine (Tokyo) February 2000 at <http://www.nyu.edu/globalbeat/usdefense/May0200.html> accessed on January 6, 2005.
15. See Dai Xu, *Shengshi Langyan* (Heyday of Approaching Smoke Signals) (Beijing: Xinhua Publications, 2009).
16. See Dai Xu, "U.S. building 'Asian NATO' to encircle China" August 11, 2010 accessed at <http://www.china.org.cn/opinion/2010-08/11/content_20687335.htm>
17. Yin cited by Malcolm Moore, "China may build Middle East naval base" *The Telegraph* December 30, 2009 at <http://www.telegraph.co.uk/news/worldnews/asia/china/6911198/China-may-build-Middle-East-naval-base.html>
18. See the opinions of several Chinese, including from the navy, Yu Dong, "Where Will the Chinese Navy Build its Overseas Supply Points?" *Guoji Xianqu Daobao* April 14, 2010 NewsEdge Document Number: 201004141477.1_1bd10359d1406ce4 World News Connection File Number 985 Accession Number 297401581
19. See Peter Brown, "The PLA raises its voice" *Asia Times* March 9, 2010 accessed at <http://www.atimes.com/atimes/China/LC09Ad01.html>
20. Giri Deshingkar, *Security and Science in China and India (Selected Essays)* (New Delhi, Samskriti Press, 2005) Edited by Manoranjan Mohanty and Mira Sinha-Bhattacharjea.

1

CHINA'S GROWING MILITARY POWER: IMPLICATIONS FOR INDIA

GURMEET KANWAL

India is conscious and watchful of the implications of China's evolving military profile in the immediate and extended neighbourhood.

Ministry of Defence, Annual Report for 2010-11

CHINA'S STRATEGIC OUTLOOK

China is making steady progress on its long march to acquiring world power status. China's long-term grand strategy is clearly to be recognised as the pre-eminent economic and military power in the Asia-Pacific region in the short-term and as a major global power in the long-term. Its strategy of "four modernisations", formally adopted in 1978, is bearing fruit and is leading to fairly rapid, though regionally skewed, economic development and military modernisation. In recent years, the Chinese have stressed the importance of "comprehensive national strength" in determining the country's role in international affairs. Their concept of national defence is no longer limited merely to the defence of territory but has been expanded to include the seaboard and outer space. In maritime security, the erstwhile strategy of "Coastal Defence" has been converted to a strategy of "Oceanic Offensive". The emphasis on bolstering naval and air forces stems from a desire to project power well away from China's shores.

Whether China's rise will be entirely peaceful, as its leaders have repeatedly professed, or one that may be marked by turbulence and chaos, as some analysts fear, is a vexing issue. History is witness to the fact that major powershifts have never occurred without large-scale upheavals. Managing the rise of China successfully is the most important fundamental challenge confronting the international community in the 21st century. Writing about China's rise, Michael D. Swaine and Ashley J. Tellis have said:[1] "This process is significant not only because it promises the internal transformation of one of the world's oldest civilisations, but also because *if concluded successfully* it could result in a dramatic power transition within the international system."

China is without doubt a revisionist power and has formulated a meticulously crafted, though not formally stated, grand strategy to chart its course towards achieving its goal of becoming a global power. China aims to become the dominant economic and military power in the Asia-Pacific region by 2010-15 and a major power internationally by about 2030-40. China's grand strategy is aimed at "firmly preserving China's core interests, strengthening its relations with neighbouring countries, consolidating friendships with the broad majority of developing countries and improving relations with developed countries."[2] In order to emphasise the benign nature of its grand strategy, China points out that its major themes are "peace and development," the non-use of force in settling international disputes, non-intervention in the internal affairs of other countries, the defensive nature of China's military strategy, its "no-first-use of nuclear weapons" declaration and its support for nuclear-free weapons zones. China claims that it will never deploy its military forces on foreign soil. However, Deng Xiaoping's 24-character strategy "keep cool-headed to observe, be composed to make reactions, stand firmly, hide our capabilities and bide our time, never try to take the lead, and be able to accomplish something" suggested a conscious desire to downplay China's ambitions. However, the present Chinese leadership has clearly gone beyond Deng's advice and appears to be eager to flaunt its military muscle at every available opportunity.

Development of Comprehensive National Power

China's grand strategy seeks to preserve national independence and increase national power through the balancing of two competing objectives: the development of Comprehensive National Power (CNP—*zonghe guoli*) and the exploitation of existing "strategic configuration of power" or "shi".[3] China's grand strategy affirms that national unity, sovereignty and stability guarantee the survival of the state, and the development of a national strategy with China at the centre of Asia. Incorporated in this strategy is Chinese patience or willingness to live with ambiguity before considering the employment of force such that advantage is obtained, moral high ground is occupied and supporters or non-supporters are identified. China's national security policy objectives, 'dynamic stability' and 'economic growth', are directly linked to the maintenance of unity through preservation of the regime, domestic order and territorial integrity. In a RAND study Michael Swaine and Ashley Tellis have written that China's grand strategy seeks to achieve the following three interrelated objectives:[4]

- The preservation of domestic order and well being in the face of different forms of social strife.
- Defence against persistent external threats to national sovereignty and territory.
- The attainment and maintenance of geopolitical influence as a major and, perhaps, primary state.

China's grand strategy, as China defines it, consists of maintaining balance among competing priorities for sustaining momentum in national economic development; and, maintaining favourable trends in the security environment within which such economic development can occur.[5] Khadong Oh Hassig of the Institute of Defence Analyses has described China's primary strategic objectives as the protection of China's sovereignty, maintaining China's security and preventing Taiwan's independence.[6] Michael Swaine and Ashley Tellis are of the view that China's strategic objectives include "assuring domestic order and social well-being, maintaining an adequate defence against threats to the heartland, increasing the level of influence and control over the periphery with an eye to warding off threats that may eventually menace the political regime and, restoring China to regional pre-eminence..."[7]

China's strategic planners evaluate and measure China's national standing in relation to other nations through CNP. The yardsticks for CNP include qualitative and quantitative measures of territorial size, economic capability, military power, natural resources, diplomatic influence, quality of domestic governance and the extent of China's cultural influence. Of all the yardsticks, China's strategy to build its CNP lays maximum emphasis on economic development. "China's 11th Five-Year Plan (2006-10), ratified during the March 2006 session of the National People's Congress, calls for a 20 percent reduction in per capita energy consumption by 2010, a doubling of China's 2000 Gross Domestic Product (GDP) by 2010, and an overall GDP of $4 trillion by 2020. (China's GDP in 2010 was US$ 5.87 trillion.) The plan stresses coordinated, sustainable development and greater investment and urbanisation in the rural interior to address widening income disparities and resultant social unrest."[8] However, as China's economy expands, its interests will also expand and China will perceive a need to upgrade its military capability to protect those interests

China's attempts to advance its concept of a "peaceful rise", also called "peaceful ascendancy", are consistent with its belief that is was historically a great empire (the Middle Kingdom) and deserves to be a major world power in the modern era. The Chinese are constantly looking for ways in which they can ensure that China's rise and integration with the world order is orderly and peaceful. Japanese columnist Y. Funabashi quotes a member of Chinese People's Political Consultative Conference as having asked him: "How did historic empires and major powers rise and what reactions do they trigger? What should we do so as not to cause excessive wariness? This is what we are currently studying internally."[9]

While China's political leadership is of the view that China has never had such a secure and stable periphery and regional environment as has obtained in the first decade of the 21st century, many PLA analysts see greater sources of instability, particularly at the global level. Senior Colonel Li Qinggong, director of the General Staff Department's First Bureau, had identified the following set of factors as causing global instability soon after the Kosovo conflict:[10]

- American hegemony and the attempt to conquer the world by force.
- Western "humanitarian intervention" and the "Clinton Doctrine".
- The increasing intensification of local ethnic conflicts, as in Chechnya, Eritrea, Indonesia and Yugoslavia.
- The decline of arms control efforts and the build-up of regional military forces.
- The rise of ethno-religious separatism and increase in terrorist acts.

Other destabilising factors noted by PLA analysts include the power imbalance caused by the collapse of the bipolar system, contest and conflict between the global hegemon (US) and "regional hegemons", a surge in "national extremism", the damage done to international arms control efforts by the South Asian nuclear tests, transnational crime and drug trafficking, disputes over economic resources and environmental issues. China is also acutely conscious of the world's dwindling fossil fuel resources in the light of its own unavoidable dependency on them. It has been moving aggressively to acquire controlling interest in oil and gas fields where it can, for example in several countries in Africa, Central Asia and Myanmar, and sign long-term supply contracts where it cannot. It is likely to take even more vigorous steps in future to safeguard its energy security.

DEFENCE STRATEGY

China's Defence Policy *China's National Defence in 2006*, the White Paper issued by the Government of China in December 2006, expressed satisfaction with the overall security environment and lists it as "sound". It describes China's defence policy in these words:[11]

> "China will not engage in any arms race or pose a military threat to any other country. At the new stage in the new century, we will take the scientific development outlook as an important guiding principle for the building of national defense and military affairs, vigorously advance the revolution in military affairs with Chinese features, and strive to realize an all-round, coordinated and sustainable development in our country's national defense and military capabilities."

According to the 2006 Defence White Paper, "China's national defense policy for the new stage in the new century is defined as follows":[12]

- Upholding national security and unity and ensuring the interests of national development
- Achieving the all-round, coordinated and sustainable development of China's national defence and armed forces.
- Enhancing the performance of the armed forces with informationisation as the major measuring criterion.
- Implementing the military strategy of active defence.
- Pursuing a self-defensive nuclear strategy.
- Fostering a security environment conducive to China's peaceful development.

National Security Strategy From its published documents and policy statements China's national security strategy may be assessed to be the following:

- The primary objective is to create a security environment favourable to the country's economic development.
- Peaceful reunification of the Motherland is one of the strategic objectives set by the Chinese government.
- Safeguarding the country's territorial integrity is the foremost responsibility entrusted to the PLA.
- China will continue to claim that it will persist in the principle of non-use of force in settling boundary differences. However, it may be expected to follow a more robust policy with pre-emptive strategies, particularly in relation to Taiwan.
- Towards its regional neighbours China will continue to follow a stick

and carrot policy of enhancing friendly relations through bilateral security co-operation, military sales and aid and bilateral trade, while remaining intolerant of major dissent and alliances.
- Actively aid international efforts to prevent nuclear proliferation, particularly in respect of North Korea.
- The government guideline for the PLA's transformation in the next 15 to 20 years is to build a smaller but more modern army, navy and air force to be able to face RMA-ready Western forces.
- China's earlier People's War military strategy of 'luring the enemy in deep' will be gradually replaced completely by the present strategy of 'active defence under hi-tech conditions'.
- While China will endeavour to prevent conflict, if conflict breaks out, its military strategy is likely to be pro-active and will be designed to take the fight into enemy territory.

China has always placed immense emphasis on diplomacy as a tool to balance out security threats and challenges through intricate alliances and strategic partnerships. In Brig Arun Sahgal's view:[13] "China's growing military capabilities backed by strategic arms sales programmes, enable it to create a series of special strategic relations with friendly states (potentially with Myanmar, Bangladesh, Thailand, South Korea, Cambodia, Malaysia and Iran), quasi alliances (Pakistan, North Korea) and external military assets (Gwadar, Maldives, Chittagong). This will increasingly allow China to manipulate regional balance of power in a manner that enhances its political economic and security interests and allow it to engage in coercive diplomacy against any state in the neighbourhood that is seen to be acting against its interests. This Chinese strategy of growth of military capability and creeping influence is in no way in contradiction with stress on partnership, economic interdependence and promoting relations with neighbours and major powers. In fact it compliments regional and global engagement strategy at a period when China is preoccupied with domestic economic reforms and is still attempting to establish political structures in tune with its modernisation drive and relatively weak power base in comparison to its principal rivals."

China's Military Strategy

The PLA occupies a position of immense significance in China's regime. China's military strategy is still guided by the PLA's historical experience of "People's War". Though in its overall approach the People's War strategy is predicated on the "strategic defensive", within that rubric it is a fairly balanced blend of defensive and offensive action. "The basic military strategy Mao formulated, known as 'active defence', was one of a protracted, defensive war... The concept of active defence means taking tactically offensive action within a basically defensive strategy... The active defence strategy consists of three phases: strategic defence, strategic stalemate and strategic counter-attack."[14] Deng Xiaoping was of the view that "Active defence itself is not necessarily limited to a defensive concept... Active defence also contains an offensive element. If we are attacked, we will certainly counterattack... anyone who wants to destroy us will be subject to retaliation."[15]

Strategic defence is considered important at the beginning of the conflict as China views its forces as weaker than those of its potential adversaries. The aim in this phase is to defeat the enemy's offensive action and, in fact, ideally to pre-empt him and disrupt his preparations. The strategic stalemate phase is designed to weaken the enemy by forcing him to fight on lines of communication that have been stretched. The aim is to stabilise the situation and enable Chinese forces to begin turning the tide from defensive to offensive operations. In the strategic counter-attack phase the aim is to defeat the weakened enemy through a counter-offensive or riposte.

Since China's ignominious incursion into Vietnam in 1979, PLA doctrine evolved from Mao's "people's war", characterised by protracted, large-scale land warfare, through a "limited/local war" phase, to "people's war under modern conditions" introduced in 1993. Subsequently, after the Cold War ended and following the Gulf War in 1991, the Chinese leadership concluded that the "Big Peace" at the geo-strategic level cannot prevent local or small wars at the regional level. The PLA then graduated to thinking about fighting local or limited wars and sought to focus on the following:[16]

- Small-scale conflicts restricted to contested border territory.
- Conflict over territorial seas and islands.
- Surprise air attacks.
- Defence against deliberately limited attacks into Chinese territory.
- Punitive counter-attacks launched by China into enemy territory to "oppose invasion. Protect sovereignty, or to uphold justice and dispel threats".

Underpinning the new professionalism of the PLA is the new doctrine of "active defence" (*jiji fangyu*) that seeks to conduct "people's war under modern conditions" but is better understood as "local wars under hi-tech conditions" (*gaojishu tiaojian xia de jubu zhanzheng*). The 'active defence' doctrine calls for integrated, deep strikes—a concentration of superior firepower that is to be utilised to destroy the opponent's retaliatory capabilities through pre-emptive strikes employing long-range artillery, short-range ballistic missiles

(SRBMs) and precision guided munitions. David Shambaugh has written:[17] "Rather than conducting a 'people's war' (a strategy to 'lure the enemy in deep' into one's own territory), the PLA doctrine of 'active defence' calls for forward positioning, frontier defence, engagement of the enemy at or over the border and potential engagement in conflict beyond China's immediate periphery. Compared with China's historically reactive stance of luring the adversary deep inside and destroying him through strategic defence, this doctrine is essentially pro-active and seeks to take the battle into enemy territory." The doctrine emphasises the effective use of advanced equipment wielded by elite units, with a focus on joint operations. The overall aim in this "limited war under hi-tech conditions" doctrine is to disrupt the enemy's combat forces and logistics but not annihilate him so as to bring about a negotiated end to the conflict or dictate terms if possible. Beijing has identified five likely limited war scenarios: military conflict with neighbouring countries in a limited region; military conflict on territorial waters; undeclared air attack by enemy countries; territorial defence in a limited military operation; and, punitive offensive with a minor incursion into a neighbouring country.

The new doctrine and the strategy and tactics associated with it have been influenced by the lessons of Gulf War I in 1991 and the Iraq War of 2003. Both these wars have been extensively studied by Chinese scholars and military analysts. The doctrine demands the creation of a capability to project force across China's borders through rapid deployment, conventional SRBMs and cruise missiles, information warfare, electronic warfare, precision-guided munitions, night fighting capabilities and other advanced military technologies. The building of these capabilities, in turn, drives procurement and defence production policies, the command and control structures and training. The present doctrine represents a Chinese adaptation of the United States' (US) revolution in military affairs (RMA) concepts to achieve victory by reorganising the military to exploit rapid advances in technology. The PLA has appreciated that modern hi-tech war, whether defensive or offensive, generally has limited political goals and it is necessary to achieve political objectives as quickly as possible and with the minimum possible casualties. This is to be achieved by:[18] gaining the initiative by striking first; achieving victory with one strike; and, concentrating China's strength to attack the core of enemy defence.

The new doctrine is also more assertive than previously and is not bound by any restrictions to confine and limit future conflict to within China's national boundaries. China claims that it has only peaceful intentions and does not believe in launching aggression and that it fights wars only to defend its sovereignty and territorial integrity. According to China's White Papers on national defence, active defence is a defensive military strategy. However, it is clear from Chinese writings that the major characteristics of active defence are distinctly offensive in nature. The PLA publication *The Study of Campaigns (Zhanyi Xue)* published in 2000, highlights this offensive approach:[19] "While strategically the guideline is active defence, in military campaigns, though, the emphasis is placed on taking the initiative in 'active offense'. Only in this way the strategic objectives of 'active defence' can be realised."

Informationisation as a Tool in Military Strategy

Early in the 21st century, based on recent conflicts, the Central Military Commission (CMC) called for a detailed study of the concept of "people's war under informationisation conditions." Ka Po Ng, an associate professor at Aichi Bunkyo University, Japan, sums up the new concept in these words:[20] "...What the PLA is prepared to fight is a people's war in the form of a "local war under high-tech conditions" with increasing attention to the application of information technology." It emerges clearly that China is engaged in assessing the implications of information technology and knowledge-based warfare on the modern battlefield.

The PLA expects to fight the next war under conditions of what it calls "informationisation" or "informationalisation".[21] In the White Paper on national defence issued in 2004, informationisation has been explained only in general terms:[22] "To adapt itself to the changes both in the international strategic situation and the national security environment and rise to the challenges presented by the RMA worldwide, China adheres to the military strategy of active defence and works to speed up the RMA with Chinese characteristics."

PLA analysts have called the ongoing RMA an "informationised military revolution".[23] It emerges that informationisation "clearly relates to the PLA's ability to adopt information technologies to command, intelligence, training and weapon systems. This would include broad investment in new automatic command systems linked by fibre-optic Internet, satellite and new high-frequency digital radio systems... The PLA can also contest the information battle space with its new space-based, airborne, naval and ground-based surveillance and intelligence gathering systems and its new anti-satellite, anti-radar, electronic warfare and information warfare systems... there is increasing 'information content' for new PLA weapons as it moves to link new space, airborne and ELINT sensors to missile, air, naval and ground-based 'shooters' to enable all its services to better use new precision-strike weapons."[24]

According to the 2004 White Paper, "In its modernisation drive, the PLA takes informationalisation as its orientation and strategic focus." The PLA has adopted what it calls a "double historical mission" and a "leapfrog development strategy"—accelerating military informationisation while undergoing mechanisation.[25]

The denial of information, strategic deception and the achievement of psychological surprise have for long been an integral part of Chinese military doctrine. The Chinese find information warfare (IW) extremely attractive as they view it as an asymmetric tool that will enable them to overcome their relative backwardness in military hardware. The Chinese are devoting considerable time and energy to perfecting the techniques of IW to target the rapidly modernising Western armed forces that are becoming increasingly more dependent on the software that runs computer networks and modern communications. In Chinese thinking, IW presents a level playing field for projecting power and prevailing upon the adversary in future wars. However, it has not been possible to ascertain from open public sources whether IW is fully integrated with the doctrine of people's war under modern conditions or if it is still treated as a separate but complementary pattern of war (*zhanzheng xingtai*). There is also some confusion created by the use of the term informationised warfare (*xinxihua zhanzheng*) instead of IW (*xinxi zhanzheng*).[26] However, there is no ambiguity in the manner in which the Chinese view information operations:[27]

- Intelligence operations, which include intelligence reconnaissance and protection.
- Command and control operations to disrupt enemy information flow and weaken his C2 capability while protecting one's own.
- Electronic warfare by seizing the electromagnetic initiative through electronic attack, electronic protection and electronic warfare support.
- Targeting enemy computer systems and networks to damage and destroy critical machines and networks and the data stored on them.
- Physical destruction of enemy sources like information infrastructure such as C4ISR through the application of firepower.

The Chinese call their pursuit of information warfare and other hi-tech means to counter Washington's overwhelmingly superior conventional military capabilities "acupuncture warfare", a term that first surfaced in a 1997 PLA National Defence University publication entitled "On Commanding Warfighting Under High-Tech Conditions".[28] Acupuncture warfare (also called "paralysis warfare"[29] or "unrestricted warfare") is described as "Paralysing the enemy by attacking the weak link of his command, control, communications and information as if hitting his acupuncture point in *kung fu* combat." Acupuncture warfare is a form of asymmetrical warfare that takes its bearings from the teachings of Sun Tzu, China's pre-eminent military strategist from the 5th century BC. For quite some time now the PLA has been simulating computer virus attacks in its military exercises.

According to a US Congressional Research Service report entitled "Cyberwarfare", authored by Steve Hildreth, China is developing a strategic information warfare unit called "Net Force" to neutralise the military capabilities of technologically superior adversaries.[30] This new information warfare unit will "wage combat through computer networks to manipulate enemy information systems spanning spare parts deliveries to fire control and guidance systems." Though the PLA's research into the theoretical aspects of information warfare is fairly advanced, it does not appear to have developed a coordinated and integrated information warfare doctrine as yet.

Chong-Pin Lin, Vice Chairman of Taiwan's Mainland Affairs Council, has said that Beijing is re-directing its emphasis away from nuclear deterrence to this new asymmetrical strategy and its "overarching purpose is to deter the United States from intervening around China's peripheries and to seize Taiwan with minimum bloodshed and destruction."[31] In another five to 10 years China will develop depth and sophistication in its understanding and handling of information warfare techniques and information operations. With Indian society becoming increasingly dependent on automated data processing and vast computer networks, India will also become extremely vulnerable to such information warfare techniques. The fact that it can be practiced from virtually any place on the earth even during peacetime makes acupuncture warfare even more diabolical. India can ill-afford to ignore this new challenge to its security.

Defence analysts Timperlake and Triplett have written that economic, political and social systems are essentially unprotected against Chinese information warfare attack. In their view, China has adopted a comprehensive strategy to further its information warfare plans:[32]

- Information warfare has the support of the top PLA brass.
- The PLA's best strategists and defence scientists have had extensive open discussions about information warfare.
- The PLA is conducting military exercises in information warfare.
- It is expanding its already strong signals intelligence (SIGINT) capability in Cuba.
- The PLA is buying the hardware necessary. (As supercomputers require huge capital investments, a strong political and financial commitment is implied.)

- The Chinese are recruiting scientists and technicians.
- The PLA is building related weapons (high-powered microwave weapons).

To prepare itself for a conflict with an RMA-ready opponent, China's military thinkers recommend that China must:[33] close the information gap; network all forces; attack the enemy's C3I to paralyse it; use directed energy weapons; use computer viruses; use submarine-launched munitions; use anti-satellite weapons; use forces to prevent a logistics build-up; use special operations raids.

Compared with China's historically reactive stance of luring the enemy in deep and destroying him through strategic defence, the present doctrine is essentially pro-active and seeks to take the battle into enemy territory. It also strives to achieve surprise in a pro-active manner that is demonstrated by new "quick-strike" tactics. The aim is to catch the enemy unprepared in order to inflict substantial damage on strategic targets and disrupt logistics to gain psychological ascendancy. While the land frontier is expected to continue to generate some local tensions, the Central Military Commission (CMC) has identified space and the oceans as the new areas where future conflict might take place.

PLA's Military Capabilities

Military capabilities the world over are evolving in line with emerging threats and challenges and the changing nature of warfare. With the probability of large-scale conventional conflict receding rapidly, contemporary conflict is becoming increasingly asymmetric. The asymmetric character of contemporary conflict is challenging conventional thinking and demanding fresh responses. General Rupert Smith has identified six key trends that define modern warfare:[34] The growing role of non-state actors as well as multinational forces as combatants; looking for creative new uses for old weapons; emphasis on force protection rather than using force at any cost; the prolonged nature of modern wars; a new focus on winning the hearts and minds of people; and, a shift from absolute objectives to more flexible ones. He writes that in the Clausewitzian trinity (army, state and people), the balance between the three has changed. "There was a time when armies dominated — as they still do in the country of warlords; later, states were able to command the complete obedience of their people. Now it is the people who are in charge and the strategic objective is their hearts and minds."[35] China is no exception to the rule except that its government is relatively less concerned about the people's thinking on military issues.

For almost two decades now, the PLA has been pursuing a systematic plan to downsize its regular army and transfer some of the personnel to reserves and paramilitary forces. In December 2005 the PLA completed another round of downsizing, reducing personnel by some 200,000. This brought the size of the PLA to about 2.3 million, according to official statistics. The inclusion of the paramilitary People's Armed Police (which has upwards of 1.5 million personnel) and reserves (800,000) increases the total figure for active, reserve, and paramilitary units to over 4.6 million. The 2004 Defense White Paper also declares that China can draw upon more than 10 million organised militia members.

The People's Liberation Army's 2.25-million-strong force makes it the largest in the world, in terms of number of troops (3.25 million if active paramilitary personnel are included).[36] The ground forces comprising 1.6 million personnel (about 70 per cent of the total force) are divided into 7 Military Regions. The regular forces of the ground forces consist of 18 group armies, which are corps-size combined arms units with 30,000-65,000 personnel each. The group armies contain nine armoured divisions, three mechanised infantry divisions, 24 motorised infantry divisions, 15 infantry divisions, two amphibious assault divisions, one mechanised infantry brigade, 12 armoured brigades, seven artillery divisions, 14 artillery brigades, 19 anti-aircraft artillery missile brigades, and 10 army aviation (helicopter) regiments. In addition, three airborne divisions are manned by the PLAAF. The PLAN has two multi-arm marine brigades.[37] The PAP is organised into 14 mobile divisions, 31 provisional/municipal internal security general corps, and 23 provisional/municipal border defence general corps.[38] Srikanth Kondapalli cites Ku Guisheng, Deputy Director of Education at the National Defence University, Beijing, as having said that the PLA should undertake reforms in four fields:[39] downsizing and rationalising force structures; integrating and 'modularising' troop composition; making the command system network-based and responsive in real-time; integrating and 'informationising' support systems.

The PLA Navy's aspirations to acquire blue water capability and to eventually reach out to the Indian Ocean are well known. It is engaged in transformation aimed at information-based platforms with "stealth, 'modularisation' and intelligence-based capabilities". "The concept of a navy is no longer the traditional one of seaborne fighting strength but rather one of a comprehensive military service with high concentrations of technology and knowledge and possessing air, surface, sub-surface and amphibious strengths."[40] Recent Chinese naval operations included an "intrusion" of a Han-class nuclear submarine in Japanese territorial waters. Amphibious landings are being increasingly practiced by the Marine Corps, as witnessed during exercise "Peace Mission 2005" with Russia held in the last week of August 2005.[41]

The PLA Air Force (PLAAF) is gradually moving away from quantity to quality. It has already acquired and is now manufacturing SU-27 (J-11) fighter aircraft and has begun the process of obtaining SU-30MKK multi-role fighters from Russia as well as air-to-air re-fuelling capabilities. At the same time, it has been upgrading its electronic support measure (ESM) capabilities and acquiring beyond visual range air-to-air missiles. Plans are also afoot to acquire AWACS capability in the near future. The PLAAF has also increased its aerial footprint and Chinese fighters have been flying farther into the South China Sea.[42] However, the PLAAF still suffers from obsolescence, lack of adequate command and control capability and poor training standards and has a long way to go before it can be called a truly modern air force with RMA capabilities.

The PLA Army has been actively engaged in downsizing its regular and para-military forces, increasing the number of rapid deployment units and in improving mobility and logistics support capability, while simultaneously upgrading the ability to undertake all-weather operations, improve air defence capability and institute modern command and control systems. The PLA Army is in the process of upgrading one division in each military region to the status of a rapid deployment division. China's simultaneous efforts to gradually upgrade the PLA Navy to 'blue water' status and to acquire mid-air refuelling capability, deep penetration strike and strategic lift transport aircraft for the PLA Air Force are also significant. All these endeavours aim to create a modern fighting force capable of undertaking swift offensive operations in areas away from China's borders. According to a US Department of Defence report, the ultimate goal of the Communist giant is "parity in economic, political and military strength with the world's leading powers by the middle of the next (21st) century."[43]

Recent developments in the field of modernisation of China's Strategic Forces hinge around the miniaturisation of warheads, progress towards developing MIRV capabilities and further improvement in the design of ballistic missiles using solid-fuel propellants. The development of the DF-31A ICBM that can target any city in the US from the Chinese mainland is reported to have been completed. China has also stepped up its plans for the development of a ballistic missile system and is in the process of improving the accuracy of its land attack cruise missiles to about 5-10 metres.[44]

Some military activities during the last five years are noteworthy. A

Chinese Song class submarine that had obviously been tailing a US carrier battle group chose to make its presence known by surfacing close to the USS Kitty Hawk off Okinawa in November 2006.[45] The Chinese are also developing modern ground-to-ground and ground-to-air missiles to give shape to a new "anti-access" strategy aimed at countering the US ability to operate near its borders. China's new S-300PMU2, a surface-to-air missile with a 150-km range, will allow it to engage aircraft flying over Taiwan. This will enable China to shore up its air defences against US aircraft aiding Taiwan in a future confrontation. All of these apparently belligerent activities are indicative of an emerging China that is becoming increasingly more comfortable with flaunting its military power.

Expeditionary Ambitions The PLA's expeditionary forces include three airborne divisions, two amphibious infantry divisions, two marine brigades, about seven special operations groups, and one regimental-size reconnaissance element in the Second Artillery. Besides training for an invasion of Taiwan, these forces are being prepared for employment to seize or regain the Spratly and Paracel Islands in the South China Sea and, in future, to guarantee China's uninterrupted access to the sea lanes through the Malacca Straits for oil and gas supplies and maritime trade. At present, Chinese access to the Malacca Straits depends on US acquiescence as the US Navy dominates and controls the oceans outside China's territorial waters. As freedom of the seas has become a fundamental national interest for China, it would prefer to safeguard vitally important sea lanes on its own rather than be dependent on the goodwill of another major power, which it sees as inimical to its interests. It can be said with a fair degree of certainty that China's military buildup is broadening the reach of its forces in Asia and poses a long-term challenge not only to Taiwan but also to other military forces operating in the Pacific and to regional powers such as India and Japan.

Domination of Space On January 11, 2007, China launched an anti-satellite rocket that intercepted and physically destroyed an ageing Feng Yun 1C weather satellite belonging to China in low earth orbit in outer space.[46] It appeared to have been a kinetic strike that physically hit the satellite and shattered it into thousands of pieces, spraying the space around with a huge cloud of debris. Though this spectacular event cannot be classified as a statement of intent, it was certainly a statement of capability. It sends out a clear signal that China will thwart the growing US desire to deploy ballistic missile defences by asymmetric means. Chinese anti-satellite capabilities have been suspected for many years. It has now emerged quite clearly that China is engaged in developing space warfare capabilities and has acquired the expertise necessary to destroy satellites in low earth orbit where most military reconnaissance satellites are normally deployed. It would be reasonable to deduce that China will use this capability to offset its conventional asymmetry with the US and its allies that are so heavily dependent on space-based C4ISR for their military operations.

Assessment of Capabilities and Implications for India

The PLA Army is still very largely a force that is rooted firmly in the "people's war" mindset of the past. Its weapons and equipment are still primitive by modern standards and it is decades away from becoming a truly capable force that can stand its ground against a modern military machine organised and equipped with genuine state-of-the-art RMA capabilities like the US Army. Integrated joint operations and amphibious warfare are still alien concepts that will take years of painstaking effort to successfully absorb and implement. The mere acquisition of modern technology is never enough. It is much harder to develop and adapt the necessary doctrinal changes and implement new tactics, techniques and procedures for the optimum employment of technological advances in hardware.

At the same time, fields such as information warfare and command and control warfare are new and though the West has a head start, it is certainly not light years ahead. Also, these fields are dominated by software superiority rather than a hardware edge and software excellence is something that China can hope to attain fairly quickly since it is not dependent so much on imports. Hence, it can be predicted with a reasonable degree of assurance that China will soon catch up with the West in these new military technologies and close the overall gap. By about 2015-20, China may be expected to gain a formidable conventional military capability that will assume even greater significance when the nuclear warheads of the US and Russia are reduced under START III and perhaps other disarmament treaties to levels close to the Chinese warheads. China's much larger conventional forces will then give it a superpower status to rival that of the US.

Though China does not at present have the technological capability and industrial capacity to translate many of its ambitions into reality, it is undeniable that there is a clear sense of purpose and confidence in its ability to gradually close the gap with the West. Besides Sun Tzu and their other military thinkers, the Chinese are well-schooled in the teachings of Clausewitz who emphasised that a good commander must apply his maximum against the enemy's minimum where the enemy least expects it. It is reasonable to assume that the Chinese would follow that course in waging asymmetric warfare against their adversaries to overcome their own technological shortcomings while they are still experimenting with new technologies. Chinese technological ambitions must be analysed and carefully evaluated to assess their impact on India's security. Professional assessments must be made to deduce realistic time frames in which these ambitions may be turned into reality and suitable action must be taken to counter these advancements effectively.

The PLA Army has been actively engaged in downsizing its para-military forces, increasing the number of rapid deployment units and in improving mobility and logistics support capability, while simultaneously upgrading the ability to undertake all-weather operations, improve air defence capability and institute modern command and control systems. China's simultaneous efforts to gradually upgrade the PLA Navy to 'blue water' status and to acquire mid-air refuelling capability, deep penetration strike and strategic lift transport aircraft for the PLA Air Force are also significant. All these endeavours aim to create a modern fighting force capable of undertaking swift offensive operations in areas away from China's borders. According to a US Department of Defence report, the ultimate goal of the Communist giant is "parity in economic, political and military strength with the world's leading powers by the middle of the next (21st) century."[47]

The Gulf Wars of 1991 and 2003 have convinced Chinese military strategists that the war of the future is most likely to be localised, fought to achieve limited political objectives and won by whichever side is better able to concentrate high-technology forces at some distance from the national borders in a decisive strike.[48] Another 1998 Pentagon report to the US Congress highlighted that the present Chinese doctrine, though defensive in nature, requires the PLA to develop a limited offensive and force projection capability, including the option of a pre-emptive military strike.[49] The report also brought out the PLA's exceptional interest in information warfare at the operational and tactical levels of war in recent years, as also its belief in electronic warfare as the fourth dimension of ground, naval and aerial combat.

China's Communist rulers are well versed in the art of *realpolitik* and understand quite well that the use of force to achieve political objectives is always a conceivable option. Beijing has often used force in the past, although primarily to counter perceived threats to territorial borders.[50] This vital aspect cannot be ignored while carrying out a threat assessment for the first few decades of the 21st century. China's new strategy focuses on fighting limited, short duration conflicts along China's periphery, including economically important maritime areas. Such concerns call for a smaller, more versatile and mobile military, with a markedly improved yet limited capability to operate beyond China's territorial boundaries.[51]

In the ultimate analysis, a pragmatic threat assessment must take note of "capabilities" and not of "intentions" as the latter are subject to change. China loses no opportunity to emphasise that its defence policy is defensive in nature, that China will neither try to occupy an inch of foreign territory nor pose a threat to any country, that China will never seek hegemony, that China's prosperity will only benefit world peace and stability, that the threat from China to India is totally groundless and that China is now fully engaged in its economic construction. It is with this aim in view, say Chinese officials that China is attempting to consolidate her diplomatic ties with neighbouring countries, including India, and is also attempting to develop an understanding on the global plane, including with the US. All this seemingly points to a stable and peace loving China stepping gently into the 21st century as a responsible nation.

However, concurrently, China has embarked upon the consolidation and development of her military capabilities and this fact needs to be vectored into India's national security calculations. As against inflation and Rupee-Dollar parity adjusted average annual decline of more than 10 per cent in the Indian defence budget over the last 10 years of the 20th century, the Chinese defence expenditure showed a net increase of 12 to 20 per cent per year over the same period. China's defence expenditure for 1998-99 was approximately US $ 39.8 billion (Yuan 334.32 billion)[52] and is expected to be US $ 91.5 billion during the year 2011-12. The US Defence Secretary, Donald Rumsfeld, had estimated that China's defence expenditure was likely to exceed US $100 billion in 2005.[53] It is also significant that unlike India's defence budget, which is maintenance intensive, the sub-allotment in China's defence budget is fairly balanced between modernisation and maintenance.

In this context, aspirations to gradually upgrade the PLA Navy to a 'Blue Water' status, to acquire mid-air refuelling capability, deep penetration strike and strategic lift transport aircraft for the PLA Air Force, are relevant. The PLA Army has also been engaged in increasing the number of rapid deployment units and in improving mobility and logistics support capability, while simultaneously upgrading the ability to undertake all-weather operations, improve air defence capability and institute modern command and control systems. All these endeavours aim to create a modern fighting force capable of undertaking swift offensive operations in areas away from China's borders. All the indicators point to a growing military gap between India and China. While at present the gap is quantitative rather than qualitative, unless immediate steps are taken by the government to enhance the Indian armed forces' combat potential and the technology base significantly, the present gap will soon become a qualitative one as well and will become unbridgeable.

Though mountain warfare is generally perceived to be less technology-dependent than war in the plains, India's recent experience during the Kargil conflict bears witness to the force multiplier impact of hi-tech weapons and equipment even in the mountains. Concentrated artillery firepower had played a major role in destroying the intruders' *sangars* (improvised bunkers) and in eventually breaking the Pakistan Army's will to fight through relentless bombardment. Had precision guided munitions, long-range rocket launchers like Smerch and high-altitude UAVs been more freely available, the contribution of firepower to the Indian Army's victory would have been still higher by an order of magnitude. In specific terms, India needs to enhance its defence spending and R&D on improving precision strike, C4ISR, information warfare, night fighting, air-to-ground strikes, rapid reaction and special operations capabilities if it is not to be found wanting in another border war with China. As long as the territorial and boundary dispute between India and China is not resolved amicably, a border war, though improbable, cannot be ruled out.

China continues to be in occupation of and lays claims to large areas of Indian territory. An un-delineated LAC and the unresolved territorial dispute are long-term destabilising factors. A border conflict, though improbable, cannot be ruled out. The recurrence of Wangdung type incidents remains likely. The China-Pakistan nexus in the nuclear, missiles and military hardware fields poses both economic and military threats. China's attempts at the strategic encirclement and containment of India are a potential source of competition and rivalry and, perhaps, even conflict. China's growing power and influence in Asia is a strategic challenge for India as, eventually, Indian and Chinese economic interests will clash.

While China professes a policy of peace and friendliness towards India, its deeds clearly indicate a concerted attempt aimed at the strategic encirclement of India. For the last several decades, China has been engaged in efforts to create a ring of anti-Indian influences around India through military and economic assistance programmes to neighbouring countries, combined with complementary diplomacy. Pakistan, Bangladesh, Nepal and Sri Lanka have been assiduously and cleverly cultivated towards this end. China has gained strategic advantage over India by progressively making India's neighbours dependent on her to a large extent for their defence supplies. It has supplied Pakistan with technical assistance in the joint development of the F-7 fighter aircraft and MBT-2000 (Al Khalid). In addition, the Chinese have supplied T-59/T-69/T-85 tanks, heavy artillery guns, anti-aircraft gun systems, SAM and other defence related equipment to Pakistan, Bangladesh and Myanmar. China's supply of critical nuclear technology and M-9 and M-11 missiles to Pakistan has been well documented. China may even have supplied the design of a nuclear warhead to Pakistan.

In recent years, Chinese involvement in Myanmar has escalated substantially. China has also supplied a variety of arms and missiles to Iran and even to Saudi Arabia. While China's direct support for counter insurgency movements in India's north-eastern region has definitely dwindled, China is seeking to keep India strategically 'engaged' through its neighbours. The large-scale supply of cheap small arms (rifles, hand grenades, rocket launchers, pistols, ammunition and even SAM-7 surface to air missiles) to regimes inimical to India is a clever method of indirect involvement as these small arms are eventually supplied by agencies such as the Inter Services Intelligence (ISI) of Pakistan to insurgent groups in Jammu and Kashmir and the north-eastern states of India. The developments in Myanmar are of particular concern as they give the Chinese the potential to deploy their sea power in India's maritime areas of interest, and to eventually directly threaten India's eastern flank. The establishment of a Chinese electronic listening post on the Coco Islands, just off the northern tip of the North Andaman Island and military assistance to the Government of Myanmar to improve and develop naval ports and facilities on the Arakan coast, have been well documented.

It is in India's interest to focus its diplomatic efforts to expedite the delineation of the Line of Actual Control (LAC) on the Indo-Tibetan border and urge China to resolve the territorial and boundary dispute in an early time frame. In conventional weapons and present force levels, the Indian Army has adequate combat capability to defend the border, but not sufficient to deter war. The gap between India and China in overall military potential, particularly the gap in strategic weapons, is increasing rapidly in China's favour. China is also actively engaged in substantially upgrading the military infrastructure in Tibet. The all-weather railway line to Lhasa, being extended further to Shigatse and later to Kathmandu, will enable China to build up rapidly for a future conflict. New roads and military airfields have also been built. Military camps are coming up closer to the border. China has inducted a large number of SRBMs into Tibet and can rapidly induct another 500 to 600 SRBMs for a future conflict by moving them from the coastline opposite

Taiwan. China's erstwhile capability of building up and sustaining 20 to 25 divisions in Tibet over two summer seasons has gone up to 30 to 35 divisions. The PLA's rapid reaction divisions can also significantly enhance its combat potential over a short period of time. As China's military power in Tibet grows further, it will be even less inclined to accept Indian perceptions of the LAC and the boundary.

Another factor of concern to India is the emplacement of Chinese nuclear-tipped missiles in Tibet, reportedly first brought to the Tibetan plateau in 1971.[54] While these missiles may have been targeted against the Soviet Union till recently, the present Russia-China rapprochement would make such targeting illogical. The mere presence of Chinese nuclear-tipped missiles in Tibet poses a direct and most serious threat to India as these missiles (DF-2, DF-3, DF-4 and, possibly, DF-5) are capable of reaching all Indian cities.[55] Beijing has been very effective in hiding details of the number of missiles actually deployed and India is only now acquiring the technological means to track and pinpoint the exact locations of these missiles or any others in the Lanzhou-Chengdu region and at the Datong and Kunming missile bases which may have the potential to reach and target Indian cities. This shortcoming needs to be overcome as early as possible through an Indian military intelligence satellite and by humint means.

India, therefore, needs to build up adequate military capabilities to thwart the threat from China. In the short-term, the requirement is to ensure that there are no violations of the LAC through effective border management while maintaining a robust dissuasive conventional posture. India must step up its diplomatic efforts to seek early resolution of the territorial dispute, particularly the immediate delineation of the LAC physically on ground and map. Efforts to develop military infrastructure in the border areas for the speedy induction of forces need to be stepped up. India must maintain a strong capability to defend island territories in the Bay of Bengal and to safeguard national interests in the Exclusive Economic Zone. Diplomatic efforts to increase India's influence in the CARs, Myanmar, Nepal, Bangladesh and with the ASEAN countries should be pursued vigorously.

The long-term requirement is to match China's strategic challenge in the region and develop a viable military deterrence capability against the use of nuclear and missile weapon systems. Threats posed by nuclear-tipped ballistic missiles cannot be countered by the deployment of land forces and conventional air power alone. Nuclear weapons are best deterred by nuclear weapons and as a logical corollary only missiles can deter missiles. Hence, India must develop, test and operationally induct the Agni-III and Agni-IV

IRBMs so as to be able to upgrade its present strategic posture of 'dissuasion' to one of credible 'deterrence' against China.

Henry Kissinger has written:[56] "China has always dealt with foreign dangers with extraordinary tenacity. It has survived 5,000 years of turbulent history by making patience its weapon and time its ally." There is no reason to believe that China's behaviour in the 21st century will be any different. China is well aware that to achieve its grand strategy it must avoid conflict—particularly with the US—while it is still engaged in its military modernisation. China knows that the abiding lesson of history is that those who have challenged the current hegemons have always failed; those who have cooperated have succeeded. There is an old Chinese saying that a single mountain cannot accommodate two tigers. China takes it for granted that it is destined to dominate the Asian mountain forever. In this quest lie the seeds of future competition and, perhaps, conflict between these two major powers in Asia.

NOTES

1. Michael D. Swaine and Ashley J. Tellis, *Interpreting China's Grand Strategy: Past, Present and Future* (RAND: Santa Monica, CA, 2000), p. 1. (Emphasis in the original).
2. Yang Jiemian, "International Environment and Sino-US Interaction: Strategic Thinking and Policy Planning", *China International Studies*, Winter 2005, p. 61.
3. *Military Power of the People's Republic of China* (Office of the Secretary of Defense, United States Department of Defence: Annual Report to Congress, 2002). The report explains "shi" as the "alignment of forces," the "propensity of things," or the "potential born of disposition," that only a skilled strategist can exploit to ensure victory over a superior force. Similarly, only a sophisticated assessment by an adversary can recognise the potential exploitation of "*shi*".
4. Swaine and Tellis, n. 1, p. x.
5. *Military Power of the People's Republic of China* (Office of the Secretary of Defense, United States Department of Defence: Annual Report to Congress, 2006).
6. Khadang Oh Hassig, "Northeast Asian Security Environment", Defence Threat Reduction Agency Study, August 22, 2001.
7. Swaine and Tellis, n. 1, p. 112.
8. Ibid.
9. Yoichi Funabashi, "China is Preparing for Peaceful Ascendancy", International Herald Tribune, December 30, 2003. Also see Note 10.
10. Li Qinggong, "A Review of and Prospects for the World Military Situation", *International Strategic Studies*, January 2000, pp. 29-33, cited by David Shambaugh, n. 12, p. 295. For other PLA views, see David Shambaugh, pp. 295-297.
11. *China's National Defence in 2006*, White Paper on national defence published by the Government of the People's Republic of China on December 30, 2006.

12. Ibid.
13. Personal interview with the author on April 30, 2007.
14. Kenneth W. Allen, Glenn Krumel and Jonathan D. Pollack, *China's Air Force Enters the 21st Century* (Santa Monica, CA: RAND, 1995), p. 24.
15. John Wilson Lewis and Xue Litai, "China's Search for a Modern Air Force", *International Security*, Vol. 24, No. 1 (Summer 1999), p. 78.
16. Ibid, p. 29.
17. David Shambaugh, "China's Security and Military Policy and Potential for CBMs in the Region", *Asian Security Series*, Henry L. Stimson Centre, Washington, D.C., December 1996.
18. US DoD report to Congress Pursuant to the FY2000 National Defense Authorization Act, http://www.defenselink.mil/news/Jun2000/china06222000.htm
19. United States Department of Defence, *Annual report to Congress: The Military Power of the People's Republic of China 2004*, Section II: Trends in Military Strategy, Doctrine and Training – China's Military Strategy.
20. Ka Po Ng, *Interpreting China's Military Power: Doctrine Makes Readiness"* (Abingdon, Oxon: Frank Cass, 2005), p. 21.
21. Western governments and analysts are using both the terms "informationisation" and "informationalisation" inter-changeably. It has not been possible to get an exact equivalent to the corresponding Chinese phrase from an authoritative source. From the point of view of language aesthetics and phonetics, the term informationisation is preferred here.
22. *China's National Defence in 2006*, White Paper on national defence published by the Government of the People's Republic of China, p. 5.
23. Zhou Fangyin, "The Impact of Information Revolution upon Military Affairs and Security", *Contemporary International Relations,* 7 (2001), p. 28.
24. "China's Military Power: An Assessment from Open Sources", Testimony of Richard D. Fisher, Jr., International Assessment and Strategy Centre, before the Armed Services Committee of the US House of Representatives, July 27, 2005; www.strategycenter.net.
25. n. 20, p. 109.
26. n. 20, p. 110.
27. n. 20, p. 111.
28. Barbara Opall-Rome, "PLA Pursues Acupuncture Warfare", *Defense News*, Springfield, Virginia (USA), March 1, 1999.
29. "According to the Taiwanese Ministry of National Defence, China is shifting from deterrence-based strategy to pre-emptive strike strategy… 'Paralysis warfare features web-based information warfare, saturation ballistic missile attacks, joint precision strikes and seizure of the enemy's capital city by special operation units… Such tactics will become major options for the Chinese military in its choice of modes of modes of attack…" Srikanth Kondapalli, *A Great Leap Forward Modernisation: China's Armed Forces in 2003"*, Centre for China Studies, National Chengchi University, Taiwan, 2005, p. 27, cited from Brian Hsu, "China Developing 'Paralysis Warfare", Taipei Times, October 8, 2003, FBIS-CHI-2003-1008, October 10, 2003.

30. Jason Sherman, "Report: China Developing Force to Tackle Information Warfare", *Defense News,* November 27, 2000.
31. Robert Karniol, "Power to the People", *Jane's Defence Weekly,* Surrey (UK), July 12, 2000.
32. Edward Timperlake and William C. Triplett III, *Red Dragon Rising: Communist China's Military Threat to America* (Washington, D.C.: Regnery Publishing Inc., 1999).
33. J. S. Bajwa, *Modernisation of the PLA: Gauging its Latent Future Potential,* (New Delhi, Lancer Publishers, 2002), p. 216. (Cited from Michael Pillsbury, "PLA Capabilities in the 21st Century: How does China Assess its Future Security Needs?" Article in Larry M. Wortzel, ed. *The Chinese Armed Forces in the 21st Century,* pp 113-114.
34. Rupert Smith, *The Utility of Force: the Art of War in the Modern World,* (London: Allen Lane, 2005), reviewed by C. Raja Mohan, "Ways to War", *Indian Express,* June 18, 2006.
35. Robert Cooper, "The Utility of Force by General Rupert Smith", *Sunday Times,* September 18, 2005, http://www.timesonline.co.uk/article/0,,23112-1779750,00.html
36. http://en.wikipedia.org/wiki/People's_Liberation_Army
37. Ibid.
38. Ibid.
39. Srikanth Kondapalli, *A Great Leap Forward Modernisation: China's Armed Forces in 2003",* Centre for China Studies, National Chengchi University, Taiwan, 2005, p. 27, cited from Ku Guisheng, "The New Change in Ml Affairs Calls for the Renewal of the Organisational Set-up of China's Military", *Liaowang,* July 28, 2003, FBIS-CHI-2003-0805, August 15, 2003.
40. Ibid, cited from Zhong Hailin, "Naval Development Trends of the New Century", *Liaowang,* July 21, 2003, FBIS-CHI-2003-0730, October 6, 2003.
41. "Russia-China Joint Military Exercises", Worldpress.org, http://www.worldpress.org/Asia/2138.cfm, accessed October 30, 2005.
42. Ann Scott Tyson, "Chinese Buildup Seen as Threat to Region", Washington Post, July 20, 2005.
43. Anil K. Joseph, "PLA to Project Chinese Power in Asia: Pentagon", *Times of India,* December 8, 1998.
44. Kondapalli, n. 39.
45. "China Sub Stalked US Fleet", *Washington Times,* November 13, 2006. http://www.washtimes.com/national/20061113-121539-3317r.htm
46. For an analysis from an Indian point of view, see "ASAT Test and China's Strategic Ambitions", *Strategic Comments,* Institute for Defence Studies and Analyses, New Delhi, February 13, 2007, http://www.idsa.in/publications/stratcomments/JagannathPanda120207.htm
47. Anil K. Joseph, "PLA to Project Chinese Power in Asia: Pentagon", *Times of India,* December 8, 1998.
48. Ron Montaperto, "China as a Military Power", *Strategic Forum,* (Washington: Institute for National Strategic Studies, Number 56, December 1995).

49. T V Parsuram, "China Building Pre-emptive Military Strike Capability", *Observer of Business and Politics,* 5 November, 1998.
50. Michael D. Swaine, "Don't Demonise China", *Washington Post,* 18 May, 1997.
51. Ibid.
52. Jasjit Singh and Rahul Roy-Chaudhury, "Trends in Defence Expenditure", *Asian Strategic Review 1998-99,* (New Delhi: Institute for Defence Studies and Analyses, November 1999), p. 45.
53. Donald Rumsfeld, "Rumsfeld says China Lying about Army", *Hindustan Times,* October 19, 2005.
54. W P S Sidhu, "India's Security and Nuclear Risk Reduction measures", (Washington: *The Henry L. Stimson Centre Report,* November 1998).
55. Ramesh Chandran, "New Chinese Missiles Target India", *Times of India,* 11 July 1997.
56. Henry Kissinger, "Outrage is not a Policy", *Newsweek,* Tokyo, November 10, 1997.

2

CHINA'S GRAND STRATEGY

SRIKANTH KONDAPALLI

We must enhance independent innovation capabilities and build an innovation-type country. This is the core of the national development strategy and the key to increasing comprehensive national strength.

—***President Hu Jintao*** at the 17th Party Congress in 2007[1]

INTRODUCTION

After the United States, China today is increasingly focusing on grand strategic principles. This appears to be obvious as China had become the second largest economy in the world and despite reports about slow down due to the Euro Zone crisis and the effects of global financial crisis specifically on China's exports, several stakeholders in China have been emphasising on grand strategy. Broadly, the major drivers in China's grand strategy today are enhancing its comprehensive national power (*zonghe guoli* -CNP), protecting its minimalist aspects of state identity (viz., its territorial claims and sovereignty aspects),[2] jockeying for great power status (*daguo xintai*) and retaining its strategic autonomy in the international system. In trying to achieve these goals China had made concerted efforts to seize "strategic opportunities" in the international system and implemented the four modernisation programmes in agriculture, industry, science and technology and defence and followed three and then five pillar international strategy of evolving relations with major powers, neighbouring countries, developing countries, multilateralism and soft power as reflected in the Communist Party congress reports.

While China had not issued any explicit grand strategic outline of its current and future course of action domestically and internationally, several recent pronouncements by the Chinese leadership and other stakeholders indicate that certain interpretations could be made of these statements. Initially, as the Common Programme of September 1949 and subsequently the four constitutions (till 1982, and since amended) indicated China's objectives domestically are to consolidate the Communist Party's rule in the country and enhance substantially GDP figures. Although this blueprint had substantially altered—given the political movements related to Great Leap Forward and Cultural Revolution- a common threat among these "two line" struggles indicated to the relevance, nay centrality, of the Communist Party's rule as well as the necessity for furthering the agricultural and industrial output, while at the same time protecting perceived claims on Tibet, Xinjiang, Inner Mongolia and Taiwan, Hong Kong and Macau issues.

In the 1980s, Deng Xiaoping emphasised on "economic development at the centre" and advocated "hiding capabilities and biding for time" [*taoguang yanghui*].[3] Several Chinese premiers and presidents had mentioned that the GDP figures would be quadrupled. As President Hu Jintao mentioned in his address to the Bo Ao Forum for Asia in April 2004, the Chinese government intends to "quadruple the 2000 GDP to 4 trillion US dollars with a per capita GDP of 3,000 US dollars".[4] As the 16th Chinese Communist Party (CCP) in 2002 and reiterated by the 17th Party Congress in 2007, further emphasised, China's goal is to build a "well-off society" [*xiaokang shehui*] by 2020—that of reaching the socio-economic standards of the developed western European countries. All these are to convert the nation into a "rich country and strong army" [*fuguo qiangbing*].[5] To some extent these were met—not only were Hong Kong and Macau united under China in 1997 and 1999 respectively, but also that the GDP had been increased to an estimated $4.6 trillion in 2009—making China as the third largest economy after the United States and Japan. Next year, China displaced Japan in these economic figures as the second largest economy with nearly $6 trillion in GDP. Chinese government statistics indicated that, despite the global financial meltdown in 2008-09, China in 2009 was able to maintain 8.7 percent economic growth rate and exported $2 trillion worth of goods (while Germany exported $1.17 trillion). Also, surging exports contributed to the enhancement in the coffers of China—estimated at more than $2.2 trillion by 2009 and $3.2 trillion by mid-2011. Militarily as well, China made significant progress and with the $78 billion in official defence budget allocations in 2010 and $112 billion in 2012 it becomes the largest spender in Asia, next only to the United States.

Internationally, China had emphasised, for a long time in the past, on minimalist foreign policy goals of stressing and protecting its perceived sovereignty and territorial integrity and maintaining its perspective. As a consequence, it was only after Taiwan was displaced from the United Nations in 1971 that the People's Republic of China (PRC) was able to take its "right full" place at this international forum with veto power. Considerable diplomatic pressure was mounted on Hong Kong, Macau, Tibet, Xinjiang and Inner Mongolian issues as well. Also, foreign policy was made to serve the national strategy of economic development—by attracting foreign direct investment, technology and sustaining exports. However, as a consequence of the rise of China in hard and soft power aspects, new approaches are noticed in China's external responses that point towards moving into maximalist foreign policy perspectives, viz., active role in international political and economic institutions, "Beijing Consensus", G-2, etc. These provide scope for the flowering of more articulate China's grand strategy formulations in the future.[6]

This paper analyses the main strands in the Chinese debates on China's grand strategy, its rise in the recent two decades, and argues that although China's sights are now set at the strategic levels and it has been concertedly preparing for the realisation of "strategic opportunities", its ability to realise these goals are likely to be challenged by rising countries in the region, in addition to the US. Nevertheless, a few caveats are in order. While the concept of grand strategy originated in the US,[7] and while very few Chinese historically delved on such subjects with the exception of some Chinese scholars in the last decade, a few Chinese concepts come closer to this phenomenon, viz., "grand strategy" (*da zhanlue*), great power diplomacy (*daguo waijiao*) strategy (*zhanlue*), etc.[8] Secondly, it appears that the Chinese discourse on the subject has similar themes as in the western literature, although several Chinese still consider that they have to further develop the theoretical contours of such a phenomenon.[9] In this sense, as a developing country, China is yet to unveil full-fledged and comprehensive grand strategic formulations and can be said that this is still in the making.[10]

As a country which insists on learning from the ancient strategies, China is legion in attracting global attention in terms of grand strategy, although as a relatively developing country in the recent period, it is still in the process of unveiling major aspects of such a strategy.[11] In the pre-modern and modern periods, several Chinese have indicated to their interest in grand strategy, although largely not cohesive and 'grand' in scale. Thus, Sun Zi in the sixth century BC is credited to have triggered the Chinese minds on overcoming the adversaries through strategy and without using force. Wei Yuan, in the light of the battering with which China was subjected by the western powers during the late Qing dynasty period, had proposed principles for the rejuvenation of the country. The Hundred Days of reform of 1898 proved to be inconclusive in the fast changing fortunes of the empire. Likewise, the May Fourth Movement, while galvanized several sections of the population, proved inconclusive. Dr Sun Yat-sen, considered by both CCP and the Kuomintang (KMT) as their founding father, proposed Three Principles of People's Livelihood (with nationalism democracy and livelihood), which appeared comprehensive solutions for those times. Subsequently, the country became a victim of the Japanese inroads and civil war, which forbid any grand strategy formulations. After the People's Republic of China (PRC) was established in October 1949, conditions were conducive for such strategies, although the country was soon drawn into wars with the United States in the Korean Peninsula (1951-53), with India (1962), the then Soviet Union (1969) and with Vietnam (1979), even as intermittent skirmishes with Taiwan confined China to the East Asia box.

Mao Zedong, Zhou Enlai and others did provide for strategic thinking and inputs between 1949-76 as reflected in the "leaning to one side"(towards the then Soviet Union), Five Principles for Peaceful Co-existence or "good neighbourliness" policy and Three World construct. Yet, the weak material base for such grand design proved costly for China till Deng Xiaoping's reform and opening up provided for certain concrete inputs such as is reflected in the concept of "*taoguang yanghui*" [hiding capabilities and biding for time/ maintaining a low profile]. Essentially, this slogan, unveiled in 1989, called for focusing on economic development, engaging all countries for the smooth flow of investments and technologies into China and even postponing conflicts for a long time except on core sovereignty issues.

In the last three decades of reform and opening up, China debated the grand strategic contours. Essentially including the minimalist foreign policy positions of Mao and others (viz., the core interests- sovereignty over Taiwan, Hong Kong, Macao and "lost territories"), Deng's China (inclusive of Jiang Zemin from 1989-2004 and currently under Hu Jintao), emboldened, as it were, with the increases in comprehensive national power of the country, unveiled a grand strategy.[12] Although still in the making, such a vision envisaged firstly enhancing the material wealth of the country—with economic development at the centre and under the CCP's rule. Disintegration of the Soviet Union that reduced military threats from the north, favourable reform policies, engagement with the outside world, multilateral efforts with several "partners" globally and changes in the CCP policies[13]—all provided for inputs into the Chinese grand strategy and implementation.[14] Indeed, China had—with relative successes—had unveiled several concepts and initiated steps in this regard.[15] Mention should be made of the occupation of the Paracels from Vietnam in 1974, Mischief Reef from the Philippines in 1988, expansion in the exclusive economic zone in 1992, commons security concept, new security concept, and multilateral initiatives in the political and security fields (such as with Shanghai Cooperation Organisation and East Asian Summit) and in the economic fields (Bo Ao Forum), conducted grand events such as Beijing Olympics in August 2008 and Shanghai Expo in 2010,[16] etc.

To summarise and outline the major components of China's grand strategy, in brief, the Chinese leadership believes in enhancing firstly its economic and military profile in the international system so as to form the foundation for its concerted role in the international order. Three concepts recur in the Chinese debates, viz., international system, international pattern and the international order. While the first two indicate to an objective situation of interactions between states (and also non-state actors), the third concept—order—indicates to the subjective desires of the country concerned. In China's case, as reflected in the seven white papers issued on national defence and the 16th and 17th Party Congresses reports,[17] it can be argued that China currently wants to maintain and support the current international strategic situation so as to build a "well-off society" by 2020 in China. At the same time, it wants to retain its autonomy in the international relations and even become a great power, specifically in the light of the decline of the US in events such as Iraq and Afghanistan.[18] China's premier Wen Jiabao, during the dinner meeting with the US President during the latter's visit to Beijing in November 2009, also rejected the idea of G-2 on the above assumption, although US-China relations today have acquired strategic dimensions. Indeed, when the US Secretary of State Hillary Clinton said at Beijing during the strategic and economic dialogue in 2012 that the US is engaged in re-writing the rules of power transition in the 21st Century, she was acknowledging the majors strides made by China in its comprehensive rise.

Comprehensive National Power (CNP)

One of the major components of China's grand strategy includes ways and means to enhance comprehensive national power (CNP). The CNP calculations include a country's power ranking in the world and include sustained economic growth rates over a long period of time, defence allocations, human resources development, science and technology prowess, innovative capability and the like. These aspects are also taken as primary indicators in calculating the CNP. This concept of CNP in the Chinese lexicon is only of a recent origin. This reflects to the emphasis China places on acquisition of power and its standing in the international arena. Although till about the 19th century several Chinese had articulated the view that the Middle Kingdom held sway and contributed substantially to the global economic growth figures, subsequently due to the Maoist self-sufficiency experiments in the 1950s and 1960s, China declined to be a part of any major global attention on economic growth rates. Ideologically the Maoist project was closer to the Third World theory and its attendant international approaches—such as affinity with the developing countries, raising issues of inequality, intervention, etc. Recently, with thirty years of reform and opening up, China had engaged the world in extensive trade, investments and other market exchanges—underlining the importance China places with the metropolis. Another aspect, military capabilities are also emphasised by China as a part of the reform efforts and learning from the debacle in the Vietnam War of 1979. Therefore, it could be argued that CNP aspects are rebounding in the Chinese calculus from about the 1980s and intensified in the last decade.

In the backdrop of the current debates about G-2 (Group 2 with the US and China, first noted by Zbiginew Brzezinski) and extended G-8 (of industrialised countries) or G-20 in the last few years, studies on China's CNP have become more extensive within China and outside. Within China, these coincided with the comprehensive rise of China in international economic, political and strategic relations and the need to further reduce the gap with the more advanced countries. To some extent this phenomenon in China reflects to the urge to "catch up" or even involve in a race, with countries having more CNP indicators. Outside China, in general, such interest in China's CNP is a reflection of a certain awe (to be replicated if possible) or with concern in the medium to long term perspectives.

The following section traces the main arguments in China related to CNP calculations and efforts, trace the triggers for such a phenomenon and reflects on the impact at the domestic and regional geo-strategic levels. The emphasis here is to evaluate Chinese perceptions on the CNP and concludes that these are pervasive in the Chinese establishment in the recent period.

Evolution and Key Motivations

It can be argued that the current Chinese interest in the CNP calculations have historical moorings in the Confucian world order and in the strategic culture propounded by Sun Zi and others, while current considerations of the Chinese leadership indicates to its "great power mentality" (*daguo xintai*) —sometimes also termed as rejuvenation of the Chinese nation.

First is the Confucian hierarchy and ranking in the society as a part of the "five great relationships". Thus, in general at the societal level, for ushering in social stability, the ruling elites historically prescribed strict observance of laws of obedience by a son to his father, by a wife to her husband, by a student to his/her teacher, by the people to their ruler and between a friend and a friend. However, for the ruling elites, the Chinese culture prescribed Legalist principles of law. The advantage of this system is that for centuries there was relative social stability and the continuation of centuries' long rule of the Middle Kingdom, only to be punctured by the entry of the "barbarian" western powers in 19th century. Nearly a decade ago, former President Jiang Zemin initiated the debate about "spiritual civilisation" and followed this up with "three represents" principles. That is, the communist party of China henceforth should represent the broad masses of the people, advanced productive forces (implying private entrepreneurs) and advanced culture (implying, along with "spiritual civilisation", neo-Confucian trends). In the last few years, President Hu Jintao's slogan of building "Harmonious World" has traces of the Confucius world order which remained hierarchical and unequal, interwoven, as it were, into tight cultural controls from the elite.

Secondly, in the sixth century BC, Sun Zi observed closely the Warring States condition and had prescribed several tenets that became popular with most ruling dynasties in the Chinese history. The Chinese Communist Party (CCP) had utilised extensively such historical writings in waging wars or formulating military strategies. After 1949, the Chinese military had extensively introduced Sun Zi's writings in the military academies. In the context of the CNP debate, Sun Zi had warned that the outcome of war depends on the correct assessment of power through calculations and estimates of enemy strengths and weaknesses.[19]

Thirdly, a series of events in the recent past in China indicates that the Chinese state had been making concerted efforts to become a global power to reckon with in the 21st century and that, as the 16th and 17th Party Congresses had stressed in 2002 and 2007 respectively, it has to seize "strategic opportunities" provided by the relative decline of several existing powers such as Russia, Japan, Germany, UK, France or even the United States. For instance, the fourth plenary session of the 16th CCP Central Committee issued its decisions on September 26, 2004. It stated:

> We must tightly seize the period of important strategic opportunity, concentrate efforts on construction, wholeheartedly pursue development, and continually strengthen comprehensive national strength and improve living standards. In accordance with the demands of comprehensively building a well-off society and embarking on a new-style road of

> industrialisation, with economic restructuring as the main thread and reform, opening up, and science and technology progress as the driving force, we must focus efforts on transforming the economic growth mode, and comprehensively improve the overall quality and competitiveness of the national economy. We must vigorously implement the strategy of building the country through science and technology, speed up the building of the state innovation system, and give full play to the role of science and technology as the first productive force.[20]

This effort to seize opportunities and enhance CNP started with the 1980s obsession to increase the country's gross domestic product (GDP) figures by leaps and bounds. This was reflected in the comments made by the previous Chinese premiers Hu Yaobang and Zhao Ziyang on increasing the GDP. In February 1990, Deng Xiaoping suggested that national power should be viewed in comprehensive terms. Likewise, President Hu Jintao mentioned in his address to the Bo Ao Forum for Asia in April 2004, the Chinese government intends to "quadruple the 2000 GDP to 4 trillion US dollars with per capita GDP of 3,000 US dollars".[21] Subsequently, on the eve of the 55th anniversary of the foundation of the PRC in 2004, Premier Wen Jiabao stated

> The Chinese people, who have mastered their own destiny, have displayed unprecedented innovative vitality and turned the long poor and weak old China of the past into a prosperous New China. Following the enhancement of comprehensive national strength, improvement of the people's livelihood, and increase in international exchanges, China's international status has been raised markedly, and all the Chinese people at home and abroad are deeply proud at the increasingly powerful motherland![22]

Hu Jintao, addressing the National Congress of Brazil on November 12, 2004 stated the increase in GDP, utilisation of FDI, etc, thus:

> Twenty-five years ago, the Chinese people, under the leadership of Mr Deng Xiaoping, set off on a historical journey of reform, opening up and building socialism with Chinese characteristics. In the past 25 years, China's economy has grown rapidly in a sustained manner, all social undertakings have developed comprehensively, the social productive forces and the comprehensive national strength have made a historical leap forward, and the people's living standard have, on the whole, reached a well-off level.[23]

Further, at the 17th Party Congress in October 2007, Hu declared that China would make efforts to enhance the GDP figures. By 2009, China had already overtaken Germany in GDP figures and is a few notches below Japan, at about $4.8 trillion. The Chinese government statistics indicated that, despite the global financial meltdown in 2008-09, China in 2009 was able to maintain 8.7 percent economic growth rate and exported $1.2 trillion worth of goods (while Germany exported $1.17 trillion). By 2011, China's GDP has surpassed that of Japan and became the second largest economy in the world. Also, surging exports contributed to the enhancement in the coffers of China—estimated at more than $2.2 trillion by 2009 and $3.2 trillion by June 2011. The foreign exchange reserves provide for enormous clout for the Chinese leadership not only in its relations with major powers but also to correct the imbalances in China and to import the much-needed advanced technologies. Indeed, on the eve of his visit to Europe, Premier Wen Jiabao suggested that increase in foreign exchange reserves in China had enhanced the CNP. China had utilised these reserves to import advanced technologies and products, reform the financial sector and reorganise the enterprises.[24]

Interlinked to the GDP increases is the phenomenon of China rise, more starkly visible during the Jiang Zemin's rule from 1989-2002. According to an official praise of the period, marking the release of Jiang Zemin's writings, the People's daily observed:

> ... we persisted in the strategic policy of observing coolly, tackling calmly, refraining from taking the lead, and doing what we could, while at the same time standing for fairness and justice, thereby forming a good image in promoting world peace and development. We worked hard to reinforce our comprehensive national strength, create a favourable strategic posture, increase the country's strategic capability, and extensively carry out reciprocal cooperation. We never yielded to any external pressure on the issues related to national interests and state sovereignty, thus further consolidating and developing a favourable peaceful international environment, particular a peaceful surrounding environment.[25]

This trend continued under the current President Hu Jintao as well—with more dimensions further considered and added by the establishment. As several neighbouring countries had viewed such a rise with unease, there was an attempt by the Chinese elite to mollify such concerns by suggesting that China's rise is going to a peaceful one and that it would avoid the consequences of the rise of Japan and Germany of the 1930s. In this context, the concept of "peaceful rise" was proposed by Zheng Bijian, vice president of the Chinese Communist Party's Central Party School at Bo Ao Forum for Asia in 2003. Following these injunctions are a series of Chinese TV shows, serials and writings on learning from the rise and fall of several empires from Rome to the current period. These efforts had furthered the concept of CNP in the elite imaginations of China in the last decade and triggered more debates on how to further consolidate the rise of China.[26]

Another crucial aspect that became evident to China is the military dimension, especially the blowing winds of revolution in military affairs (RMA) and the advancements made by western countries or even some of China's neighbours in this field. The interlink between CNP and war preparations are reflected in the following statement by the People's Daily which suggested that the 2003 Iraq war is a trigger to further enhance the CNP of China. The People's Daily stated:

> The war in Iraq serves as a warning to the peace-loving people, that is, peace should not merely be an aspiration. The Chinese people have learned penetratingly from their own historical experience that in an era when hegemonism and power politics are prevailing, it is of utmost importance to concentrate efforts to take good care of our own affairs. Only by exerting efforts to make China strong and concentrate attention on building up our comprehensive national strength will we be able to defend ourselves and our peaceful live and contribute more to safeguarding world peace.[27]

When the Chinese leadership initiated reform and opening up policies in 1978, the four modernisation programme included agriculture, industry, science and technology and defence—not necessarily in that order of priority. However, it had been stated that for enhancing the defence sector, firstly the economic sector should be refurbished. In this context, at the 16th Party Congress held in 2002 it was suggested to usher in coordinated development of the economic and defence sectors of the country. Hu Jintao, elaborating the crucial linkage between the two at the 15th collective study session of the Politburo on July 24, 2004, stated:

> Economic construction is the basic prop of national defence construction; there can be no question of national defence construction if economic construction is not done well. National defence strength is an important component of comprehensive national strength, and if national defence construction is not done well, a secure environment for economic construction can hardly be assured. Hence, while concentrating efforts to carry out economic construction, we must tangibly strengthen national defence construction and ensure the coordinated development of national defence construction and economic construction, forming a good situation of mutual promotion between the two.[28]

METHODOLOGIES

As mentioned above, while there has been an increase in the literature and new-found interest on the CNP in China, there is neither universally acceptable nor uniform method to calculate such indicators. However, there has been a proliferation of literature on the subject in China in the last decade, mostly by the strategic community—indicating not only to the international dimensions but also to the long-term implications of such a phenomenon.

Chinese assessments on CNP trace their inspirations to the realist/neo-realist perspectives of the western countries, specifically in the US. Hans Morgenthau, of classical realism, described the "elements of national power" to include geographical features, natural resources, industrial capacity, military preparedness, population, national character and morale, and the quality of government and diplomacy.[29] Another author that Chinese trace CNP studies or phenomenon is to Kenneth Waltz who belonged to structural realism school of thought and had emphasised on relative distribution of power that determines the international system.[30] Stephen Walt, after studying alliance formations in West Asia from 1955 to 1979, had argued that aggregate power (which includes population, individual and military capabilities, technical prowess), geographic proximity, offensive power, and aggregate intentions—all affect the level of threat to a state.[31]

Several of these studies during the Cold War period emphasised on military power,[32] while in the post-Cold War period, due to the blowing winds of globalisation and the emergence of non-traditional security challenges, the scope of power had been expanded to include economic, multipolarity and other factors such as the extent of territory, natural resources, social conditions, stability of the domestic government and its regulations, foreign policy initiatives and relative international influence.[33] The following table provides for the different indicators in calculating the CNP of major powers in the world.

Chinese assessments on CNP cite Michael E. Porter's 1990 publication *The Competitive Advantage of Nations* which identified five main elements of resources, viz., physical, human, infrastructure, knowledge and capital as crucial for enhancing competition between nations/regions and their prosperity.[34] Klaus Knorr in his work *The War Potential of Nations* had argued that there crucial factors that determine potential military power, viz., economic capacity, administrative competence, and motivation for war.[35] Yet another study is by Clifford German, with the index, G = National power = N (L + P + I + M) [where N is for nuclear capability, L is for land, P is for population, I is for industrial base, and M is for the size of military forces].[36] Closer to this study, but also including emerging importance of the energy issues is the study by Wilhelm Fuchs in 1965. Population size, energy production and steel output are predominant in calculating the CNP. Other studies identified hard and soft power aspects. For instance, Ray Cline's study

Table 1: CNP of Several Countries

Sl.No.	Country	经济力 Economic	科技力 Tech	军事力 Military	资源力 Energy	社会发展 Social Dev	政府调控 Govt Regu	外交力 Foreign	年增长率 Growth rate	综合国力 CNP
1	**US**	**3251**	**1718**	**2249**	**547**	**559**	**185**	**131**	**0.43%**	**8639**
2	Japan	2158	1111	806	226	416	169	100	0.26%	4986
3	France	1588	994	814	201	419	184	119	0.31%	4319
4	UK	1602	856	830	217	400	171	112	0.75%	4188
5	Germany	1762	854	623	191	419	184	107	0.48%	4139
6	**China**	**1321**	**312**	**508**	**483**	**245**	**133**	**116**	**2.98%**	**3119**
7	Russia	598	504	863	521	332	157	118	2.20%	3092
8	Canada	836	227	176	532	423	174	99	1.92%	2467
9	Italy	743	252	227	228	397	161	97	1.97%	2106
10	Australia	554	147	130	375	410	148	89	2.56%	1852
11	Brazil	551	211	169	382	253	110	85	2.21%	1762
12	Spain	621	157	114	209	364	124	85	2.08%	1674
13	**India**	**588**	**176**	**170**	**334**	**189**	**104**	**87**	**1.79%**	**1650**

Source: No Author; No date (possibly 1990s) accessed from <http://www.cwrank.com/prime/data.php?id=537>

in 1975 proposed the equation P = (C + E + M) × (S + W), where the latter two sets of the equation connote hard and soft power components. Here C stands for land and population; E for economic strength and national income, non-fuel mineral resources, energy, food, trade and the manufacturing sector; M for military capabilities and inclusive of strategic balance and combat capability; S for national strategy and W for the political conditions, level of national integration, leadership capacity and national stakeholders strategies.[37]

While many of the above methodologies were developed during the Cold War, reflecting to the times and with emphasis on the military capability in general, the nature of the collapse of Russia and Iraq, despite their military capability had ushered in new assessments. Ashley Tellis in his 2000 study for the RAND Corp. argued that "National power can be defined simply as the capacity of a country to pursue strategic goals through purposeful action".[38] He emphasised on three components, viz., national resources, national performance and military capabilities.

Within China there are a series of assessments on calculating the CNP. Apart from the Academy of Military Science (AMS) estimates, the civilian think-tank for the Communist Party, Chinese Academy of Social Sciences (CASS) and others have been cited to in the literature on CNP. The CASS study in 1996, as cited by Michael Pillsbury, suggested the following:

> We believe that Comprehensive National Power is the organic sum of the different powers of a sovereign state during a certain period of time, it is the base which all countries rely on for existence and development, and it is the foundation on which world powers establish their international position and give full play to their influence and roles. Specifically, it is the condensed sum of the entire calculations of societies' various existence and development factors at a certain time, space, and under certain conditions.[39]

Eight major areas of CNP include: natural resources, domestic and foreign economics, science and technology, military affairs, government and foreign affairs capability, and social development. The AMS estimate by Col Huang Shuofeng is different from the CASS estimates in terms of identifying systems and sub-systems. Cited by Michael Pillsbury in his "China Debates the Future Security Environment", Huang divides the CNP index system into four major index subsystems—the material power (hard—inclusive of natural resources, economics, science and technology, and national defence), the spirit power (soft), the coordinated power and the environmental index subsystem. The CASS and AMS projections of the CNP of major powers is reflected in the following table 2.

According to a study conducted in Hunan province and edited by Wang

Table 2: China Scholars CNP Projections

Country	1970	1980	1989/90		2000		2010		2020	
	CASS	CASS	Huang	CASS	Huang	CASS	Huang	CASS	Huang	CASS
U.S.	100 [1]	100 [1]	100 [1]	100 [1]	100 [1]	100 [1]	100 [1]	100 [1]	100 [1]	100 [2]
China	25 [9]	33 [8]	37 [6]	34 [8]	53 [5]	42 [7]	72 [3]	52 [7]	97 [2]	61 [5]
Germany	42 [3]	52 [3]	64 [3]	58 [3]	68 [3]	67 [3]	72 [2]	77 [3]	77 [3]	85 [3]
Japan	34 [4]	50[4]	62 [4]	58 [3]	66 [4]	76 [2]	69 [4]	97 [2]	73 [4]	119 [1]
India	15 [10]	19 [10]	24 [9]	18 [10]	34 [8]	22 [10]	44 [6]	26 [10]	57 [5]	30 [10]
France	33 [6]	46 [5]	47 [5]	46 [5]	47 [6]	59 [4]	48 [5]	70 [4]	48 [6]	82 [4]
Brazil	-	-	26 [8]	-	33 [9]	-	39 [7]	-	47 [7]	-
England	34 [4]	42 [6]	36 [7]	42 [6]	34 [7]	48 [6]	33 [8]	54 [6]	32 [8]	60 [6]
Canada	33 [6]	35 [7]	23 [10]	36 [7]	22 [10]	38 [8]	21 [9]	40 [8]	20 [9]	42 [8]
Australia	26 [8]	29 [9]	19 [11]	28 [9]	18 [11]	29 [9]	17 [10]	31 [9]	17 [10]	32 [9]
USSR	64 [2]	77 [2]	65 [2]	66 [2]	79[2]	-	-	-	-	-
Russia				(50)	-	54 [5]	-	57 [5]	-	56 [7]

(as a Percentage of U.S. CNP by Year, U.S. = 100) [*rank*]

Source: The scores for 1989 and 2000 are from Huang Shuofeng, *Zonghe guoli lun* (On Comprehensive National Power) (Beijing: Zhongguo shehui kexue chubanshe, 1992), 220-221. Scores for 2010 and 2020 were generated by Pillsbury. Table combines the Tables 9 and 10 in Pillsbury, *China Debates*, 248-249. Huang = projections to 2020 of AMS (Academy of Military Science) GNP statistics. CASS = Chinese Academy of Social Sciences. Ranks for the 1970 and 1980 scores contain ties, because Pillsbury only provided percentages (of US CNP) for those years; actual CNP scores were provided for later years. [The author thanks Wang Wei-cheng for sharing this information.]

Songfen, the CNP index should have the following aspects. As cited by Michael Pillsbury, the framework includes natural resources, socio-economic capability, military components, regulatory mechanisms etc as shown in table 3.

Table 3: The Comprehensive National Power Index Framework

Natural Resources
- *Man Power Resources:* total population; life expectancy; the proportion of the economically active population in the total population; the number of university students per 10,000 people
- *Land Resources:* the area of national territory; the area of cultivatable territory; the area in forest
- *Mineral Resources (reserves)*: iron; copper; bauxite
- *Energy Resources (reserves)*: coal; crude oil; natural gases; water energy

Economic Activities Capability
- *Actual Economic Strength (total)*: gross domestic product (GDP); industry production capability (electric energy production, steel output, cement output, logs output); food supply capability (total grain output, degree of self-sufficiency in grain); energy supply capability (volume of energy production, volume of energy consumption, crude oil processing capability); total cotton output
- *Actual Economic Strength (per person):* GDP per person; industry production capability (electric energy production, steel output, cement output, logs output); food supply capability (total grain output, average calories per person); energy supply capability (volume of energy consumption)
- *Production Efficiency:* social labor production rate; industry labor production rate, agriculture labor production rate
- *Material Consumption Level:* volume of energy consumption based on GDP calculations
- *Structure:* the proportion of the tertiary industry in the GDP

Foreign Economic Activities Capability
- Total import and export trade; total import trade, total export trade
- Total international reserves; international reserves (not including gold); gold reserves

Science and Technology Capability
- Proportion of research and development in the GDP; number of scientists and engineers; the number of scientists and engineers per 1,000 people; proportion of machinery and transportation equipment exports in total exports; proportion of high-technology intensive exports in total exports

Social Development Level
- *Education Level:* education expenditures per person; proportion of people studying in higher education; proportion of people studying in secondary school education
- *Cultural Level:* adult literacy rate; number of people per one thousand who get a daily newspaper
- *Health Care Level:* health care expenditures per person; number of people doctors

are responsible for; number of people nurses are responsible for

- *Communications:* number of people who have a telephone per 100 people
- *Urbanisation*: Proportion of the urban population in the total population

Military Capability

- Number of military personnel; military expenditures; weapons exports; nuclear weapons (the number of nuclear launchers; the number of nuclear warheads)

Government Regulation and Control Capability

- Proportion of final government consumption expenditures in the GDP; proportion of central government expenditures in the GDP; investigation through interviews asking nine questions

Foreign Affairs Capability

- Uses ten factors in a "nerve network model" to carry out a broad assessment.

Source: Wang Songfen, ed., *Shijie zhuyao guojia zonghe guoli bijiao yanjiu* [Comparative studies of the comprehensive national power of the world's major nations] (Changsha: Hunan Publications, 1996), 69 as cited in Michael Pillsbury, ed., *Chinese Views of Future Warfare* (Washington, DC: National Defense University Press, 1997)

The above CNP studies indicate to the *relative* ranking of a country vis-à-vis other countries and indicate to either its rise or decline in the power matrix in comparison with the other countries. Since these are relatively static at a given point of time of the study, the relative changes in CNP or the actual gaps are difficult to calculate accurately. At the same time, the historical changes in that specific country as well as subjective and contingency factors (based on external or internal stimuli) needs to be taken into consideration. Also, calculations of power need to factor in changing equations. For instance, while manufacturing sector is considered to be the backbone of the industrial age, today per capita output value in the knowledge economy far outweighs that in the manufacturing sector.

The above brief discussion points to the predominant interest in China on CNP calculations.[40] While several of these are critical of some of the western estimates in calculating CNP indicators and ranking, as a rising country among the industrialised countries (and above developing countries), China is keen to further develop CNP methods. More importantly, these efforts also indicate to the sustained intentions to become a global power in the long-term perspective. For this to happen, China needs to further revamp its internal structures and external contacts.

CNP for National Power Building

For revamping the domestic sector, a number of declarations and decisions were made by the Chinese leadership. Hu Jintao speaking at the 6th plenary session of the 16th CCP in late 2006, said:

> Our development is standing on a new historic starting point; the development opportunities facing us are unprecedented, and this also applies to the challenges facing us. While seeing the rare historic opportunities, we must strengthen our awareness of danger and soberly perceive the severe challenges facing us. Looking at the international scene, the factors of instability and uncertainty affecting peace and development have increased, and competition in comprehensive national strength is intensifying by the day, and we will continue to face for a long time the pressure of the developed countries' economic and science and technology superiority. Looking at the internal scene, with the profound transformation of the economic structure, profound changes in social structure, profound readjustment in the interest pattern, and profound changes in ideological concepts, deep-seated contradictions are gradually becoming apparent, and there is a marked increase in the number of problems affecting social harmony, including unbalanced development, difficult living conditions for some of the masses, widening income distribution gaps, and the growth of negative corruption phenomena, and so on.[41]

For Hu Angang, director of the National Information Research Centre at Tsinghua University, speaking at the First China's Competitiveness Forum on March 22, 2003,

> In order to achieve the strategic goal of making our people wealthy and our nation strong and continuously enhance the proportion of China's comprehensive national strength in the entire world, China will give full play to its strategic dominance, turn its inferior position into a strategic superiority, and advance from an economically huge country to an economically strong country in the world.[42]

Hu, along with Men Honghua, had suggested that to enhance CNP should emphasise on six goals in the next two decades, viz., "high growth, great national power, affluent people, national security, improvement of international competitiveness and sustainable development".[43] The emphasis, in most of the CNP calculations had been on the hard power, specifically on enhancing the economic strength of the country. In contrast to the Maoist emphasis on production relations, Deng faction focused on productive forces. According to an article published by the Central Party School,

> Only when a country has a sufficient economic volume, corresponding comprehensive national strength, and fairly high living standards for its people will it enjoy a material foundation and a prerequisite in terms of national strength that are essential for basically realising modernisation.[44]

Apart from the GDP growth rates, manufacturing sector, etc, that China had been able to post successes in the last three decades of reform, China realised of late that, like in the western countries, China needs a large battery of qualified personnel to tackle complex issues of development. Reflecting to this position, Premier Wen Jiabao, attending the State Council executive meeting on September 21, 2005 stated:

> ...implementing the strategy of revitalising the country by means of education and the strategy of making the country strong by means of training more capable people and making great efforts to develop vocational education and speed up the development of human resources are an important move to enable our country to move forward on the road of a new type of industrialisation, solve the "the three rural issues [the issues of agriculture, peasants, and rural areas]", and expand employment and re-employment; are an important way to comprehensively improve the quality of the nationals and increase the comprehensive national strength of our country; and are the inevitable requirement in following the laws governing education, implementing the principle of teaching students in accordance with their aptitude, and promoting the coordinated development of basic education, vocational education and general higher education.[45]

Interconnected to the above aspect is the science and technology prowess of the country, which was underlined as the 3rd modernisation aspect, as a part of the four modernisation programme, which began in 1978. Several schemes were drawn from the 1980s to further this process, including the "863 programme", "967 plan" and others which emphasised on new technologies such as automation, information, energy, space, bio and nano technologies. Emphasising this aspect, Hu Jintao stated at the 34th collective study session of the Politburo,

> In the world today, knowledge has more and more become a factor determining the increase in comprehensive national strength and international competitiveness and human resources have more and more become strategic resources promoting economic and social development. To continuously meet the increasing material and cultural needs of the people and realize the modernisation of our country, it is necessary to comprehensively improve the science and culture quality and the ideological and moral quality of all the people.[46]

More significantly, if China were to further enhance its CNP, independent innovation efforts have to be unleashed across the board. For instance, outlining priorities of the Eleventh Five Year Plan, the People's Daily suggested that

> In today's world, human society is in the middle of a global scientific and

> technological revolution. Competition among enterprises, the development of economies, and the contest among countries in the area of comprehensive national strength have been manifested in scientific and technological competition in an increasingly concentrated manner. In view of such a situation, we have no alternative but to regard independent innovation as a strategic foundation for our future scientific and technological development, and to greatly improve our independent scientific and technological innovation capability.[47]

The results of the above statements and initiatives are seen in the several successes that China achieved, specifically in the space programme—a difficult technology to master. The unmanned and then manned spacecraft launches have been the major events recently. According to a commentary of the People's Daily on the eve of the successful launch of the manned spacecraft in 2005,

> The "Shenzhou VI" manned space flight will carry out China's first scientific experiments in space with human participation in its real sense. It also marks the start of the second-step tasks in China's "three-step" strategy for its manned space programme. Now, the space programme of our country has entered a new stage. The successful launch of the "Shenzhou VI" manned spacecraft has shown China's characteristics and technological progress. It has manifested China's comprehensive national strength and international competitiveness and boosted the national confidence and solidarity of the people of the whole country. Because of this, the Chinese people are inspired and feel proud.[48]

Further, according to Hu Jintao, on the successful launch of the Shenzhou VI, this highlighted the CNP increases of the country, thus:

> The complete success of the Shenzhou VI manned space mission, which is an important manifestation of China's continuously rising comprehensive national strength and scientific and technological level in the past more than two decades since reform and opening up, has great and far-reaching significance in boosting China's international status and further inspiring all party members and the people of all ethnic groups throughout the country in the struggle for building a well-off society in an all-round way....we should always put the improvement of the capability of independent innovations in a prominent position and enhance China's scientific and technological strength substantially. Scientific and technological strength is the key component and foundation for the comprehensive national strength, while independent innovations are the core of a country's competitiveness. A country or nation, which wants to achieve development and bring benefit to mankind in a real sense, must pay close attention to independent innovations......we should always foster a concept

> that talented people are the primary resources and go all out to train and bring up a high-quality contingent of qualified scientists and engineers. The competition for comprehensive national strength in the world today is essentially a competition for talented people. In the final analysis, the competition in science and technology is also a competition for talented people. The key to enhancing China's scientific and technological strength and national competitiveness lies in accelerating the development of educational undertakings and scientific and technological undertakings and constantly building up the contingent of talented people.[49]

Later, in October 2006, China issued a white paper on China's space programme, one of whose aims is to "build up the comprehensive national strength." of the country.[50] Luan Enjie, chief commander of the lunar satellite project said in October 2007,

> Launching the lunar probe has enormous practical implications and far-reaching historic significance for raising China's international stature, further promoting the peaceful use of outer space, and enhancing the nation's cohesiveness and its comprehensive national strength.[51]

Successful space launches, as the launching of the lunar probe indicated, rests on building scientific talent and resources, as pointed out above. According to a commentary:

> Capable personnel are the foundation of the country, the country is governed by capable personnel, and the prosperity of our cause depends on capable personnel. In the final analysis, the competition of comprehensive national strength of the world today is the competition of capable personnel.[52]

Another facet of the CNP is the huge amounts of resources catered to improve the infrastructure projects of the country. China initiated gigantic projects such as East-West gas pipeline connecting Urumqi with Shanghai and extended to Kazakhstan; river diversion projects from south to north; laid down Tibet railway, built superhighways, fibre optic networks, etc.[53] In this context, marking the opening of the Tibet railway on July 1, 2006, Hu Jintao stated:

> ...we must firmly grasp development, the most important task of the party in governing the country and making it strong, and continuously increase the comprehensive national strength of our country. The difficulty in the construction of the Golmud-Lhasa section of the Qinghai-Tibet Railway and the high demands on the reliability and safety of the equipment are unprecedented in the world's history of railway construction. Under special geographical and climatic conditions, we have spend only five years on

> completing this more than 1,100 km long plateau railway. This tremendous achievement is an important expression of the constant increase in the comprehensive national strength of our country in the past 20 years and more since the beginning of reform and opening up. This fact has once more fully proved that so long as we firmly grasp development, the most important task of the party in governing the country and making it strong, and constantly increase the comprehensive national strength of our country, we definitely shall be able to constantly score new victories in socialist modernisation.[54]

Significantly, for the first time in the history of China, such infrastructure projects integrate far-flung minority inhabited areas with China proper and boost China's market and political integration. For instance, speaking on the eve of the 50th anniversary of the founding of Ningxia, politburo member He Guoqiang stated:

> Supporting the minority ethnic groups and areas inhabited by them in speeding up development is a basic central policy and is an important task of the general development of the western region. With the increase in financial revenue and the growth in the comprehensive national strength, the central authorities will make greater supportive efforts to create more favourable conditions for the good and fast economic and social development of Ningxia.[55]

Apart from these statements to enhance "hard" power, China is also emphasising on soft power build up.[56] Consequently, China is planning to set up more than 2,000 Confucian studies centres all over the world to further its soft outreach. Internally, China is also in the process of reforming the cultural structures. In mid January 2006, the People's Daily published a commentary on reforming the cultural structure of China. It stated:

> Making the advanced socialist culture prosperous and promoting the comprehensive development of man as well as promoting economic growth, increasing the comprehensive national strength, taking part in international competition, cultivating the national spirit and promoting social progress have urgently required that we must liberate and develop the cultural productive forces and properly build and develop the advanced socialist culture.[57]

Again, an unattributed report in Xinhua suggested that China should expand its soft power aspects of the CNP. For,

> A culture's soft strength is an important component of comprehensive national strength and international competitiveness. If China wants to win the initiative in the fierce international competition, it must make the

> national culture's soft strength rise greatly while expanding economic and technological strengths and strengthening national defence power at the same time.[58]

Interlinked to this in terms of enhances the CCP control is the "patriotic education" programme, necessary for the CCP stability in Han-dominated areas battered by income inequalities and rising public protests in the last decade, but also in the minority areas of the country. According to a commentator in People's Daily, China should enhance its "patriotic education" campaign.

> The era that we face is the era of an increasingly deepening trend of economic globalisation. It is the era of increasingly intense competition in comprehensive national strength among states. It is also the era displaying a bright prospect for the great rejuvenation of the Chinese nation.[59]

The above statements by the Chinese leadership make it amply clear that the different aspects of CNP need to be pursued with seriousness in order to become a major power. One indictor to gauge China's success in this field is to consider the state's response to the natural calamities or other related issues. For instance, while China had been relatively slow in setting up a national disaster relief mechanism in May 2008, when Sichuan earthquake devoured more than 100,000 people, China on the whole had mobilised troops and others on a massive scale for relief operations subsequently. According to a commentator in the People's Daily,

> Without the comprehensive national strength resulting from the wholehearted pursuit of development and achievements over the past 30 years, there would have been no such strong technological guarantees and ample material support for this earthquake control and relief operation.[60]

CNP for Geostrategic and Regional Political Advantage

Recent enhancements in the CNP figures for China are providing rich dividends for the country. Not only is the "manufacturing hub of the world" image enhancing the country's image, but the GDP increases are galvanising the country at the high table. As a permanent member of the United Nations Security Council, China is also being wooed by a large number of countries. In the recent years, more than half of global heads of states had visited Beijing, while China is also unveiling new initiatives such as Special Envoys to the Middle East and Africa, climate change proposals, peacekeeping operations, etc. China is also being praised by several leaders. For instance, despite following a "juche" (independent/self-sufficient) philosophy, North Korean leader Kim Jong-Il, during his visit in January 2006 to Hubei, Guangdong, and Beijing, observed:

> We have seen with our own eyes that China's comprehensive national strength is continually rising and its social appearance is being transformed, and we have a more all-round understanding of China; we have a deeper appreciation of the policies of the Chinese party and government such as emancipating the mind, attaching importance to talent, basing efforts on self-determined innovation, and making efforts to promote all-round, coordinated, and sustainable development.[61]

One of the implications of the extensive propaganda about the rising CNP is the awe it could create among the neighbourhood of China. While China had been engaged in mutually beneficial economic interdependence with a number of its neighbours, at the same time its CNP increases have made several of its neighbours fall in line with Beijing on a number of issues. These include a variety of subjects such as counter-terrorism, border trade, free trade agreements, building regional security complexes, cooperating on non-traditional security issues, multilateral networks, etc, while at the same time questioning or marginalising other regional powers (such as Japan, Russia, India and others) or global powers (such as the US).

In this context, explicitly, several statements from the Chinese establishment reassure the outside world of its benevolent intentions and that China would be a "responsible power". For instance, attending the 4th conference of the Shangri-La dialogue process at Singapore in 2005, Cui Tiankai, the then director-general of Asian Affairs of the foreign ministry said:

> As a big country in the region, China has in recent years maintained a stable and healthy development and its comprehensive national strength has greatly improved. China is willing to make contributions to promoting regional peace, security and harmony with responsible action and a scientific understanding of the current security issue.[62]

According to Wang Yizhou, of the CASS, in the recent period, China had adapted to the international system by undertaking several initiatives on counter-terrorism, six party talks, relief operations etc. With these,

> ...China has appeared on the international stage with a diplomatic stance that is more open, more confident, more rational and more pragmatic. It has gradually established an excellent image as a responsible power with a constructive role to play, and its diplomatic influence grows along with the rise in our country's comprehensive national strength.[63]

The relief aid by the Chinese government across the globe is also depicted as a reflection of CNP, although China's efforts in this field are only in the preliminary stage as compared with other states.[64] Nevertheless, Zhang Guoqing of the College of Government Administration at Peking University stated in an interview, reflecting on the Chinese aid to Indonesia after Tsunami hit that country: "In a sense, at present international aid has become a kind of peaceful rivalry as it has become a display of comprehensive national strength and national image."[65]

Another account suggested that China will adapt to the international system. According to Wang Yi, secretary of Ministry of Foreign Affairs CCP Committee and vice foreign minister,

> ...as China's comprehensive national strength is continually growing, and its international influence is continually increasing, we are also considering how, as a socialist power following the path of peaceful development, to adapt to the changes in our international status and role and how to respond to the expectations of the international community, especially the developing countries, and make still greater contributions to world peace and development.[66]

Yet others suggested that increases in the CNP will not make China falter its course by neither joining the Soviet experience nor confronting the west. According to Zheng Bijian, the architect of the China rise theory, attending a seminar in Shanghai in September 2006:

> With respect to building up the country's comprehensive national strength, China will never dream the "Soviet dream". Instead of going all out to join the arms race and "exporting revolution" in a big way like the Soviet Union did in the past, China has chosen to develop itself. We only export computers, not revolution.[67]

Others, however, had taken head-on the argument that China poses challenges to the international system. For instance, according to Wang Xinjun, of the Academy of Military Science,

> ...there is the assumption that China's rapid development threatens the geopolitical order of East Asia which is dominated by the United States. Given the sustained and rapid growth in China's economy, its comprehensive national strength as a whole, and its international influence, certain forces in the United States and Japan have begun changing the common "China threat theory" into a "China military threat theory". Thereby, they exaggerate China's military spending and military modernisation drive. Under the backdrop of this kind of public sentiment, the purpose of China's military modernisation is questioned, and Sino-US

> geopolitical contradictions, which have intensified due to man-made reasons, have surfaced.[68]

Wang, however, acknowledged that due to the increase in the Chinese CNP, the US and others are increasingly engaging—including in the military field-with his country.[69] Nevertheless, the dilemma facing the Chinese decision-makers is that enhanced CNP also brings in its forth the desire to preserve or even protect the international system. One of the major challenges that the world is faced today is proliferation of nuclear weapons /ballistic missiles which could destabilise the system. China from about early 1990s had been suggesting that it would be careful on this aspect and in 1995 released a white paper on arms control and disarmament. After the AQ Khan incident was reported, partly implying Chinese role in the WMD transfer issue, China passed laws to restrict the trade of dual use technologies in early 2007. According to an official's comment:

> In recent years, important changes have taken place in the situation of international non-proliferation and antiterrorism, and the importance of preventing the proliferation of weapons of mass destruction and their carriers has become very prominent in international political and security affairs. With the further increase in the comprehensive national strength of our country, perfecting the non-proliferation export control structure and standardizing the export of sensitive items and technologies are of great significance to protecting national security and social common interests, performing international obligations undertaken, and establishing a responsible international image.[70]

Thus, it could be concluded that the CNP considerations are extensive in China today, indicating to the extensive interest on the subject and the intentions to pursue such goals of enhancing its power in the international system. The above statements, reflecting to not only official but also the press, think-tanks and the academy, amply make clear that China's three decades of reform had catapulted the country on to the international scene and that despite problems—such as sustainability of growth rates, ageing society, income and regional inequalities, political stability, constraining influences of US-led alliances, etc—the country's CNP could bring back the memories of the Middle Kingdom.

Impact on India

China's grand strategy, as outlined above, directly does not mention about the possible strategy towards India. Although both countries are large neighbours, with huge populations, rising CNP's and profiles in the international system today, there appears to be a disjuncture in their approaches.[71] After the bonhomie of the 1950s in which India facilitated China's entry into the multilateral process such as Bandung conference, bilateral relations suffered due to the territorial as well as the Tibet issue. The 1960s witnessed the setting of cold war in the bilateral relations, only to be normalised diplomatically in the late 1970s. Till April 2005, China viewed India in more tactical terms and since Premier Wen Jiabao's visit to Delhi that year, "strategic and cooperative partnership" had been announced between the two countries. This was partly re-iterated in President Hu Jintao's visit to Delhi in November 2006 and during Premier Wen's visit in December 2010. Yet, today strategic relations between China and India are mostly confined mostly to the multilateral process such as at the climate change talks at Bali, Copenhagen and Durban or in the institutions such as BRICS (Brazil-Russia-India-China- South Africa) and others. While such interactions have been beneficial for both countries, the impact of such "strategic" relations is hardly noticeable on the bilateral relations. While China had prioritised relations with the US as crucial in its grand strategy, despite signing "strategic partnerships" of various hues with nearly a dozen countries, India had recently indicated that its relations with the US, Russia, European Union, Japan and China in that order are significant.

As a rising country in the international system with potential power transition contest with the US in the global power matrix, China's grand strategy vis-à-vis India could have the following broad trajectories. While the future international and regional dynamics could hardly be predicted, based on the previous policy prescriptions and ground reality, it could be surmised that the following could be China's strategies towards India.

A dominant school of thought in China today, partly under the influence of its military constituencies, is for balancing New Delhi through a series of diplomatic, economic and military arrangements. These include applying the strategies of "*hexiao kongda*" [i.e., supporting the weak to counter the strong]. This posture envisages cooperating with the smaller South Asian countries to build leverages against India which is seen as enhancing its CNP and hence could be a potential challenger to China in Asia and beyond. While China's CNP is higher than compared to that of India, and clearly asymmetries of power are widening between the two despite India making strides in "catching up" with China, building leverages against India could provide rich dividends to China in the future. The military components in China have viewed India through three dominant assessments, viz., that India intends to dominate South Asia [*chengba nanya*], control the Indian Ocean [*kongzhi yindu yang*], and strive to be a world class military power [*zheng dang shijie yiliu junshi qiangguo*]. Countering these through balancing New Delhi and entering into the Indian Ocean through its "two ocean strategy" could provide for leverages to China and possibly allies and friends for the Middle Kingdom in the 21st century. Sections of China's foreign ministry, steeped in the Cold War mentality, also concur with such a policy prescription as Tibet issue has not been resolved completely to the satisfaction of Beijing. As Tibet had been configured as a "core interest" and Arunachal Pradesh had been viewed as a part of "southern Tibet" since early 2000s, the Cold War warriors in China are inclined to postpone territorial dispute resolution, deploy military forces or enhance military logistics facilities for any swift operations in future. Rising nationalist sentiments in China today also dovetails with this section who argues for "teaching" India another lesson.

A second scenario is that of enhanced economic interdependence with or without reducing tensions in the bilateral relations. Leaving aside the larger issue of who benefits what and to what extent in such a relationship, today bilateral trade had substantially increased between the two to make China as the largest trading partner for India. China considers that India has an inherent advantage of over 300 million middle class who can constitute a huge market for its products, specifically as the global financial crisis is affecting its exports. A section in China's foreign ministry as well as the Shanghai Chamber of Commerce subscribes to this school with exploration of markets, expanding trade in goods and services, increasing investments, tourist potential and people-to-people contacts. Although increasingly India had been raising the issues of lack of market economy status in China, debilitating trade deficits and the like, to what extent China will take recourse to the old adage of *yimin weigong* [influencing official policy through the people] or *yishang weizheng* [influencing the polity through the business groups] vis-à-vis India is not clear and needs to be carefully studied and analysed.

A third scenario in the making is that of a cooperative and constructive one of building identities between these two developing countries in Asia. Emerging, but still nascent, civil society constituents and others in China have been advocating people-to-people understanding and NGO cooperation in finding alternative solutions to the problems facing these two countries. Nevertheless, this trend has been the most weakest in the bilateral context, although has potential to grow in the coming years.

End Notes

1. "Full text of the political report delivered by Chinese Communist Party General Secretary Hu Jintao at the opening of the 17th CCP National Congress at Beijing"

China Central TV-1, October 15, 2007 at British Broadcasting Corporation, Selected World Broadcasts, Asia Pacific (hereafter BBC).

2. For a comprehensive coverage of the subject see Yan Xuetong, *Zhongguo guojia liyi fenxi* [Analysis of China's national interests] (Tianjin, Tianjin People's Publication, 2002).
3. On the other hand, China's scholars argue that Deng's formulations should be translated as "keep a low profile".
4. See for the full text of Hu Jintao's speech on April 24, 2004 at <http://www.boaoforum.org/boao/2004nh/cd/t20040424_733981.shtml> accessed on December 20, 2004.
5. For an extensive discussion on this topic see Hu Angang ed. *Zhongguo Da Zhanlue* [China's Grand Strategy] (Hangzhou: Zhejiang People's Publications, 2002) pp. 3-37.
6. See Yan Xuetong, Jin Canrong and Liu Yuan, "Diplomacy faces shifting currents of new era" *The Global Times* April 24, 2012.
7. See Paul Kennedy (ed.), *Grand Strategies in War and Peace* (New Haven: Yale University Press, 1991).
8. See, for instance, Xiao Jialing and Tang Xianxing eds. *Daguo Waijiao: Lilun, juece,tiaozhan* [Great Power Diplomacy: Theory, decision-making and challenge] (Shishi Publications, Shanghai, 2003) 2 volumes; Hu Angang ed. *Zhongguo Da Zhanlue* [China's Grand Strategy] (Hangzhou: Zhejiang People's Publications, 2002) and Shi Yinhong, *Zhanlue Wenti Sanshi Bain – Zhongguo Duiwai Zhanlue Sikao* [Thirty Studies on Strategy—Reflections on the External Strategic of China] (Beijing: People's University Publications, 2008).
9. Avery Goldstein had argued that such a grand strategy started emerging in the Chinese thinking from 1996 after several ad hoc measures before by the leadership. See "The Diplomatic Face of China's Grand Strategy: A Rising Power's Emerging Choice" *The China Quarterly* (2001) pp. 835-64.
10. According to David Finkelstein, crucial to understanding the subject are a few fundamentals, viz., well defined objectives; development of concepts, approaches and concrete policies to achieve these objectives; development of capacities for implementation; coordination and adjustment. See his "Commentary on China's External Grand Strategy" *38th Taiwan-U.S. Conference on Contemporary China*, The Brookings Institution & National Chengchi University, July 14-15, 2009.
11. See Michael D. Swaine and Ashley J. Tellis, *Interpreting China's Grand Strategy: Past, Present, and Future* (Santa Monica, CA: RAND, 2000).
12. See Di Dongsheng, "Continuities and Changes: A Comparative Study on China's New Grand Strategy" *Historia Actual Online* No.12 (2007), pp. 7-18 and Chen Mumin, "Going Global: The Chinese Elite's Views of Security Strategy in the 1990s" *Asian Perspective*, vol. 29 no. 2, pp. (2005) 133-77.
13. These latter included Deng Xiaoping's Four Cardinal Principles of making the CCP as the focus; Jiang Zemin's ideas on "three represents" to broad base the CCP; and currently Hu Jintao's "harmonious world" to reduce tensions domestically and internationally.
14. Liselotte Odgaard had argued that in the post-Cold War period, China, taking a

cue from Matternich's grand strategy, is struggling with the outside world in order to avoid being labelled as a secondary power in the international order. See "Metternich and China's Post-Cold War Grand strategy" Institute for Strategy, Faculty of Strategy and Military Operations, Royal Danish Defence College, Copenhagen, 2009.

15. See Philip C. Saunders, "China's Global Activism: Strategy, Drivers, and Tools" Institute for National Strategic Studies, US NDU Occasional Paper 4 October 2006.
16. On this aspect and how Olympics contributed to enhancing China's public diplomacy, see Qiu Huafei, "Public Diplomacy: China's Grand Foreign Strategy" *PD Case Study: Beijing Olympics* (Issue 1 Winter 2009) at <www.publicdiplomacy magazine.org>
17. See for the white papers at <http://www.china.org.cn> or <http://english.chinamil.com.cn> See also the US Department of Defense papers on the military power of China at <http://www.dod.gov>
18. See Wang Yuan-Kang, "China's Grand Strategy and US Primacy: Is China balancing American power?" The Brookings Institution July 2006.
19. For an useful study of the concept of Shi in the ancient Chinese strategy, see David Lai, *Learning from the Stones: A Go Approach to Mastering China's Strategic Concept, Shi* (Carlyle Barracks, Strategic Studies Institute, May 2004).
20. See "Chinese Communist Party Plenum 'Decision' " *Xinhua Domestic Service* September 26, 2004 at BBC.
21. See Aki Mori, "Rich Country, Strong Armed Forces? The Sources of China's Comprehensive National Power" accessed at <http://www.rchss.sinica.edu.tw/capas/publication/newsletter/N38/38_01_02.pdf>
22. "Chinese premier's speech at State Council's National Day reception" *Xinhua Domestic Service,* September 30, 2004 at BBC.
23. Hu Jintao, "Work hand in hand to create a new situation of Sino-Latin American friendship" *Xinhua Domestic Service* November 13, 2004 at BBC.
24. Wen cited at "Chinese currency exchange rate not to be readjusted 'unexpectedly' - PM" *Xinhua* September 6, 2006 at BBC.
25. See Zhong Yan and Wen Shi, "On the great significance of the 'Selected Works of Jiang Zemin" *People's Daily* August 17, 2006 at BBC.
26. For the Chinese assessments, see Yan Xuetong, "The Rise of China in Chinese Eyes" *Journal of Contemporary China* (2001), vol. 10 No. 26 pp. 33–39 and Yan Xuetong, "The Rise of China and its Power Status" *Chinese Journal of International Politics,* Vol. 1, 2006 pp. 5–33.
27. "China's People's Daily says US war against Iraq without legitimacy" *People's Daily* March 21, 2003 p 5 at BBC.
28. Hu cited at "Chinese president stresses coordinated defence, economic construction" *Xinhua Domestic Service,* July 24, 2004 at BBC.
29. Hans J. Morgenthau, *Politics Among Nations: The Struggle for Power and Peace* (New York: Alfred A. Knopf, 1967), pp. 106–158.
30. Kenneth Waltz, *Theory of International Politics,* (Reading: Addison-Wesley, 1979) p. 192.

31. Stephen M. Walt, *The Origins of Alliances* (Ithaca: Cornell University Press, 1987).
32. See Karl W. Deutsch, *The Analysis of International Relations* (Englewood Cliffs: Prentice-Hall, 1968) and Inis L. Claude, *Power and International Relations* (New York: Random House, 1962).
33. See Yong Deng and Thomas G. Moore, "China Views Globalization: Toward a New Great-Power Politics?" *The Washington Quarterly* Vol. 27 No.3 (Summer 2004) pp. 117–136.
34. See "*Zonghe guoli*" [CNP] accessed at <http://baike.baidu.com/view/59009.htm> [hereafter *Zonghe guoli*] and Ou-yang Guo-hua, "The Comparison Model of the Comprehensive National Strength under the Globalization" *International Journal of Business and Management* (Wuhan) June 2006 pp. 70-85 accessed at <http://www.ccsenet.org/journal/index.php/ijbm/article/view/3165/2908>
35. Klaus Knorr, *The War Potential of Nations* (Princeton: Princeton University Press, *1956*) pp. 40-42.
36. Clifford German, "A Tentative Evaluation of World Power" *The Journal of Conflict Resolution*, vol. 4 (1960) pp. 138–144.
37. This is based on *Zonghe guoli.*
38. Ashley Tellis, *Measuring National Power in the Postindustrial Age,* MR-1110-A (Santa Monica, RAND Corp, 2000) p. 4.
39. Michael Pillsbury, ed., *Chinese Views of Future Warfare* (Washington, DC: National Defense University Press, 1997).
40. For a few predictions about the CNP till 2025 in China's discussion forums and blogs see "*2025 niande shijie qiangguo zonghe guoli paiming yuce*" [Predicting Global CNP ranking of strong states in 2025] accessed at <http://bbs.tiexue.net/post_4133799_1.html>; CASS report in December 2009 ranked China 9th in the global CNP rankings. See "*Zhongguo zonghe guoli quanqiu di qi junshi shili di er*" [China's CNP globally is No. 7 and Military Power No. 2] December 24, 2009 accessed at <http://news.163.com/09/1224/09/5R9PB2O5000120GU.html>
41. "First part of speech by Comrade Hu Jintao at Second Plenary Meeting of sixth plenary session of 16th CCP Central Committee on 11 October 2006" *Qiushi* January 1, 2007 at BBC.
42. Hu cited at "Chinese economist Hu Angang on ways to "enrich people, strengthen nation"" *Zhongguo Xinwen She* March 22, 2003 at BBC.
43. See Hu Angang and Men Honghua, "The Rising of Modern China: Comprehensive National Power and Grand Strategy" *Strategy & Management*, No. 3, 2002 accessed at <http://www.irchina.org/en/pdf/hag.pdf>
44. " 'Four Unswervinglys' Are of Utmost Importance to Ensuring an Overall Smooth Development in the Cause of the party and the State" *Qiushi* September 16, 2007 at BBC.
45. "Chinese PM sets out tasks to reform vocational education" *Xinhua Domestic Service,* September 21, 2005 at BBC.
46. Hu cited at "Chinese president stresses education development" *Xinhua Domestic Service,* August 30, 2006 at BBC.
47. "Chinese agency outlines priorities for 11th Five-Year Plan" *Xinhua Domestic Service,* October 7, 2005 at BBC.

48. "People's Daily celebrates China's successful launch of manned spacecraft" *Xinhua Domestic Service,* October 12, 2005 at BBC.
49. Hu Jintao, "Speech at the Rally Celebrating the Success of the Shenzhou VI Manned Space Mission" *Xinhua Domestic Service,* November 26, 2005 at BBC.
50. See Information Office of China's State Council "China's Space Activities in 2006" *Xinhua* October 12, 2006 at BBC.
51. Huang Quanquan, "China's First Lunar Probe Has Profound Significance" *Xinhua Domestic Service,* October 24, 2007 at BBC.
52. "Implement Strategy of Making Our Country Strong by Training More Capable Personnel, Carry Forward Spirit of Seeking Truth and Being Pragmatic - Second Commentary on Studying and Implementing Comrade Hu Jintao's Important Speech at Meeting To Celebrate Complete Success of First Lunar Exploration of Our Country" *Xinhua Domestic Service,* December 14, 2007 at BBC.
53. See John W. Garver, "Development of China's Overland Transportation Links with Central, South-West and South Asia" *The China Quarterly* No. 185 (March 2006), pp. 1-22.
54. See "Hu Jintao's speech at a rally to celebrate putting the Qinghai-Tibet railway into service on 1 July 2006" *Xinhua Domestic Service,* July 1, 2006 at BBC.
55. "Speech by He Guoqiang at a Meeting To Celebrate the 50th Founding Anniversary of the Ningxia Hui Autonomous Region (23 September 20098)" *Xinhua Domestic Service* September 23, 2008 at BBC.
56. See Li Mingjiang, *Soft Power: China's Emerging Strategy in International Politics* (Lexington-Rowman & Littlefield, 2009), Joel Wuthnow, "The Concept of Soft Power in China's Strategic Discourse" *Issues & Studies,* Vol. 44, no. 2 (June 2008) pp. 1-28; Falk Hartig, "Confucius Institutes and the Rise of China" *Journal of Chinese Political Science* (2012) No. 17 pp.53–76 and James F. Paradise, "China and International Harmony: The Role of Confucius Institutes in Bolstering Beijing's Soft Power" *Asian Survey,* Vol. 49, No. 4 (July/August 2009), pp. 647-669.
57. See "Gain a Deep Understanding of the Spiritual Essence of Deepening the Reform of the Cultural Structure - Second Commentary on Studying and Implementing 'Several Opinions of the CCP Central Committee and the State Council on Deepening the Reform of the Cultural Structure" *Xinhua Domestic Service,* January 14, 2006 at BBC.
58. "Raise National Culture's Soft Strength" *Xinhua Domestic Service* December 28, 2007 at BBC.
59. "Let Patriotism Shine with the Brilliance of the Era" People's Daily as published in *Xinhua Domestic Service,* April 14, 2009 at BBC.
60. Ren Zhongping, "A Great China Stands Tall Amid the Disaster—Written as the Chinese People Battle the Great Wenchuan Earthquake" *People's Daily* June 21, 2008 at BBC.
61. Qian Tong, "General Secretary Kim Jong-il pays unofficial visit to China at General Secretary Hu Jintao's invitation; Hu Jintao holds talks with Kim Jong-il and gives banquet for him" *Xinhua Domestic Service* ,January 18, 2006 at BBC.
62. Cui cited at "Chinese official expounds on new security concept at Asian conference" *Xinhua Domestic Service* June 4, 2005 at BBC.

63. Wang cited at Zhao Cheng, Li Bin, and Liu Zheng, "Five Years of Glory and Five Years of Progress - Experts Interpret Major Events Since the 16th CCP National Congress " Xinhua Domestic Service, October 9, 2007 at BBC.
64. See Srikanth Kondapalli, "Tsunami and China: Relief with Chinese Characteristics" *Asian Affairs* February 2005, also posted at <http://www.niaslinc.dk/gateway_to_asia/Asia_insights/Tsunami_disaster.as>
65. "Scholar views China's international aid effort" *People's Daily* January 4, 2005 p 5 at BBC.
66. Wang Yi, "Unswervingly Follow the Path of Peaceful Development" *Qiushi* December 1, 2007 at BBC.
67. Zheng cited by Ji Ming, Zhang Qiang and Cai Hailiang,, "Zheng Bijian says: China will not export revolution and pattern of development " *Xinhua* September 21, 2006 at BBC.
68. Wang Xinjun, "China's peaceful development must cope with the challenge of a US-Japan 'military alliance' " *Zhongguo Tongxun She,* (Hong Kong) January 18, 2006 at BBC.
69. See Wang's comments on the eve of Sino-US joint naval operation in September 2006 at Tao Shelan, "Military expert: First joint exercise of Chinese, US navies marks one step forward in bilateral military relations" *Zhongguo Xinwen She* September 22, 2006 at BBC. See also Jeffrey W Legro, "What China Will Want: The Future Intentions of a Rising Power" *Perspectives on Politics* Vol. 5, No. 3 (September, 2007), pp. 515-534.
70. Zhang Yi, "Relevant Official Responsible for the Ministry of Commerce Answers Reporter's Questions on Amendments to the 'Regulations of the People's Republic of China on Export Control of Dual-Use Nuclear Goods and Related Technologies'" *Xinhua Domestic Service,* February 17, 2007 at BBC.
71. For an interesting, but predictable, study comparing the CNPs of China and India see Su Yang, "*Zhongguo yu Yindu de zonghe guoli bijiao*" [Comparison of China's and Indian CNP] accessed at <http://www.globalview.cn/ReadNews.asp?NewsID=1308>. See also "*Zhongyin zongheguoli de bijiao*" January 8, 2008 [Comparison of China India CNP] accessed at <http://hi.baidu.com/rgoogle/blog/item/af1ca8d747c1a7d9a044df68.html/cmtid/1bec0386f0e1613366096e4c> ; and Hu Mao, "*Zhongyin zonghe guoli yu junshi de bijiao*" [Comparison of China India CNP and military] May 24, 2005 accessed at <http://military.china.com/zh_cn/critical3/27/20050524/12338986.html>. Noted South Asia specialist Amb Cheng Ruisheng observed, after comparing the political and economic systems and the geo-political contexts of China and India that the CNP of China is larger than that of India and is also expected to further expand in the next two decades. He argued that in the long-term perspective India is constrained by its socio-political and economic contradictions. See Cheng Ruisheng, "*Zhongyin guoji diwei de bijiao*" [Comparison of the international standing of China and India] accessed at <http://yataisuo.cass.cn/Bak/nyyj/9802-1.htm>.

3

Chinese National Military Strategy and Modern Trends

NAVNEET KUMAR

Introduction

China's employment of her military in her quest for enhancing her Comprehensive Military Power (CNP) is a well known fact. What is not well known is People Liberation Army's (PLA) military strategy. While there are numerous indicators and eye catching developments in the military hardware modernisation sphere e.g. its missile development programmes, acquisition of latest fighter aircrafts and its nuclear submarine programs, there are hardly any such clear contours defining PLA's military strategy. True to the mysticism surrounding Chinese approach to multifarious spheres of politics, diplomatic and economics, its sphere of military strategy too is mired with speculative as well as informed guessing with military strategists' world over trying hard to connect the proverbial dots.

It is not difficult to imagine the predicament of students of PLA military strategy. Lately, there has been a deluge of Chinese literature, made available by Chinese authorities helping the researchers with useful information on the subject. In addition to translations of these primary sources, a number of Chinese military writings in the form of discussions and analyses are available more freely in various newspapers, magazines and internet. The practice of publishing its military thought process in the form of Defence White Papers (DWP) once in every two years starting from 2002 along with various official websites has further contributed to increased military transparency. All this has helped the academic community to have a closer look at the PLA military affairs. But here comes the catch. This perceived enhancement of transparency runs counter to the somewhat unflinching assumption of China's 'double speak' on almost all its issues concerning national development, politics, economy and most importantly national security. So ,the 'other` popular school of thought in the world academic community and students of PLA see these elaborate Chinese efforts towards military transparency as part of a bigger exercise of Perception Management and Public Diplomacy targeting international audience.. Frequent references from Sun Tzu like "Hide your intentions and bide your time" and "All war is deception" are used to substantiate this hypothesis. This approach urges the military thinkers to look deeper through the surface and not get distracted by what is obvious. This approach views most of the Chinese military activities through the prism of its unpredictable 'intentions', thereby assigning a mystic motive to its every activity in a particular manner.

The fact of the matter is that 'China sells'. The study of Chinese issues—be its economy, politics, military, sports, human rights, disaster management, stock market, reality prices, violation of intellectual property rights—everything sells. There is an entire 'Think Tank Industry' around the world which is working overtime to draw important inferences on various such issues. While it is extremely beneficial for the world population to be informed about such issues, its implications on shaping up the public opinion and its consequent impact on governmental policies have to be kept in mind. Wrong input from military thinkers, acting purely as 'advocacy groups' in order to support the government policies or public diplomacy exercises, is fraught with dangerous implications. Such 'opinionated researches' may result in wrong policy choices, thus proving to be risky propositions in the long run. China is (as well as India and many others) too important a country to run such risks.

So, what is the suggested way to arrive at correct PLA military strategy? Since there are numerous military strategy students who express their views on PLA military strategy by putting the 'intentions prism' before studying every PLA activity, I have tried to adopt a different approach. I have attempted to study what China is officially saying loudly through open sources, find coherence in her thought process and analyse it. After drawing out implications of its official version, I have attempted to assess the probable future, opportunities and risks attached to its official military strategy. If the projected 'signposts' do not confirm to this futuristic projections, military analysts are welcome to revert back to alternative line of thought which may point to clash of interests and probable conflict. My intention is to find futuristic opportunities in order to alter the futuristic conflict projections.

The aim of this paper is to study Chinese National Military Strategy (NMS) and emphasise that PLA is gradually moving towards conduct of non war missions. This shift is bound to impact the relationships amongst the Chinese Communist Party (CCP), PLA and Chinese people. In addition to internal ramifications, it has the potential to create major opportunities to the international stakeholders. How well the external world manages these opportunities is deeply dependent on our understanding of these changes.

In order to understand PLA military strategy, or for that matter NMS of any country, it is extremely important to understand as to what is the meaning and implications of National Security Strategy (NSS). NSS, also called National Strategy or Grand Strategy is "The art and science of developing, applying and coordinating the instruments of national power (diplomatic, economic, military, informational, legal, technological, cultural etc.) in order to achieve objectives that contribute to national security. Ideally, NSS should be the *core document* for a nation describing its national aims and objectives (The Ends), its broad strategic concepts (The Ways) and its strategies to employ its resources (The Means) in order to achieve its objectives. From this document all the instruments and elements of national power like diplomacy, information, military, economy, law enforcement and technology etc. derive out their sub strategies which are implemented through synergized, time bound and monitored plans. NMS of any country flows out of NSS. NMS therefore, is art and science of distributing and applying military power to attain/support national objectives, as laid down in NSS, in both peace and war. It is not necessary that the military strategy is formulated only for its actual application; the mere knowledge of a strong military force itself may achieve its purpose towards overall NSS. The possibility and extent of application of military power would be contingent on numerous factors like the history, culture, national pride, present and future security scenario(s) as well as likely gains accruing out of its application. The NMS is spelt out as broad directives concepts and they serve as planning guidance. The most important inference for us is to understand that NMS is closely linked to the NSS; in fact, it is the sub strategy of the latter. Any modification in the NMS is a clear indicator of such modification in the NSS and vice-versa.

Many countries like US and UK do publish their NSS as well as NMS in open public domain.[1] It has immense advantages. Not only these documents serve as important tools for policy makers across an inter agency spectrum by conveying their thought process clearly to their domestic target audience i.e. policy implementing agencies at operational and tactical level but also these documents help in achieving the very important task of conducting strategic communication with global agencies including states, NGOs and organisations like UN, IMF, World Bank etc. China does not publish her NSS or NMS in open public domain, but owing to various reasons including international pressure for military transparency has forced China to publish official Defence White Papers (DWP) since 1998. The six DWP published so far do not ***clearly*** mention about Chinese NMS under which PLA is currently operating but their detailed study does point out to a reasonably clear framework of their NMS with adequate flesh. In addition to DWP, since 2000 the availability of primary sources of PLA thought process in the form of official publications, commentaries, discussions in the public domain has increased exponentially. These sources provide valuable inputs in the form of fillers and confirmations to the information available in DWP. In the context of Chinese NMS, a very important development took place in 2003 when Jiang Zemin's speeches, directives, and guidance to the PLA were granted the status of 'enduring thought' in the hierarchy of CCP political theory. Since Chinese NMS transformed radically during Jiang Zemin's tenure as Chairman of Central Military Commission (CMC), these writings, when made publically available in the form of three-volume selected works of Jiang Zemin (2006),[2] proved immensely useful in interpreting Chinese NMS.

A word here about transparency and authenticity of these open sources would not be out of place. There is a general sense of disbelief among students of Chinese strategy about the degree of transparency displayed by the Chinese military publications, especially the DWP. In this context, it is pertinent to refer to a Study conducted by Centre for Strategic Research Institute for National Strategic Studies(CSRINSS), National Defence University, Washington, USA in June 2010 'Assessing Chinese Military Transparency'.[3] This institute evaluated changes in transparency amongst six Chinese DWPs and compared its 2008 DWP with that of DWPs or equivalent documents published by 13 other Asian Pacific countries including India, Japan, South Korea and Australia. They developed a methodology to evaluate DWPs of 14 countries[4] by choosing 19 categories under major headings of security environment, National Security Goals, General Defence Policy, major areas of concern, current defense posture, defence management and international activity. They found that "there has been a gradual but *modest increase* in the transparency of China's DWP overtime and China's degree of transparency is roughly comparable to that of most Southeast Asian countries and to India, but significantly less than Asian-Pacific democracies such as Japan and South Korea." Another important point to note is that one of the most transparent areas found by the study team in Chinese DWP is their statement of Doctrine under General Defence Policy. Their assessment of international and regional security environment has also been graded as having medium transparency.

So, what should be construed as present PLA NMS? Detailed studies of available Chinese literature clearly suggest that Chinese leaders issue their NMS in the form of *Military Strategic Guidelines (MSG).* These are the fundamental military policies of the Chinese Communist Party (CCP) and the Chinese nation and are issued to the PLA by the Central Military Commission (CMC) and accordingly detailed programmes and plans are developed by it. MSG are "the fundamental military policies (*junshi zhengce*) of the party and the nation. They are the overall principles (*zong yuanze*) and guiding principles (*zong gangling*) for planning and guiding the development and utilisation of the armed forces."[5] MSG are issued to the PLA by the CCP CMC. Since new guidelines are issued by the Chairman CMC (often also the CCP secretary general and state president) it has only been done four times since 1949. Significant changes to the MSG are initiated by a major speech delivered by the CMC chairman to the leadership of the PLA at an expanded meeting of the CMC. These speeches serve as indicators of any major changes in the contents of the NMS. In keeping with these traditions, on 13 January,1993, Jiang Zemin, the then chairman of the CMC promulgated a new set of MSG known as "MSG for the New Period".

It is felt that while *MSG for the New Period* (issued in 1993 referred now as MSG 93) represents the basic Chinese NMS, some important changes are happening since 2004, when Hu Jintao, the present Chairman of the CMC expounded a set of "New Historic Missions". Later publication of 2006 and 2008 DWPs have further modified these missions to include Diversified Military Tasks (DMTs) and Military Operations Other Than War (MOOTW). Simply put, MSG 93 acts like a 'Rolling National Military Strategy' with additional inputs, missions, statements serving to further clarify various elements of the NMS and new programmes are added or modified as the case may be. This paper will now try to explain the present Chinese NMS with MSG 93 as the basis for explaining its various elements and emphasising the latest thinking of PLA on these. The key concerns or the strategic issues covered in MSG 93 and also the present Chinese NMS are mentioned in the succeeding paragraphs.

Major Strategic Issues in Chinese NMS

The major strategic issues covered in Chinese NMS are as follows:

(a) Presenting the Strategic Assessment.
(b) Articulating the Strategic Missions and Strategic Objectives.

(c) Issuing Guidance for Military Combat Preparations.
(d) Active Defense Strategy.
(e) Determining the focus for Army Building.

Presenting the Strategic Assessment (*Zhanlue Panduan*)

The strategic assessment is akin to 'environmental scan' which forms an essential part of any strategy formulation. The most important issue concerning strategic assessment is its being both a political as well as military assessment. It forms the basis for not only the NMS, but also for the NSS. It usually provides assessment of state of international relations and global order, trends in relations among key national powers and other important groups of nations. It clearly brings out China's position in overall international relations, its impact on China's Comprehensive National Power (CNP) and national objectives and expresses China's view on employment of its military power towards enhancement of its CNP. In the field of security affairs, this assessment clearly states out the global security environment, emerging traditional and non traditional threats, challenges and opportunities and their impact on China. It is in this context that in mid-1980s China 'Strategic window of opportunities' during which threat of world war between US and USSR receded and 'peace and development' were correctly identified as the main trends in global security scenario by Deng Xiaoping.

As regards military matters, the strategic assessment provides inputs on the aspects of contemporary warfare. It links up global developments on economic, political and security front and provides key insights to the national military about what kind of warfare they can expect in future. It also highlights the specific combat operations they would be required to train for, emphasising the kind of Revolution in Military Affairs (RMA), role of technology and information superiority as well as emerging new frontiers of aerospace and cyber warfare. This assessment also highlights the domestic security, economic and development issues and the role Chinese security forces are expected to play towards achieving national objectives concerning these. Since the assessment regarding military matters accrue out of political assessment and even given out by the Chinese political heads, it ensures a great degree of synergy between NSS and NMS, thereby making it easier for military leadership to develop relevant military programmes towards achieving national objectives as well as for political leadership to adequately support such programmes through adequate allocation of funds.

Current Strategic Assessment

There is a remarkable continuity displayed by Chinese political hierarchy since mid 80s regarding correctly identifying *'peace and development'* as the 'principal theme of the times'. This has helped them not only in carrying on full throttle with their economic development but also with military modernisation. Current assessment also talks about "economic globalisation, multipolarisation, industrialisation and informationisation"[6] and low risk of worldwide, all-out and large scale wars for a relatively long period of time. It also talks about challenges to this trend of peace and development in the form of struggles for strategic resources, strategic locations and strategic dominance. It identifies existence of hegemonism and power politics and emergence of local conflicts and wars. Non traditional threats like terrorism, environmental disasters, climate change, serious epidemics, transnational crime and piracy are also highlighted.

China is concerned about the impact of increasing influence of military power on international relations as well as CNP. She is worried about "some major powers" (US) building up their alliances, accelerating the transformation of their armed forces with advanced technology weapons and equipment. Strategic nuclear forces, astronautics, ballistic missile defence systems and global and battlefield reconnaissance and surveillance are among the top priorities of these powers. "Some developing countries" (India?) were seen as seeking and acquiring advanced technology capabilities to increase the strength of armed forces. Coupling all this with policy of supporting diplomatic strategy with military power has resulted in regional arms race and posing grave challenges to the international arms control and non proliferation regimes.

The Asia-Pacific security situation, though stable, holds many uncertainties. These include current financial crisis impact on regional economic development, political instability in some countries, ethnic and religious discords and conflicting claims over territorial and maritime rights and interests. US increased strategic focus on the region, strengthening its military alliances and enhancing its regional military capabilities is viewed with caution. Terrorist, separatist and extremist as well as non traditional threats do exist in the region. China's security situation was perceived to be improving but still confronted with long term, complicated and diverse security threats and challenges. China views all aspects of traditional, non traditional, domestic and international existence and development security as interwoven and interactive.

After having carried out 'crystal gazing', the next component of strategy formulation is defining clear missions and objectives for the military instrument of power. The current strategic assessment by Chinese political and military leaders led to a definite 'tweaking in' of PLA missions and objectives over the years. It is therefore interesting to analyse the transformation of multiple missions and role assigned to PLA and their impact.

Articulating the Strategic Missions (*Zhanlue Renwu*) and Roles of the Armed Forces

The strategic missions and roles assigned to the PLA have been listed in various biennial editions of the PRC DWPs as well as in their MSGs. It is pertinent to note that these missions have undergone changes depending upon the larger security context prevalent and also the then strategic thought process of the political leadership. Until the tenure of Jiang Zemin as chairman of the CMC, these missions listed in any permutation and combination essentially involved the following major tasks for the PLA:

(a) Defending national territory and sovereignty.
(b) Securing the nation's maritime rights and interests.
(c) Maintaining the unity of the motherland.
(d) Ensuring internal stability.
(e) Maintaining a secure and stable external environment, especially China's periphery.

The above mentioned tasks basically translated into two basic roles for the PLA—war fighting and deterrence. PLA further interpreted these roles into various modernisation programmes and worked overtime to improve its capabilities in these two fields under its Defence Five Year Plans. A slight hesitation in PLA leadership came when the present Chairman of the CMC, Hu Jintao in December 2004 realigned the PLA's priorities by expounding *"New Historic Missions"* (NHMs) during his inaugural speech to CMC on assuming its chairmanship. Termed as "three provides and one role", they are as follows:

(a) Provide an important source of strength for consolidating the ruling position of the CCP.
(b) Provide a solid security guarantee for sustaining the important period of strategic opportunity for national development.
(c) Provide strong strategic support for safeguarding national interests.
(d) Play a major role in maintaining world peace and promoting common development.

The Chinese leadership further built upon the NHMs by introducing a new term *"Diversified Military Tasks"* (DMT), a term first introduced at National

People's Congress in March 2006 and later referred in DWP of 2006 and 2008. As per DWP 2008[7] they include "counter terrorism, stability maintenance, emergency rescue and international peacekeeping" The introduction of terminology DMTs attempted to clarify the doubts which arose in PLA ranks due to the broader and intangible canvass of term NHMs. The NHMs gave an impression that PLA roles are shifting away from their basic role of winning local war under conditions of informatisation and non war missions like participation in national development, world peace and common development are assuming greater importance. It seems that term DMT was introduced to give a military like touch to additional peacetime responsibilities. This term of PLA also worked as an umbrella concept to cover both NHM as well as WLWUMIC.

In addition to above mentioned terms, a new term "*Military Operations Other Than War*" (MOOTW) was also introduced and liberally used in DWP 2008. It further emphasised the importance of non war missions of PLA. It included internal as well as external security missions involving use of armed forces in non violent manner or with including limited violence like military deterrence, military diplomacy, peace-keeping operations, counter terrorist operations, maintaining social stability, response to natural disasters and safeguarding national interest. This alphabet soup in relation to each other in terms of time and relevance can be explained in simple terms by following *Doctrinal Algebra:*[8]

DMT = WLWUMIC + NHM [MOOTW]
(2006) (2002) (2004) (2008)

The next step in Chinese NMS after enunciation of missions and roles for the PLA is giving guidance regarding the kind of warfare for which PLA should prepare itself. Similar to the process of 'mission evolution' the evolution process of this aspect also makes an interesting study.

Guidance for Military Combat Preparations (*Junshi Douzheng Zhunbei*)

Guidance for Military Combat Preparations refers to the type of warfare the PLA must be prepared to fight and therefore also constitutes an official assessment of next type of war that is most likely to be fought by the PLA.[9] This guidance contained in the NMS clearly makes a capability based assessment of the future warfare which PLA must prepare for. Students of PLA strategy have been using various lexicons under this head e.g. 'people's war', 'limited or local war', 'local wars under normal conditions', 'local wars under modern hi-tech conditions' or 'local wars under informatised conditions'. Similar to the Strategic Assessment, this guidance given by the highest political leadership is of immense importance to the military hierarchy. Once it comes from the fountainhead of the leadership of the country, its following is more or less assured both from the political as well as military apparatus of the country.

It would be important to understand here as to how Chinese political leaders guided PLA in the past regarding its military combat preparations. In 1930s and 1940s, Mao Zedong propagated the concept of *People's War* for the defence of the Chinese mainland from a more advanced invader. At the heart of this concept was taking advantage of China's inherent strengths of a large population and vast land mass while employing traditional Chinese fighting skills of speed, surprise and deception. This concept urged PLA to emphasise the role of man over weapons, mobilisation of the population and use of guerilla tactics until enough combat power could be mustered for a transition to conventional operations. Post independence, when China developed technologically and especially after development of nuclear weapons, modern weapon systems including air, naval missiles and nuclear forces were incorporated into this concept and the name was changed to *'People's War Under Modern Conditions'.*

In 1985, Deng Xiaoping declared categorically that the likelihood of a major war was remote and local war would be the most likely form of future combat, thereby emphasizing the lexicon *'Local War under Modern Conditions'* for PLA. Jiang Zemin was greatly impressed by US forces performance in 1991 and in 1993 clearly assessed that PLA must cease focusing its modernisation efforts on late industrial age warfare and technology and shift to the future warfare and technology of 20th and 21st century. This was clearly governed by understanding the possibility of enemy using precision attack missiles as well as long range aircraft to launch surgical strikes at the strategic targets throughout the country. PLA was thus guided to prepare for *'Local Wars under Modern High-Tech Conditions'.* The proof that the PLA NMS is a kind of 'rolling strategy' in which regular adjustments and modifications are carried out owing to changes in perceptions as well as general, geopolitical and technological environment is no better exemplified than changes in description of future warfare by PLA political and military leadership. The description of 'Local Wars Under Modern High-Tech Conditions' was officially changed to *'Winning Local War Under Modern Informatised Conditions'* (WLWUMIC) in 2002, when it was felt that 21st Century warfare would entail a complete informatisation of the entire range of sensor, to firing weapon systems.

PLA is following the guidance of WLWUMIC for combat preparations till date and continuously developing modern programmes for building its national defence and armed forces as part of this overall guidance. It has set itself the objectives of "laying a solid foundation by 2010, accomplish mechanisation and make major progress in informationisation by 2020 and by and large reach the goal of modernisation of national defense and armed forces by mid 21st century".[10] PLA refers to mechanisation as equipment up gradation, acquisition and modernisation whereas information refers to networking of these equipment so that all arms and the services (ground, air, naval and nuclear forces) can operate their surveillance , information, intelligence, command, control and firing system on common platforms.

The Chinese NMS, after discussing strategic assessment, PLA missions and roles and guidance of combat preparations would be incomplete unless a vital component of 'Active Defence' is added in it. It is perhaps the most important component of Chinese NMS.I deliberately chose to discuss it after some basic components of NMS have been discussed earlier in the paper.

Adjustment to the Active Defense Strategy (*Jiji Fangyu Zhanlue*)

In the plethora of lexicon used to describe Chinese NMS, terms like 'Active Defence', 'Active Defence Strategy' and 'Military Security Guidelines of Active Defence' are clearly, the most confusing and misunderstood among international academic community. Strategic thinkers across the world interpret them differently. The term "Active Defense" (jiji fangyu) originates from "Mao Zedong Military Thought", especially Mao's 1936 essay "The Problems of Strategy in China's Revolutionary War". It defined[11] it as:

> Active Defense is also known as offensive defense, or defense through decisive engagement Passive defense is also known as purely defensive defense or pure defense. Passive defense is actually a spurious kind of defense, and the only real defense is active defense, defense for the purpose of counter-attacking and taking the offensive....Militarily speaking, our warfare consists of the alternate use of the defensive and the offensive. In our case *it makes no difference whether the offensive is said to follow or to precede the defensive,* because the crux of the matter is to break the "encirclement and suppression".

This later on became popular as 'Active Defense Strategy' (ADS). It could be seen that essentially, the terminology established a set of *broad strategic concepts and principles* and a set of very general *operational concept* for *prosecuting war* at the strategic level of conflict. In 1956, ADS became linked to MSG when Marshall-Peng Duhai linked the two at an expanded meeting of the CMC by adding a political component to the ADS (i.e. strategically, China does not attack until it is attacked) and declaring that China would adopt the 'Military Strategic Guidelines of the Active Defense'.[12] Lately, the scope of this terminology has been further expanded to the 'Military Security Guidelines of the Active Defense for the New Period' and used extensively in DWP 2008. Presently this 'omnibus' term not only *covers the strategic and operational concepts* for *prosecuting war* (by WLWUMIC) but *also covers the principles of deterrence, nuclear strategy of no first use, PLA modernisation and army building* in view of DMTs (including NHMs and MOOTW) *and strategic concept of people's war.*

Three important conclusions can be drawn from this evolution of the terminology of 'Active Defense' to 'ADS' to 'MSG of Active Defense' to 'MSG of Active Defense for the New Period'. Firstly, the levels of concepts mentioned have graduated from the operational or strategic to national level. Secondly, the contents of MSG of ADS have progressively been broadened from war fighting to the all encompassing national level military concepts (mentioned earlier) as part of NMS. In fact, *'MSG of Active Defense for the New Period' essentially is the present Chinese NMS.* Thirdly and more importantly, the realignment of PLA's missions in terms of DMTs, NHMS and MOOTW is clearly an added emphasis in the latest terminology as compared to Jiang Zemin's era, as also the concept of People's War. The essential concepts highlighted in 'MSG of Active Defense for the New Period' (now referred as ADS) are covered under subsequent paragraphs.

The first and foremost important component of the ADS is explanation regarding *prosecuting war.* DWP 2008 clearly states that "strategically, China adheres to the principle of featuring defensive operations, self defense and striking and getting the better of the enemy only after the enemy has started an attack."[13] After careful analysis of other available military literature, this general statement can easily be expanded to include following broad deductions:

- (a) Overall, China's military strategy is defensive. It attacks only after being attacked. But the operations are offensive in nature.
- (b) China's counter offensive will not be limited by space or time.
- (c) It will not put boundaries on the limits of its offensives.
- (d) China will wait for the time and conditions that favour its forces when it does initiate offensive operations.
- (e) It will focus on the opposing force's weaknesses.
- (f) It will use own force to eliminate the enemy's forces (i.e. not depend on others).

(g) Offensive operations against the enemy and defensive operations for its own force protection will be conducted simultaneously.
(h) China will maximize its advantages against the opposing forces.

ADS *also* points out towards the *doctrinal component* of prosecution of war. In order to WLWUMIC, it will follow basic approach of integrated joint operations and bring the operational strengths of all arms and services in full play, combine offensive and defensive operations and make the best use of their strong points to attack the enemy's weak points. It also talks about refining the joint command, training, logistics and organisational structure in order to WLWUMIC. ADS focuses on enhancing the capabilities of the armed forces accomplishing DMTs with focus on NHMs, WLWUMIC and MOOTW. These have already been explained in detail previously in the paper.

The *second important component of ADS is deterrence.* It lays stress on deterring crises and wars through close coordination among military, political, diplomatic, economic, cultural and legal endeavors. China aims to shape a favourable security environment, thereby preventing and defusing crisis and deterring conflicts and wars. It believes in building a lean and effective deterrent force and the flexible use of different means of deterrence. As regards nuclear strategy, it believes in policy of 'No First Use' and self defensive nuclear strategy.

The *third most important component* ADS specifically addresses is about "carrying forward the strategic concept of people's war".[14] It talks about the importance of people in building of national war potential and defense strength. It mentions about "striving to make innovations in the content and forms of people's war, exploring new approaches of the people in participating in warfare and support for the front and developing new strategies and tactics for people's war in conditions of informationisation.[15] PLA subordinates its development to the overall national construction, supports local economic and social development and consolidates the unity between PLA and government, and between PLA and people."

Determining the Focus for Army Building (*Jundui Jianshe*)

The final important component of Chinese NMS is actually laying down the important modernisation programmes (or Army Building) which will prepare PLA in achieving its 'war and non war missions'. In strategy terms this comprises of the 'ways and means' of the NMS construct. The PLA uses the term Army Building (jundui jianshe) when it speaks of modernisation and reform effort. In addition to the modernisation objectives, PLA reforms, capabilities to be developed and required institutional superstructure are covered under this head.

The MSG 93 expounded by Jiang Zemin identified following key areas for pursuing Army Building:

(a) Development of science and technology for national defence and development of weapon systems and supporting technologies.
(b) Enhance the overall quality of officers and enlisted personnel. This included strengthening of unit training, army instruction military research, development of military academies and schools developing doctrines and unit level tactics to WLWUMIC.
(c) Bring about organisational changes including Rapid Reaction Forces (RRFs), reserve forces and improving mechanisms for rapid national defense mobilisation.
(d) Strengthen and improve the military ideological and political work by developing Military- Party organisations at all levels, guaranteeing Party's absolute leadership over the military and collective unity within units.
(e) Strengthen the development of military logistics from the unit level up to national level mobilisation mechanisms through formation of a joint civil-military logistics support system.

Based on these guidelines CMC in December 1995 issued the 'Outline of the Plan for Army Building the 9th Five Year Plan' covering 1996-2001, which coincided with state's ninth Five Year Plan ensuring requisite funding for PLA. In addition to the above mentioned general areas, each of the PLA services and branches were issued new Army Building Missions based on the future hi-tech requirements in WLWUMIC. 'Control of the air', 'control of the sea' and 'strategic strike' capabilities were emphasised for PLA Navy, Air Force and the Second Artillery Corp respectively, thereby giving clear building directives to these services in addition to ground forces.

In view of the abundance of available data on PLA modernisation programmes, details of various service specific programmes have not been mentioned in this paper. Suffice to say that the 'mechanisation' (equipment acquisition) and 'informatisation' (networking of equipment) of the PLA in important areas of weapon system and combat capabilities, institutional, structural, systematic and personnel reforms and doctrinal adjustments are progressing extremely well. In fact, the pace of PLA modernisation clearly has given rise to suspicion in the regional and global circles about the 'peaceful development' objective of PRC.

The above mentioned components of Chinese NMS, in my view do fulfill the conditions of a workable and forward looking 'rolling military strategy' which any country matching the size and aspirations of China should have. It is one thing to have an NMS, but totally different to ensure its smooth implementation as per the intended desire of highest political and military leadership. Though unity of national effort in terms of iron rule of CCP has certainly facilitated in effective strategy formulation and implementation process, it would be naïve to assume that this process would be without major challenges. In succeeding paragraphs, I have attempted to identify the future trends in Chinese NMS and their likely implications.

FUTURE TRENDS AND IMPLICATIONS: BROADENING SCOPE OF PLA MISSIONS

The most important trend in Chinese NMS is the broadening scope of PLA missions. While WLWUCOI is retained as the desired core capability, non war missions and tasks are assuming more importance under the rubric of NHMs, DMTs and MOOTW. It is very important to understand as to why such tinkering with the terminology of PLA missions like NHMs, DMTs,WLWUMIC and MOOTW has been done and what hidden message(s) does it convey to various audience, in a typical subtle Chinese manner.

Expounding of NHMs could be seen both as an external as well as domestic compulsion for Hu Jintao. The blistering PLA modernisation programmes since late 90s were creating a lot of apprehensions in the region as well as across the globe. However hard China was trying to assuage the world about her peaceful intentions, the PLA modernisation programmes were giving a different perception altogether to the external audience. This anxiety in the neighbourhood had the potential to be a spoiler in the overall strategic picture of 'peace and development' for PRC. The last thing China wants is increased presence of US military in their 'sphere of interest' on the pretext of providing 'security umbrella' or capability to react to any contingency (Taiwan). These pin pricks were bound to deny China the erstwhile 'strategic window of opportunity' during which it utilised free US security insurance cover to focus on its economic development. Therefore, China deliberately tried to tone down the perceived PLA's hegemon image by assigning it new non war missions towards its efforts to contribute to 'world peace' and 'common development'. Hu JinTao through expounding NHMs tried to project China's image of responsible member of international community committed to ensure global peace and security and simultaneously aimed to synergise with its foreign policy objective of sustaining an international environment conducive to continued economic growth.

The other important compulsions for expounding NHMs were purely domestic in nature. The changing security environment actually warranted additional emphasis to be given to non war missions. With the possibility of a local war receding and improving relations with Taiwan, the continued justification for accelerating PLA modernisation programmes required new and expanded missions which went beyond the traditional geographic frontier and secure the 'interest frontier'[16] of PRC around the world, across various mediums. The 'strategic window of opportunity' enjoyed hither-to-fore by China in carrying out relentless economic development and pursuit of national interests could no more be taken for granted. It even made economic sense to re-orientate the expensive military tool's effort towards issues providing cost effective spin offs e.g. internal stabilisation, national calamities management and counter terrorism. In view of the perpetual high budgetary demands made by military leaders to carry out their 'war fighting modernisation', political leaders always have to balance such allocations and try to maximize PLA's efforts towards war as well as non-war missions. In addition, the enhanced PLA modernisation programmes were giving rise to increasing political aloofness amongst military cadre, which was thought to be an essential requirement to achieve rapid expertise in pure military matters, thus resulting in diminishing control of the party over the military cadre. A need was therefore felt by the political leadership to realign the priorities of PLA towards people oriented missions supporting the overall national development .Owing to all above mentioned reasons, Hu JinTao expounded the NHMs as part of his overarching concept of 'scientific development' thereby delivering a strategic masterstroke targeting international audience and domestic stakeholders especially PLA, CCP and the people. This important strategic realignment had its own repercussions in the various echelons of PLA, which has been discussed subsequently in this paper.

Future Trends and Implications: PLA's role in the Society and Concept of People's War

The second most important future trend in NMS is the PLA's changing role in Chinese society and the concept of People's War. Traditionally, Chinese people and the PLA enjoy a mutual relationship which is often described as "Mutual Support" (shuang yong), defined as "civilian work units to support the military and to provide favoured treatment terms to families of military professionals in service...and military work units to support the civilian government and to love civilian people."[17] The visible programs displaying these bonhomie become prominent around New Year's Day (January 1), during Chinese New Year (Spring Festival between January 21 and February 16) and on Army Day (August 1).

This 'love the people' concept is displayed by PLA in number of ways including participation in variety of infrastructure projects e.g. building highways, bridges, airports, ports, pipelines and railroads etc., providing medical support in the form of PLA doctors, nurses and hospitals in remote areas, blood donation, environment protection programs like tree plantation, pollution control as well as responding to national emergencies like Severe Acute Respiratory Syndrome (SARS), earthquakes, snow storm etc. In fact, the disaster relief provided by PLA during Wenchuan earthquake of May 2008 and snow and ice disaster in January-February 2008 was appreciated by all sections of society as well as political leaders.

For the civil authorities, the concept of mutual support involves supporting PLA in terms of recruitment, helping out family members of serving PLA personnel, assisting demobilised PLA soldiers in finding jobs and supporting various PLA units in cantonments in co-ordination with civil departments like electricity, construction, provisions etc. These efforts and assistance to PLA units and demobilised personnel help PLA in cutting costs and thus achieving budgetary savings from the overall allocation through central budget. In terms of resource mobilisation during wartime, the system of National Defense Mobilisation Committees, actively assist PLA and form important component of civil-military mutual support.

However, there are modern trends which are affecting the Chinese society and in turn PLA, its modernisation and its NMS. One such trend is changing socio-economic profile of the country. In view of better economic opportunities offered by the private sector, it is providing competition to the potential officers' entry to PLA. Similarly better educational and job opportunities elsewhere are restricting youth to enlist in PLA. Though the rural and poor youth do prefer to enlist in PLA, latter is not getting the recruits as per desired standard. Secondly, China's 'one-child policy' is also proving to be a challenge to PLA. Surprisingly 'one-child soldiers' tend to exhibit normative behaviors including reluctance to engage in high-risk training, problems in cooperating with peers, and a sick call rate twice that of soldiers with siblings. This demographic trend is turning out to be interesting challenge for PLA.

There are peculiar trends displaying complex changes in civil-military relations at the local administrative level also. As explained earlier, local civilian authorities are responsible for the provision of requisite recruitment quotes for the PLA. The recent trend shows that in rural China, the liberalisation of traditional household registration system (*Hukou* system), large scale selling of agricultural land by small farmers for profit and migration of rural population to urban centres for jobs and higher wages is resulting in non-availability of qualified candidates for PLA recruitment. Therefore, the unqualified candidates in terms of their criminal records, medical and physical fitness and educational records are able to find their way into the PLA, by bribing the civilian officials. This trend is hitting at the 'mutual support' and trust shown hither-to-fore between the PLA and local civilian officials. Similar problems are being faced by the 'enlisted men' and officers on their demobilisation. Their smooth absorption in the society in terms of guaranteed job placement and preferential treatment for various social services is the responsibility of local civilian officials. The changing socio-economic profile and imbalances fail to provide equal opportunities to this de-mobilised lot, leading to widespread dissatisfaction among these persons. In fact, a research in 2003 found out that a good number of peasant uprisings in one county of Human Province were led by males with prior service experience in the PLA.[18] This has forced PLA to get special laws passed under the authority of State Council's Ministry of Civil Affairs, in order to force civil officials to meet their obligatory duties in terms of demobilisation. The rise of private sector economy is also adversely impacting the national defense mobilisation system. Traditionally, local government provides logistical support to the PLA when large exercises are held in their locales. This is undergoing a change, as private entrepreneurs are increasingly showing their reluctance to provide resources for such tasks as it depletes their profit margins due to low or no compensation received for such resources from the local government. There also exists lack of clarity in term of legal framework supporting such assistance.

Implications of New Trends in NMS on PLA

While on one hand Hu Jintao as a political figurehead and president of CMC is busy re-alligning PLA missions and tasks owing to number of compulsions, as described, on the other hand there are a lot of debates and discourses on the possible implications of these strategic changes, thereby resulting in various "contradictions"[19] amongst Chinese military thinkers. The most important contradiction is *between the cost and the availability of resources for PLA modernisation.* With additional responsibilities thrust upon PLA in view of NHMs, PLA is finding it hard to balance the 'ends' and the 'means' required for its army

building. This is popularly being referred as *"1 Contradiction; 2 Incompatibles"*[20] by Chinese military writers, "the main contradiction in our army building will still be that our level of modernisation is

> incompatible with the demands of winning a local war under conditions of informatisation, and that our military capabilities are incompatible with the demands of carrying out the army's historic missions.[21]
>
> The *first "incompatible"* is between the process of mechanisation and the process of informatisation. In their own assessments, a number of Chinese military leaders accede to the fact that *PLA still remains a mechanised force, rather than an informatised military.* Inspite of some pockets of IT sophistication, they consider the IT penetration in PLA to be of low level.
>
> The *second "incompatible"* is between the demands of war and non war missions. The non war missions are generally manpower intensive with focus on human aptitude. They require a different doctrine altogether and have different training requirements of generally lower technological level. There are huge legal, cultural, language and societal issues involved with non war missions at home and especially abroad. The 'victory lines' are blurred and thus missions take a much longer time horizon to accomplish. It is general military belief that since achieving simultaneous expertise in war as well as non war mission is extremely resource heavy in terms of manpower, timings and material resources, the efficiency achieved in one will be at the cost of other. The existence of this 'incompatible' was so serious that Hu Jintao himself clarified that "core military capabilities (for war missions) are the foundation for military operations and MOOTW capabilities are an extension of core military capabilities; the two capabilities support each other and both are indispensable."[22]

The three services of the PLA are also displaying contradictory approach towards MOOTW. The PLA Navy, in view of being best positioned and organised to undertake MOOTW at home and abroad, has welcomed them. PLA Air Force, by virtue of its strategic mobility also favors them. In fact, its role in Wenchuan earthquake won lot of laurels from the political leadership as well as various sections of the society. On the other hand, Ground Forces have displayed an ambivalent reaction to MOOTW. No doubt, MOOTW adoption will give rise to additional manpower to PLA, but the same rise owing to extra budgetary burden may prove detrimental to their technology upgradation programmes. The different approaches by different services on MOOTW are certainly hampering its whole hearted adoption by the PLA.

On the other hand emerging trend of PLA's role in Chinese society and changing concept of People's War is forcing PLA to revisit its strategic concept of People's War. "A PLA that is perceived as a drain on society rather then a productive component of China's social structure, is not likely to receive the moral, manpower or material support from the population it needs to modernize and accomplish its missions.[23] Towards this end, in addition to various issues already mentioned in the paper as part of ADS, PLA is taking following steps:

(a) Setting up a mechanism for unified and efficient national defence mobilisation.
(b) Setting up mobilisation of economy, science and technology, information and transport.
(c) Making innovations in content and forms of People's War exploring new approaches of participation peoples in warfare and support for the front.
(d) Developing new strategies and tactics for People's War in condition of informationsation.
(e) Revision in regulation on military service of active duty soldiers issuing out detailed policies and procedures for recruitment, professional development end career management of senior enlisted personnel and offices.
(f) National Defence Scholarship Programme to attract highly educated personnel in NCO and offices rank.

CONCLUSION

It is pretty evident that China does have a 'rolling' NMS synergizing PLA reform and modernisation programs. Instead of publishing it in open domain like USA or UK, Chinese leaders convey this NMS to the PLA through issuing Military Strategic Guidelines (MSG) from time to time. These MSGs generally hold good for a very long time, with every new chairman of CMC bringing out a few modifications or realignments. The various components of MSG include 'The Strategic Assessment', The Content of the Active Defense Strategy', 'Strategic Missions and Strategic Objectives', 'Military Combat Preparations' and 'The Focus for Army Building'. The origin of every military reform or modernisation program of PLA can be traced back to some fundamental decision made and conveyed to PLA through MSG. The most recent MSGs are the ones issued by Jiang Zemin in 1993 and modified by Hu Jintao in late 2002 (the introduction of terminology of WLWUMIC), 2004 (introduction of NHMs) and in 2009 (introduction of MOOTW as expounded in DWP 2008).

We should not get unduly hassled or confused with new slogans and terminologies, each interpreted differently by different scholars of varying nationalities at various points of time. The basic tenets of MSG over the years have remained the same. The strategic assessment of identifying the 'strategic window of opportunity' and 'peace and development' as the 'principal theme',

'Active Defense Strategy', military combat preparations by 'winning wars under the focus of army building conditions of informatisation' and strategic missions in terms of 'Diversified Military Tasks (DMTs), 'New Historic Missions' (NHMs) and MOOTW—all these clearly demonstrate the remarkable continuity and continuous refinements in various tenets of NMS. *There is nothing hidden, full of suspense, exotic or strange in China NMS.* It is a purely calculated and practical 'strategy' befitting the size of the country and it's military.

It is also extremely important to analyze Chinese NMS in a different paradigm altogether. This can be done at two levels, first the relationship *within the various components* of the NMS and secondly, the relationship which *NMS enjoys with other national level strategies* including foreign, economic, information and development.

As regards the first part, NMS displays exceptional balance and coherence within its different tenets. The various components of NMS viz. the ADS, preparation for military combat, missions and objectives and the PLA modernisation programmes not only grow from each other but also display a remarkable degree of symbiosis , continuity, balance and realignment over the years. PLA political leadership have proactively and astutely assessed not only the global and regional security situations but also efficiently translated this assessment into exact *deliverables* in the form of multiple military programmes. The success of their approach can clearly be gathered from the prolonged peaceful strategic window made available to PLA to carry out its unhindered modernisation. Smooth transition from the concepts of 'People's War' to 'Local War' to 'Local War Under high tech conditions' to 'Local War under informatized conditions' bears testimony to the success of this 'rolling' NMS over the years. The latest proof of these 'informed' changes to the NMS was the pronouncement of NHMs in 2004, which clearly was an effort to realign PLA's missions to the changing global and domestic requirements, as discussed in the paper earlier. In fact, the pronouncements and implementation of long term military modernisation plans like '30 year informationisation plan'[24] ensured the larger continuity of such plans. This by no means suggests that the formulation of NMS and its implementation among military cadres was an easy task. Military cadres at all levels did show their reservations and apprehensions on NMS over the years. The fact that the internal military debates occurring at various levels of PLA are not available in open domains, does not point to their absence. But, such debates, apparently only added to the refinements at the policy making as well as implementation processes.

In my view, the most important feature of PLA NMS is the higher level coordination it could achieve with other national strategies and other instruments of national power. The foremost in this regard is the remarkable congruity and symbiosis between the Chinese military and polity. In addition to the various established institutional mechanisms prevalent in their politico-military structures in the form of CCP's Central Committee and CMC (both at the state and party level) Chinese political leadership actually succeeded not only in ensuring keeping its military instrument under check but also ensured its continued modernisation. The CCP has successfully kept 'the gun under control' and hopes to do so in future too. In spite of numerous contrarian scenarios depicted by non Chinese military experts, CCP's control over the gun has not displayed any trend reversal. Since the strategic assessment, military missions and their future warfare preparations were clearly spelt out by the political leadership themselves, the synergy among the 'ends', 'ways' and 'means' was successfully achieved including the requisite provision of funds for military.

The second most important feature of Chinese NMS, *is it subordination to the National Development Strategy*. As it is evident from the Military Strategic Guidelines of the ADS, it has been clearly brought out in words as well as acts, that the PLA modernisation in specific and PLA NMS in particular has been viewed as but one element of the nation's enhancement of 'Comprehensive National Power'.[25] The resource allocation to the PLA as part of NMS, thus, is part of the well thought out overall National Development Strategy, therefore part of the other overall national objectives. This clearly achieves the synergy of the desired level in NMS and NSS of any country. A PLA National Defense University's Army Building Research Department (2004) publication[26] clearly writes down:

> The military strategic guidelines of the new period persists with obeying and serving the development strategy of our nation....Our national development strategy (guojia fazhan zhanlue) is a strategy of comprehensive development that employs the strategy of economic development as the core , and is the general strategy (zong zhanlue) for guiding the coordinated development of our nation's economy, politics ,military, diplomacy, culture,[etc].The military strategic guidelines for the new period are a component of the national development strategy so without doubt they should obey and serve the nation's general strategy.

In my view, the subservience of NMS to national development, gradual shift of PLA missions to non-war missions and ensuing doctrinal changes, continued control of CCP on PLA and national efforts towards redefining the concept of People's War in view of societal changes point to the *long term mega trend of mellowing down of PLA* .The various 'signposts' in these 'sub-trends' have to be monitored regularly in order to confirm or reject this hypothesis. The risk management processes and contingency planning in case of trend reversal need to be in place. *But most importantly, opportunities offered by this mega trend need to be identified in civilian and military field and be exploited, as I am of the firm view that they are the best bets available to nudge China towards desired future.*

END NOTES

1. The first time US published its NMS on public domain was in 1992.
2. PLA National Defence University Army Building Research Department, *Study Guide for Jiang Zemin Thought in National Defence and Army Building.* Chinese Communist Party History Publishing House, Beijing. April 2004, 2nd edition.
3. Michael Kiselycznyk and Phillip C Saunders. *Assessing Chinese Military Transparency.* National Defense University Press Washington D.C.. June 2010.
4. The countries included: Australia, Brunei, China, Cambodia, India, Indonesia, Japan, Laos, Philippines, Singapore, South Korea, Taiwan, Thailand and Vietnam.
5. PLA National Defence University Army Building Research Department, *Study Guide for Jiang Zemin Thought in National Defence and Army Building,* Chinese Communist Party History Publishing House, Beijing, April 2004, 2nd edition.
6. China's Defence White Paper 2008.
7. Chinese DWP 2008.
8. Andrew Scobell, *Discourse in 3-D : The PLA's Evolving Doctrine, CIRCA 2009.* The PLA at Home and Abroad: Assessing the Operational Capabilities of China's Military. Strategic Studies Institute. Jun 2010.
9. David M. Finkelstein, *China's National Military Strategy: An overview of the "Military Strategic Guidelines"*, in *Right Sizing the People's Liberation Army: Exploring the Contours of China's Military.* 2006. US Army War College.
10. China's Defence White Paper 2008.
11. Dennis J Blasko, *The Chinese Army Today*, Routledge, 2010, p 96.
12. David M. Finkelstein, *China's National Military Strategy: An overview of the "Military Strategic Guidelines"*, Right Sizing the People's Liberation Army: Exploring the Contours of China's Military. 2006. US Army War College.
13. Chinese DWP 2008.
14. Chinese DWP 2008.
15. Ibid.
16. David Lai, *Introduction.* The PLA at Home and Abroad: Assessing the Operational Capabilities of China's Military. Strategic Studies Institute. Jun 2010.
17. Dennis J Blasko, *The Chinese Army Today,* Rontledge, 2010, p. 171.
18. David Finkelstein, Kristen Gunness, *Civil Military Relations in Today's China*, Pentagon Press, New Delhi 2009, Pp xiv.
19. Andrew Scobell, *Discourse in 3-D : The PLA's Evolving Doctrine, CIRCA 2009.*

The PLA at Home and Abroad: Assessing the Operational Capabilities of China's Military. Strategic Studies Institute. Jun 2010.

20. Ibid.
21. New Years Day Message (Liberation Army Daily), January 1, 2008.
22. Andrew Scobell, *Discourse in 3-D : The PLA's Evolving Doctrine, CIRCA 2009.* The PLA at Home and Abroad: Assessing the Operational Capabilities of China's Military. Strategic Studies Institute. Jun 2010.
23. Dennis J Blasko, *The Chinese Army Today,* Rontledge, 2010, p 181.
24. Chinese DWP 2008.
25. It is a Chinese concept of measuring the *general power* of a *nation state*, which can be calculated numerically, involving a wide variety of factors encompassing tangible and intangible strength in political, economic, scientific, technological, military, cultural and educational sphere. By CNP it generally means the overall impact of political, economic and military power. Yan Xuetong, *The Rise of China and its Power Status. Chinese Journal of International Politics,* Vol. I, 2006.
26. PLA National Defence University Army Building Research Department, *Study Guide for Jiang Zemin Thought in National Defence and Army Building,* Chinese Communist Party History Publishing House, Beijing, April 2004, 2nd edition.

4

NUCLEAR WEAPONS IN CHINA'S SECURITY THINKING

M.V. RAPPAI

How each country perceives its own security, to a large extend depends upon the strategic environment available to it. In the post-Second World War era this has been closely linked to the intrinsic capability of a nation and its military prowess including ones ability to defend itself. The use of nuclear weapons by US towards the end of the Second World War did make a difference in this thought process. The history of nuclear weapons is comparatively a very short one, yet the images it invokes are atrociously stark and ominous. Therefore, no discussion of nuclear weapons is free of these horridly destructive and gloomy images left behind by the first ever use of atomic bombs in Nagasaki and Hiroshima. A greater tragedy of its use lay in the fact that it was dropped at the fag end of the Second World War against a decimated Asian power like Japan whose population base was comparatively very shallow. Its survival and recuperation in the post war scenario largely depended upon these very spirited people. It also maybe time for Asian societies, especially the Japanese, to ask why the Americans did not try this weapon in Europe?

This pathetic and abominable experience shaped the post World War Asian psyche to a large extent. China, despite its adversarial relations with Japan, maybe due to its closeness to the territory took a serious note of the stupendous destructive capabilities of this weapon. How far these images influenced the thinking of late Chairman Mao Zedong on nuclear weapons needs to be probed further. As a predominant Asian nation this definitely evoked empathetic concerns even from the ordinary Chinese who otherwise would have preferred to hate the Japanese at that point of time.

However, the origins of China's nuclear strategy clearly reflect China's willingness to use such weapons as a political tool for enhancing the nation's vital interests and prestige. Some of these trends were really evident in its original thought process. This chapter only forms a part of my planned study on China's nuclear weapon force, more popularly known as the 'Second Artillery Force' (SAF). The attempt here is to study the strategy adopted by China for its nuclear weapons since its liberation in 1949.

One of the basic arguments is that China clearly used the possession of Nuclear weapons to gain a foothold in a totally hostile international arena and still continues to rely heavily on these weapons to enhance its *lebensraum* in the global power structure. Hence an effort is also made to understand the broad contours of China's nuclear strategy and its possible impact on China's overall national security strategy as well as on the overall international strategic scenario. Towards the end an attempt is made to briefly indicate the possible impact of this strategy on Indian nuclear forces and its future course.

Strategic thinking is an integral part of ancient Chinese ethos. Over a period, spanning several centuries this process has been nurtured as well as flourished under the patronage and active participation by a dedicated set of bureaucrats, normally referred as the *mandarins*. Under the normal circumstances, a successful Communist revolution could have supplanted the indigenous thinking process by the new predominant ideology. Maybe partly due to the historical process of Chinese revolution, which was largely led by the peasantry; the post liberation approach in social change was also different. China's own skeptical approach to its overwhelming northern neighbour, Russia conditioned through historical experience also might have affected the process of post-revolutionary changes.

Ever since the Zunyi conference in January 1935, when Mao took over the effective leadership of the Chinese Communist Party (CCP) he also exerted a lot of influence on the decision making process in China. His trusted colleagues and lieutenants played a crucial role in this process. With regard to the foreign policy and other related areas Zhou Enlai, a longtime friend and the first Premier of China had a very key role. However, in matters relating to the strategic thinking it seems Mao believed in his own rustic wisdom.

Since earlier on his approach to nuclear weapons was by and large formed by the political use of this weapon, Mao never wanted the other big powers of that time to bully China. Therefore, he realised that the nuclear weapon is an instrument in keeping the strategic autonomy of China. One of the key nuclear thinkers of present day China Maj. Gen.Wu Jianguo traces this sort of early thinking on these weapons. Mao's thinking was more guided by his rural background and the mental make up of an able peasant leader. Gen. Wu wrote "the study of issues concerning warfare can be conducted in the same way. Comrade Mao Zedong said a long time ago: 'investigation and study are very important. When we see someone hold something in his hand, we should look into the matter. What is he holding in his hand? It is a knife. What is the use of a knife? It can kill a person. Whom will he kill with the knife? He will kill the people. After probing into these matters, we should further the investigation: the Chinese people also have hands, and they can hold knives too. They can forge one if have none…."

Mao's thinking on atom bomb was also linked with China's prevailing strategic doctrine, 'the people's war', a concept developed by Mao over a period of time. For him the broad masses of people were everything. The people are the key factor, which decides the outcome of a war. Therefore, "the atom bomb is a paper tiger which the U S reactionaries use to scare people. It looks terrible, but in fact it isn't. Of course, the atom bomb is a weapon of mass slaughter, but the outcome of a war is decided by the people, not by one or two new types of weapon."

Another important factor, which played a key role in the thought process of Chinese leadership, seems to be the then prevailing conditions. With the end of the Second World War the imperialist powers felt that to keep the urge for independence and democracy in the erstwhile colonies was becoming more and more troublesome. On imperialism Mao wrote, "imperialism has prepared the conditions for its own doom. These conditions are the awakening of the great masses of the people in the colonies and semi-colonies and in the imperialist countries themselves. Imperialism has pushed the great masses of the people throughout the world into the historical epoch of the great struggle to abolish imperialism." This objective historical background also influenced China in its search for nuclear weapons.

Almost parallel to this, at the same time a big churning process was going on among the scientific community. By unleashing the destructive forces of atom they gave a potentially destructive weapon in the hands of unscrupulous politicians. Therefore, one counterstrategy thought by several scientists was the proliferation of the very same weapons to break the monopoly of weapon powers at that point of time. It may be only a mere coincidence that the scientific community which helped both India and China in setting their first experimental labs for nuclear technology turned out to be the French nuclear physicists.

This influence of international scientific community also seems to have played a crucial role in forming the nuclear strategy of liberated China. "In October 1951, Frederic Joliot Curie in Paris urged the Chinese radio-chemist Yang Chengzong to seek out Mao upon Yang's return to China. "Please tell Chairman Mao Zedong," he said, "you should oppose the atomic bomb, you should own the atomic bomb. The atomic bomb is not so terrifying." He noted that the "fundamental principles of the bomb had not been discovered by the Americans." Irene Joliot-Curie then gave Yang ten grams of radium salt standardized for radioactive emissions, because she wanted "to support the Chinese people in their nuclear research."

By 1955, this French advice and assistance had helped raise the level of consciousness in Beijing about the bomb and its potential significance for China. Mao characterised that significance for his senior colleagues in 1958, when he told them that without atomic and hydrogen bombs, "others don't think what we say carries weight."

Throughout the fifties the aim of the Chinese leadership was to acquire basic technology and amass enough material and facilities to project to the world that they are serious about making these weapons in order to avoid bullying and blackmailing by other nuclear powers. Therefore, one line of thinking about the nuclear weapons was very clear. The Chinese leadership was well aware about the potential clout of these weapons; not only as a disastrous weapon but it also is a powerful diplomatic tool which can be utilised for ending China's isolation at that point of time. This maybe, one of the major difference with India's nuclear strategy since the beginning. India always looked at this as a defensive weapon to protect once own sovereignty and territorial integrity.

Rather, the earlier Nehruvian approach laid more stress on gaining scientific and technical know-how. Hence we hardly come across any obvious reference on Indian side to use nuclear weapons as an offensive diplomatic tool in early periods of post independent India. Further, throughout the fifties and sixties Indian approach to nuclear weapons was more driven by moralistic passion and an urge to use it as a scientific tool. The defeat in 1962 war and the subsequent 1964 test by China might have added to the list of vows of modern India. Yet nobody gave a serious thought to use this weapon as a political and diplomatic tool. This by and large remains so even today, merely two years after India declared its intention to be a full fledged nuclear weapon power.

Towards the end fifties the differences between the two largest cold war allies, China and Soviet Union, had become more evident. These differences among erstwhile Soviet Union and China started ever since the involvement of Russian advisors in the Chinese Communist movement in early 1920s. Due to varying perceptions and interpretations about the fundamental nature of a society and the resulting approach towards revolution, there existed a difference of opinion among the two socialist giants. However, beyond all these polemical rhetoric one of the fundamental causes for the Sino-Soviet split in the late fifties was their differences on the nuclear cooperation.

As per the New Defence Technical Accord signed between these two countries on October 15, 1957 Soviet Union promised to supply China with blueprints and a working prototype atomic missile. However, due to acute power struggle within the Soviet hierarchy this specially assembled prototype was never delivered to China. The, "Sino-Soviet relations had considerably deteriorated by 1958 and Khrushchev decided to postpone the transaction. Unaware of this decision, the Chinese continued to build a room suitable for exhibiting the prototype for instructional purposes. Russian scientists in China even forced several modifications in the design of the room. Until the middle of 1959 Chinese workers repeatedly went to the railway station to collect the prototype that never arrived." This really aggravated the bilateral relations and gave way to the final split.

However, in different ways this helped the Chinese in pursuing their strategic goals single handedly, they knew this is going to be a tough path. The sixties saw China emerging as an independent global nuclear player.

The sixties witnessed a steady progress in China's nuclear goals. On October 16, 1964, she tested her first atom bomb, it also succeeded in testing the first nuclear capable missile on October 27, 1966. On June, 17, 1967 China exploded its first hydrogen bomb. In the meanwhile it reconstituted the special Artillery corps founded in 1958 as the strategic missile force. The Second Artillery Corps (SAC) of China was formally established on July 1, 1966 under the direct control of the Central Military Commission.

Throughout the sixties China's main thrust was to oppose any kind of restriction on its efforts to enter into the elite club of nuclear weapon powers. The first hurdle was the adoption of Partial Test Ban Treaty (PTBT) by the existing weapon powers. All nonproliferation efforts was generally looked with suspicion, therefore, it vehemently opposed all such efforts. The official declaration after its first ever nuclear test on 16 October 1964 it declared, "in developing nuclear weapons, china's aim is to break the nuclear monopoly of the nuclear powers and eliminate nuclear weapons."

The basic strategy of Chinese nuclear weapons more or less still remains as it was enunciated in its official declaration immediately after the first test. This predominantly remains as a defensive doctrine based on 'no first use. The key operative part is contained in its 'solemn proposal' for a summit conference be held to discuss "the complete prohibition and through destruction of nuclear weapons and that nuclear weapon states commit themselves not to use nuclear weapons against non nuclear weapon states and nuclear weapon free zones or against each other."

"In developing nuclear weapons, China's aim is to break the nuclear monopoly of nuclear powers and to eliminate nuclear weapons." After it acquired the position of a 'status quo nuclear weapon power' it conveniently forgot some of its good intentions. Throughout the 1960s and the 1970s, China also tried to project its weapons as a shield against imperialist forces of the world in the interest of the 'toiling masses'. China has so far conducted 45 nuclear tests and it is estimated that it has about 400-500 warheads. It is also reported to have a stockpile of 1.7 to 2.5 tonnes of weapon grade plutonium. China also relies on the highly enriched uranium route for its nuclear weapons programme.

While, it is very difficult to get any accurate data on nuclear weapons and stockpiles in open democracies, getting such information and being sure of the veracity of its sources in a country like China is close to impossible. Yet, odd statements from Chinese sources to the effect that it will be ready to consider serious strategic arms limitation talks when the major weapon powers reduce their number of warheads to the levels of one thousand, give some clues in this regard.

China's efforts to develop her delivery systems can be assessed more predictably. As of now, it has a fairly advanced arsenal of delivery systems among the medium level nuclear weapon powers. Along with its decision to make nuclear weapons, China began to think about the possibilities of developing its own delivery systems. This effort resulted in the setting up of a dedicated small group under the leadership of Marshal Nie Rongzhen and famous Chinese Physicist Qian Xuesen on October 8, 1956.

One of the fundamental differences between China's space programme and that of other countries, which have reached a certain level of development in their space programme, is noteworthy. On the basis of this difference it can be safely said that China first developed her missiles and then started thinking of converting those capabilities and knowhow into a successful space programme. Now China has emerged as a frontline competitor for launching commercial satellites in the global market. Recently, the Chinese space agency has revealed its intentions to introduce a new series of launch vehicles in the near future. This further proves the capabilities she achieved in recent times in her missile development programmes.

While we are looking into the nuclear weapons it will be useful to take a glance at the delivery systems of China. Even though China still possesses some old Russian Tu-52 bombers wired for delivering nuclear weapons, on a realistic basis it is unlikely that those will ever be used by China in an actual combat scenario. Hence it will be useful to concentrate on the missiles in their arsenal a list of the ballistic missiles is given in Table 1.

The above table clearly shows China's intention to modernise and enhance its delivery systems. Its new series of DF-31, its submarine-launched versions JL-2 and DF-41 are aimed at any possible NMD deployment in the near future. However, to link the entire modernisation process of nuclear weapons and their means of delivery systems to the issue of NMD will not be correct. It is well known that China's efforts to modernise the nuclear weapons in their quiver are closely linked to the overall plans of military modernisation in China. However, the missile defence debate has certainly accelerated this process. One immediate impact of this proposal is China's quest for sophisticated technologies and the urge for the survivability factor. Various developments during the past debate amply prove this need. China's search for its missile modernisation is reflected in its approach to procurement of technology and its application.

Unexpected breakdown of erstwhile Soviet Union was a real boon in this regard. According to different sources during the post-Soviet phase, China hired a substantial number of experts who had worked with different nuclear weapon establishments. According to various reports China was looking for scientists with a deep understanding of rocketry, guidance systems, specialised machine tool skills, etc. Apart from this there are also some Russian scientists who came through official exchange programmes. The efforts of these scientific and technical personnel have already started to reflect in the enhanced efficacy and accuracy of Chinese missiles.

Meanwhile, the Chinese nuclear weapons establishment, being aware of the limitations of the Russian technology in this field, has also kept abreast of the sophistication achieved by western nations especially, the United States. How China obtained these technologies including certain specifications relating to the latest US warhead W-88 and others is common knowledge. As per a study done by National Intelligence Council for CIA "by 2015 China will likely have tens of missiles targeted against the United States, having added a few of more survivable land-and sea-based mobile missiles with smaller nuclear warheads-in part influenced by US technology gained through

Table 1: China's Ballistic Missiles

	System	Year deployed	Fuel/ Basing	Range km.	Pay load Kg.	Warhead type	Number deployed
Short Range	DF-15 (CSS-6 or M9)	1995	solid/TEL	200-600	500-950	dual capable	100-150
	DF-11 (CSS-X-7 or M-11)	1995	solid/TEL	185-300	500	dual capable 350 kt	100+
Medium Range	DF3/3A (CSS-2)	1971	liquid/ transportable	2650-2800	2150	1-3 mt	50-120
	JL-1 (CSS-N-3)	1986	liquid/SLBM	1700	600	200-300kt	12-24
	DF21/21A (CSS-6)	1986	solid/TEL	1800	600	200-300kt	10-36+
	DF-25	1989	solid/TEL	1700	2000	*	
Inter-continental	DF-4 (CSS-3)	1980	liquid/ cave	4750	2200	1-3 mt	20-30
	DF-5/5A (CSS-4)	1981	liquid/ silo	12000-15000	3000-3260	3-5 mt, 4-5 MRV?	15-20+
	DF-31	tested	solid/ TEL	8000	700	200-300kt MRV/MIRV?	-
	DF-41	-	solid/ TEL	12000	800	MIRV?	-
	JL-2	-	solid/SLBM	8000	700	MIRV?	-

Source: For a more detailed list see M.V. Rappai, "China's Missile Modernisation" in *Nuclear India* edited by Air. Cmde. Jasjit Singh, (New Delhi: IDSA. 1998), pp. 214-218.

espionage." China has had the technical knowledge to develop an MRVed missile, however, the new technologies obtained from weapon labs of USA have enhanced its ability to deploy them with more precision. On the basis of this technical capability China is now in a position to develop and deploy the latest generation multiple independently targetable re-entry vehicles (MIRVs).

Capability of Chinese scientists in MIRV was further boosted by the help received from two US hi-tech companies in the mid-1990s. The almost sudden collapse of a Chinese Long March 3B (LM 3B) Rocket carrying a Loral satellite in February 1996, turned out to be a boon in disguise for their ballistic missile launch capabilities. A detailed investigation report of this failure conducted by one satellite expert from Hughes Corporation provided a series of useful data for improving Chinese technologies.

Recent reports in Hong Kong press pointed out that the PLA Navy is seriously working on improving its submarine launch capability. A series of tests conducted by PLA Navy submarine units and the Second Artillery troops since 2001 was part of this drive. Even though the development of JL2 series of SLBMs may not be on a high priority list now, yet the US decision to go ahead with BMD deployment will further hasten these efforts.

However, if one closely look at this there maybe two basic deviations which are becoming more visible in the post Cold War world scenario. The first one is that once China became a statusquoist nuclear power it has no real zeal for implementing the above solemn promise. Secondly, China also realistically understand that it cannot give up its nuclear weapons under the existing world order where these weapons still hold the strategic balance.

In late Sixties China's condemnation of Nuclear Non-proliferation Treaty (NPT) was one of the most virulent ones. It caricatured the 'Treaty' as an imperialistic tool to perpetuate the iniquities of the world system.

In different ways the evolution of China's nuclear strategy is very closely linked to its perceptions about the prevailing international atmosphere and the role it wanted to play in maneuvering such condition for its benefit. Therefore, the Chinese foreign policy making elite always tried to link up its policy goals to these weapons and its related activities. One such area is the use of international disarmament process for achieving these aims. Coming to the late eighties and nineties China also started conveniently to juggle the concept of *disarmament* with its antithesis the *non-proliferation.* According to Prof. Mingquan Zhu, "the evolution of China's nuclear nonproliferation policy can be divided roughly into three stages:

(1) emphasis on the national right to develop nuclear weapons (1949-59);
(2) acceptance of the nonproliferation norm and independence from the international nonproliferation regime (1959-84); and
(3) gradual integration with the international community (1984-present).

During the Cold War period China's approach towards disarmament was more idealistic and to a great extend dictated by the pragmatic necessities of maintaining its strategic autonomy. In the first phase it totally allied with the erstwhile socialist bloc for gaining the basic capabilities. In the later period China tried to cooperate with USA not only to gain its rightful strategic place in the world but also to get access to the more advanced scientific and technical knowledge. Despite the early advances the Soviet Union made in science and technology as well as in economy it never bothered to clearly understand the developments like the arms race as a tool to oppose the enemy economically and a deliberate retardation of scientific prowess of the enemy etc. This maybe largely due to the suppression of independent thinking under a very strict authoritarian Stalinist order.

In the post Cold War period China is also affected by this syndrome to a lesser extend. Especially this is true in the field of arms control and disarmament. For example the first ever defence 'white paper' published by China in 1995, tries to confuse the issue of arms control and disarmament. It states, "during the course of foreign policy implementation and national defence construction, China attaches importance to the active role of arms control and disarmament, holding that arms control and disarmament are conducive to reducing and eliminating the danger of war and increasing factors for international peace and security. Such controls and reductions will help improve relations and mutual trust among nations and will enable the contribution of more resources, capital and technology to economic and social development."

This is totally in contrast to the approach adopted by NATO and its allies. For them arms control is only a tool to restrict the capabilities of its opponents. But, before getting into this debate let us take a look at what China is actually doing on its own about its nuclear forces.

Some of the recent changes that are happening in the force structure of China itself show the significance attached to SAF by China. After the dramatic decision in the mid eighties to cut the strength of PLA by one million, the Chinese Communist Party again decided to reduce the strength of PLA by another 500,000 during the 15th Party Congress in late 1997.

On completion of the latest round of this reduction process the current strength of forces are given in the following Table 2.

Table 2: China's Military Strength

	1996-1997	2000-2001
Total strength of Armed forces	2,935,000	2,470,000
Strategic Missile Force	90,000	100,000
Army	2,200,000	1,700,000
Navy	265,000	220,000
Air Force	470,000	420,000

Source: The Military Balance, IISS London.

One significant change in the figures is the change in the profile of its Strategic Missile Forces, except this all other arms have reduced their strength. Therefore, the increase in this figure is very vital. In spite of the lip service paid by China to the ongoing non-proliferation measures at the international level it is well aware about the strategic capabilities of nuclear weapons. In the field of nuclear weapons and its posture towards India in this regard deserves our special attention. The real increase in the strength of its Second Artillery force has to be looked at from this point. This increase is only talking about the uniformed component of the Second Artillery. The real strength of its scientific and technical community supporting these efforts is still in the realms of guesstimates only.

In parallel to these developments China is also making a deliberate attempt to strengthen its capabilities in the field of missiles. Some of the recent developments show her attempts to strengthen the submarine launch capabilities of MIRVed JL-2 missiles, further refining of nuclear capable cruise missiles etc. The enhanced nuclear capability of China will definitely add to India's security problems. One recent report pertaining to the SAF revealed that China has taken a decision to form a specialised group of one hundred senior missile specialists to chalk out future plans. Further, the senior strategic thinkers of China still assume that inspite of the development of newer technologies and the progress in Revolution in Military Affairs (RMA) in the developed world, '*strategic nuclear weapons*' will still be the future 'high-technology warfare's overall defence umbrella'.

Indian national security establishment cannot remain oblivious to this reality, a China which has a lot more nuclear warheads and accurate delivery systems. This in conjuncture with its enhancing global profile seeks some urgent responses from India.

One main tragedy of the post Cold War era is the growing weakness of the disarmament process. Further, on the part of the established nuclear weapon states and the developed world a serious and deliberate attempt is made to destroy the efforts for disarmament. This aim is by and large achieved by juggling the old jargons and deliberately not to carry out any real reduction in the categories of weapons that matters. More than this a willful attempt is also made to confuse the rest of the world by deliberately inter-mingling the issues of disarmament and arms control partially and selectively. One of the sad facts is that there are enough apologists for these lobbies in India also. India must be championing the cause of disarmament and try to expose the hypocrisy of the nuclear haves.

The report of Gen. Shalikashvili on the Comprehensive Nuclear test Ban Treaty (CTBT) clearly brings out this position. His report states, "preventing proliferation is an enduring American interest......Over the decades, the United States has utilised a wide range of non-proliferation tools. We have entered into mutual security alliances and helped friendly states satisfy defence needs without having their own nuclear weapons. We have cooperated closely with like-minded states in threat reduction efforts, including export controls. We have negotiated and joined numerous international treaties, including the sequence of test ban treaties; the Non-Proliferation Treaty; and the SALT/START series of strategic arms accords. These and other less formal arms control arrangement convey the same message; nuclear weapons are different; they must be constrained by special rules."

This statement fully exposes the real intentions of developed western powers towards nuclear weapons. If India have to grow fully we have to fight and overcome this new tendency of confusing nations and broad masses of people my mixing the twin issues of disarmament and arms control. India have to reassert the necessity of real disarmament and fight against the selective arms control measures to perpetuate an unequal power balance. There are still powerful lobbies in both USA and China to make the question of proliferation as an issue of 'South Asia' centric one and use it as a tool to promote better relations between the two.

"For example, in the area of "high security," Washington and Beijing share interests in stemming the development of weapons of mass destruction and controlling their means or delivery; limiting the spread of fissile material and other militarily and strategically sensitive items;......reducing tensions in South Asia by bringing both India and Pakistan into the NPT and the WTO and freezing the nuclear progammes of both nations before they move to weaponisation and deployment...These are all vitally important strategic commonalities to build on."[1]

China started to understand this game well; and they are now operating at different levels, their primary concern is to safeguard the numerous advantages they gained as a *de jure* weapon power. In the meanwhile they also understand their widening technology gap with USA. This instills some fear about the strategic viability of existing weapons and missiles. Therefore, their basic aim is to diplomatically engage USA and other western bloc countries in order to gain further advantages. In the meantime they also do not want India and other newly emerging powers to get into these exclusive clubs, where power sharing is easier.

At one level China deliberately uses arms control mechanisms to keep its *statusquo* as a P5 and N5 club. Under the present dispensation the permanent members of the United Nation's Security Council and the exclusive nuclear club as defined by the NPT regualtions remains same. This gives a lot of advantages to these powers to influence the emerging new World order, especially on issues concerning nuclear weapons etc. But on a more practical sense it wants to fully utilise the loopholes within the existing international order. Among the existing N5 powers China holds the minimum quantity of accumulated weapon grade fissile material. Therefore, it intends to cover-up this gap, it argues, "....the United States and Russia still possess nuclear arsenals large enough to destroy the world many times over, it is China's position that continued nuclear disarmament and the prevention of an arms race in outer space are multilateral fora or arms control that should be given more priority than the FMCT negotiations. Therefore, the Conference on Disarmament (CD) in Geneva should not emphasize the importance of only the FMCT negotiations to the neglect of the issues of nuclear disarmament and the prevention of arms race in outer space, and should, at the minimum, give equal attention to all three issues by carrying out substantive work in a balanced manner."

The above quoted report on CTBT also substantiates the fears expressed about the real intentions of the treaty in India during the past few years. According to Gen. Shalikashvili the main advantages of the treaty are:

- "The Test Ban Treaty will complicate and slow down the efforts of aspiring nuclear states, especially regarding more advanced types of nuclear weapons.
- It will hamper the development by Russia and China of nuclear weapons based on new designs and will essentially rule out certain advances.
- It will add to the legal and political constraints that nations must consider when they form their judgements about national defence policies.

- The Test Ban Treaty is vital to the long-term health of the Nuclear Non-Proliferation Treaty, and will increase support for other elements of a comprehensive non-proliferation strategy.
- The United States is well positioned to sustain its nuclear deterrent under the Test Ban Treaty.
- The verification regime established under the Treaty will enhance the United States' own very capable nuclear test monitoring system and foster new techniques to improve verification."

This clearly gives away the diplomatic window dressing done by USA, China and other nuclear weapon powers to project CTBT as a standalone nonproliferation measure.

Before getting into the nitty-gritty of what India can do one must understand and assess correctly the current international system and where our nuclear strength can be maneuvered and bartered for larger bargains. With the end of Cold War the place of moral values and ideology have been overtaken by pragmatism and cool headed realpolitik. Therefore, it is high time for the decision making elite to think coolly and start looking for options.

In order to do this we must understand the real nature of India and its decision making community. Further, this also is a time for soul-searching and cool-headed assessment of bargain leverages. Are we onto the right track? What is the nature of our society, what we want and where we want to take the nation. Are our bureaucracy and the elite class is still stuck in the old groove of a *comprador* mental makeup? A large majority of these very same social forces collaborated with the British imperialism for advancing their own interests. Where do they stand now?

The 'virtual' reality of a surging India has overtaken these old fashioned, by and large gerentocratic, elite looking for 'kudos' from abroad. If India has to survive as an independent, self reliant and democratic entity it also needs an autonomous strategic capability. In this context the role of nuclear weapons becomes crucial. If we accept this is the '*virtual*' world which we live in, it is time for India to act before the opportunity to refine its nuclear capabilities get fully chocked.

In other words, due to the ongoing power struggle in the international arena for strategic one-upmanship there is clear window of opportunity for India to make further nuclear tests and refine the weapon and missile capability. Further, this also is a time for refining our arguments in the international diplomatic arena to use the nuclear weapons as tool for driving real bargains.

In early times technological innovations helped mankind to evolve new methods of fighting the enemy. Innovations like the use of catapults, fireballs, horses and stirrups to gunpowder—all have more or less changed the course of history and mankind's parameters of development. However, the beginning of the twentieth century saw a constant quest by mankind to fight wars with the assistance of modern technology rather than relying on time-tested traditional weaponry. This, in turn, has tremendously changed man's approach to technology itself. If, until then technology was helping to fight a war, the late nineteenth and early twentieth centuries witnessed a fundamental change. Nations states and leaders began to pursue technology to win wars. This has also radically changed the way we live and work. The impact of this constant search for technological innovation has introduced not only new ways to kill human beings but also enhanced the level of competition for markets.

At another level one can also argue that this constant search for technology emanates from the desire for absolute security. From Indian mythology one can cite examples of characters ranging from demons to gods who constantly searched for absolute security. To a great extent the need to perfect a foolproof missile defence system also formed a part of this constant search. According to late Mao Zedong, "to the present day, all weapons are still an extension of the spear and the shield. The bomber, the machine gun, the long range gun and poison gas are developments of the spear, while the air raid shelter, the steel helmet, the concrete fortification and the gas mask are developments of the shield."

The flip side of this search for absolute security is that it generally creates more insecurity. As no nation in the world will remain untouched by these developments, it will be in our interest to study how India's deterrence posture and nuclear capability can be preserved under this changing scenario.

With the indefinite extension of the Nuclear Non-Proliferation Treaty (NPT) in 1995, the nuclear weapon powers started to lull themselves into the belief that they had crossed a major milestone towards a nuclear weapons free world. On the other hand, it was very obvious to any discerning person that the Nuclear 5 powers and their allies were devoid of any noble intention about a nuclear free world. They were only trying to perpetuate their strategic superiority over the other hapless nations lacking any real means to protect themselves from a massive strike with their existing arsenals. Even at normal times, these nuclear powers coerce other nations to accept their hegemonist designs without a whimper. The tragedy was not in their belief that they were going to transport humanity to the promised land of a nuclear- weapons-free world, but, the fact that a large section of the international media, mostly owned and controlled by the developed world, began to perfect and propagate the chimera of such a world. A number of experts and scribes in their payrolls as well as some well-meaning genuine disarmament zealots all over the world, also helped to further propagate this myth. The prospect of signing the Comprehensive Test Ban Treaty (CTBT) elevated the pitch of this requiem to its crescendo.

However, soon, the world started realising that these two efforts further worsened the actual scenario. The existing nuclear weapon powers and their camp followers clandestinely took the issue of test ban to the United Nations General Assembly (UNGA) and manipulated the passing of the resolution by a brute majority. With much fanfare and media hype, the Treaty was signed by all the P5/N5 powers. China was the second to sign the Treaty after USA. However, the very next day after it signed the CTBT in 1996, China's Foreign Minister and respected senior diplomat Qian Qichen delivered a statement attaching certain conditions to China's adherence to the treaty. In his statement he reiterated that, "all states refrain from developing or deploying weapons systems in outer space and missile defence systems that undermine strategic security and stability." Since then, these two issues have become a continuing concern for China.

Most of the Chinese functionaries dealing with non-proliferation issues used to point out the salience of "missile defence" as a major factor in the ongoing process of the non-proliferation debate. Usually, this is taken as routine rhetoric, yet the reality is that the Conference on Disarmament (CD) has not transacted any meaningful business in the last so many years. According to the accepted international opinion, both scholars and larger sections of public started believing that by incorporating China into various international institutions it can be manipulated to do the bidding of the majority. On the other hand, one may assume that the real intention of China in joining these multilateral institutions was to gain legitimacy and enable itself to be in a position to manipulate these very institutions for its own benefit. Significantly, this is not only true for international non-proliferation regimes, it also applies to a vast number of multilateral economic and trade institutions including World Trade Organisation (WTO).

With the ascendancy of the Bush administration, predominantly manned by conservative cold war era fighters, the Chinese campaign against United States National Missile Defence (NMD) also got shriller. In a statement made by China's envoy on disarmament issues, Ambassador Sha Zukang, in March 2001, clarified the approach of his country in clearer terms, "China will not allow its legitimate means of self-defence to be weakened or even taken away by anyone in anyway...the US NMD programme will hamper the international arms control and disarmament process and even trigger a new round of arms race." Further, on the issue of proliferation of missiles he went on to clarify that, "NMD is not a solution to missile proliferation but will only undercut the very foundation of the international non-proliferation regime, and even stimulate further proliferation of missiles."

As per the tradition of Chinese diplomacy and policy pronouncement plans, they are not given to issue statements without proper study and detailed deliberation at the highest levels. Further, Ambassador Sha Zukang is a seasoned diplomat, a suave and smooth negotiator, normally he does not beat around the bush. Hence, from his assertion three broad conclusions can be drawn:

1. China is going to take necessary steps to strengthen her existing nuclear arsenal to defend any possible pre-emptive strike from an adversary. This means, both upgradation of existing delivery systems as well as acquiring and incorporating sophisticated technologies like MRV/MIRV for countering the adversary's missile shield.
2. As stated earlier, China's commitment to existing non-proliferation regimes is only a tactical ploy to enhance its own strategic space. It became a party to the very mechanisms (NPT, CTBT, etc) it derided in unequivocal terms at the time of their inception only shows its pragmatic approach to non-proliferation.
3. Chinese leadership has never believed in the exclusivity of the ownership of nuclear weapons by a few selected developed nations as a tool for coercing weaker nations. This was one of the underlying reasons why the Chinese leaders wanted to acquire the weapons at any cost. Even though it has graduated to being a 'status quo' nuclear power in the traditionally accepted terms of international treaty system, it has not given up its option to disseminate weapons and the technology relating to its delivery systems to its allies.

Even today, China's basic national security strategy is largely rooted in its ancient tradition of Master Sun Tzu and others, hence it will be essentially a pragmatic and cost effective one. This basic approach will mandate China to follow a nuclear policy as well as its orientation towards the challenge of NMD. Therefore, in all probability China is going to adopt a multi-pronged approach. It will invoke non-proliferation as a mantra to check India and other aspirants who are ready to bargain for a seat in the exclusive N5/P5 club, whenever its suits China. This issue as well as the overall change brought about by the September 11, 2001 terror attack on the mainland USA and other related issues will be discussed later.

China's pronouncements regarding NMD have to be taken in their broader perspective. Most of the time it uses them as a tool to achieve its overall national security interests. Hence, many a time its posturing on missile defence is only an indication of its actual intent in the larger power game.

NUCLEAR ARSENAL AND ITS MODERNISATION

Out of the existing N5 nuclear weapon states, China stands apart in many ways. It was one of the last entrants to the club after it tested its first atom bomb on October 16, 1964. It was quick to assure the world of its 'no-first-use' and minimum deterrence posture. This posture suited the existing global environment. China was operating under pressure and was being treated as a pariah in the international circles while its economy looked weak.

As noted earlier, China's approach to the issue of proliferation of weapons of mass destruction, especially the nuclear ones and their delivery systems are rooted in her pragmatic realpolitik approach to global issues. For Chinese leadership the entire argument of non-proliferation is also more or less linked to their arguments about "asymmetric warfare". If one has to fight an adversary, who is technically more advanced and financially stronger, it would be foolish to adopt a strategy of frontal confrontation. In such a scenario the strategic interest of a lesser power can be better served by the ancient teachings of Sun Tzu, "All warfare is based on deception. Therefore, when capable of attacking, feign incapacity; when active in moving troops, feign inactivity. When near the enemy, make it seems that you are far away; when far away, make it seem that you are near." Mao in his own way internalised this thought process and amalgamated the same into his own military thinking. His thinking still reigns supreme as a basic tenet in the modern day strategic establishment of PLA.

According to Chinese strategic calculations, the nuclear weapons have a larger role to play for a long time to come. It remains a fact that China was the first nation to propose a "no first use" doctrine immediately after she exploded her first atomic weapon way back in 1964. On different occasions Chinese scholars and think-tanks have pointed out the significance of nuclear weapons for strategic and diplomatic manipulation. For them these weapons are significant political tools.

On the issue of proliferation China comes across as one country which was a willing partner in proliferating both nuclear weapons and missiles. Its special relations with Pakistan and North Korea substantiate this trend. Apart from this, China used its missile sales to countries like Saudi Arabia and Iran to enhance its strategic reach to areas which are vital to its national interest.

For China, Middle East is not only an area from where it gets part of its energy supplies, but is also a region that will remain where the big power interests in both political and economic arena will stay entangled for a long time to come. Further, in the last few years, China has once again started projecting its role as the champion of the developing world and with its entry into WTO this cause is likely to get prominence. This also suits its claim, at times, as the sole representative of developing nations in the P5 mechanism. In the normal course this serves as a sophisticated diplomatic tool for China.

According to a paper on "proliferation" prepared by the office of the US Secretary of Defence in January 2001, "In recent years, Chinese firms have provided some important missile-related items and assistance to several countries of concern, such as Iran, Libya and North Korea. China has also provided extensive support in the past to Pakistan's nuclear and ballistic missile programmes, and some ballistic missile assistance continues." As a consequence of the ongoing problems in Southern Asia, the US Congress has decided to waive the entire weapon related restrictions relating to Pakistan, therefore, this can further boost the nuclear and missile capabilities of Pakistan. Further, China also can utilise this as a convenient excuse to supply what has been in the pipeline so far.

In order to enhance its strategic lebensraum, China is going to continue to use proliferation as a tool in its bargains with other big powers. This is the calibrated approach of China in the ongoing discussions and negotiations about various non-proliferation measures like FMCT, weaponisation of outer space, etc. therefore, its overall approach will be based on this pragmatic approach to contemporary balance of power, articulated through comprehensive national strength and multipolarity.

Attributing China's decision to modernise and tailor its nuclear arsenal entirely to the National Missile debate on USA will be taking too simplistic an approach. Yet, if we look at various aspects of the current Chinese efforts to improve its existing limited nuclear arsenal, the main focus has shifted from routine modernisation to categorically addressing the future possible threats contained in the US proposals on NMD and TMD. As argued earlier, it is taking a multi-pronged approach. With the collapse of the erstwhile Soviet Union, the Chinese leadership under a weather-worn pragmatist like Deng Xiaoping has decided to shift its focus totally away from a bipolar global system.

At one level it can be argued that this international outlook in its essence is a textual "balance of power" approach based on national interest. But it substantially deviates from the classical western teaching on the subject. If one can use one of his own favourite phrases "the Chinese characteristics", it will be easier to explain his argument; it essentially is an approach based on "international relations with Chinese characteristics". At another level it also can be argued that, his global outlook is still largely rooted in Mao's "three world theory". Being a quintessential pragmatist, for Deng these were mere slogans. His basic idea was to enhance China's economic and political power to keep better control on the foreign policy initiatives. Hence he was very flexible in approaching the international system dominated by a group of western powers.

In order to understand China's approach to NMD, this background is very essential. China fully understands that technologically and scientifically USA is the most advanced power in the world, therefore, China can achieve its goal of becoming a modern, prosperous and independent global player only by cooperating with the US. To achieve this ultimate aim it is ready to go along with USA, while not projecting itself as a camp follower and losing its credibility among its supporters, a number of developing and underdeveloped nations. Again, this is also tempered with China's growing status as a major trading power.

During the early part of this year, while George W Bush was articulating his pet project of NMD and his eagerness to cut to size China in the foreign policy profile of the USA, China was more apprehensive about his real intentions. The technical failures of the first few experiments of Pentagon of its experimental kill vehicle and other delays coupled with the subsequent developments after Bush's coming to power, have again emboldened the Chinese leadership. Now their approach is to influence the ultimate deployment of missile defence system in a way that preserves China's own deterrence capability against USA.

One of the underlying approaches of Bush and his defence team consisting some of the veteran Cold War era warriors is to repeat their performance by offering the bait of competitive escalation of warheads and their delivery systems. This was a strategic ploy used successfully by USA in escalating the defence expenditure of the erstwhile Soviet Union. Chinese are well aware of this strategy and will avoid falling into this trap at any cost.

Owing to some of the latest developments in the field of changing security perception the world over, China has already gained substantial breathing time. The Bush administration's approach to nuclear weapons is radically different from that of the almost evangelistic approach to non-proliferation of the previous Democratic Party led Clinton administration. Due to their own domestic constituencies and their ambivalent approach to the ongoing stockpile stewardship programme, many a persons including Defence Secretary Donald Rumsfeld, are advocates of the renewed weapons tests. A recent New York Times news item further clarified this, "a senior official said this week that in the future, resumption by China of underground tests of its nuclear weapons might be accepted by the United States, which might also someday want to resume testing."

These developments show that China will be more than willing to accommodate and live with an NMD developed and deployed by USA. In private, at least, some Chinese scholars have started articulating a position that China will not have any problem with USA setting up a very limited number of intercept sites for its proposed NMD. In other words, they are ready to live with it so long as it does not affect their penetration capability. Till now, the Chinese were grudgingly or happily living with a highly asymmetric nuclear equation, with the knowledge that they would be in a position to penetrate the US mainland with at least one warhead, which would do unacceptable damage to the USA.

However, their approach to TMD (in the US scheme of things these distinctions are becoming less important) is going to remain more vehement and politically motivated. This is not really linked to their worries about technical capabilities. Rather it pertains to their approach to Taiwan as well as their long term worries about a militarily independent and strong Japan. The sudden increase in the numbers of deployed short range ballistic missiles like DF-11 and DF-15 shows this concern. Still as there is less likelihood of an open war over Taiwan, these missiles will further add to Indian worries. Further, China is also carrying on with its own research and development on missile interception capability. At least three tests have come to the public notice. It is also known that China has a fairly advanced research programme on lasers and their ability to use them as interceptors in the outer space.

The wider debate in USA after the September 11 incident did not reflect this confidence. According to Noam Chomsky, a well-known critic of US foreign policy, these "events reveal, dramatically, the foolishness of the project of 'missile defence'. Currently, not only he but many others including some influential US politicians have begun to have second thoughts about the efficacy and diplomatic use of missile defence system for the overall interest of USA. This debate, on the use of nuclear deterrence against a possible chemical or a biological attack, even the possibility of using nuclear weapon for a pre-emptive strike in order to deter the above threats was going on in USA for the last few years. The terror attacks have added a new urgency to this whole debate. It will call for a range of adjustments in the existing nuclear arsenal of USA. As some feel, "that we need to regain some capability for some low yield nuclear weapons and particularly earth-penetrating low-yield weapons."

One of the immediate fallout maybe that, in the near future, USA is likely to go for a series of tests aimed towards this end. China is looking for this chance to finish its job of refining its own arsenal. This can provide a window of opportunity for India, therefore, it is time to carry out the necessary tests required for making India's nuclear deterrent a potent one against any possible adversary.

The evolving debate on missile defence systems around the world provides a chance for India to take a fresh look at its nuclear weapons and its linkage with the overall national security strategy. The experiences of nation states ever since the World War II have adequately proved that these are not mere weapons that adorn the military arsenal of a nation, like any other heavy artillery pieces exhibited in parades. They are basically political and diplomatic tools to achieve the desired strategic goal of a nation to enhance its own national interest.

Hence it helps to have a look at what others think about India's deterrence capability. According to Sun Tzu knowing one's enemy is as equally important an element as knowing one's own self. China being India's immediate neighbour and an experienced nation with adequate deterrence capability with nuclear weapons, it is important for India to know what they think about India's nuclear weapons. Their official military mouthpiece assesses that, "to really form a nuclear deterrent force, India must not rely merely on its successful nuclear tests but should also possess two conditions; the first is making warheads smaller and the second is improving carrier systems and auxiliary facilities." This is a reasonable argument, more or less similar to the sentiments expressed by some Chinese scholars in their private conversation. This gives a clear message, that merely carrying out a few tests does not form a sufficient deterrent force.

As there is little information about Indian efforts to improve upon the nuclear weapons and their delivery systems, let us take the Chinese argument at its face value. Regarding the nuclear weapons and their deterrence posture, India has made two major mistakes, the first, not adequately using the nuclear weapons as a diplomatic and political tool in its dealings with other nations, second by focusing solely on its small western neighbour, Pakistan. A country of India's size, depth and power can easily deter it by its conventional capabilities. Therefore, a rethink on the articulation of Indian nuclear weapons in terms of Pakistan as well as signing nuclear related CBMs with that country may be needed. India should have waited patiently and prepared its ground for China to take note of its deterrence capability and initiate a nuclear dialogue with it. This way India could have gained a larger leeway in its bargains with both Pakistan and China. One major flaw in carrying on with the nuclear related discussions with Pakistan was that this undermined India's strident public posture in advertising the fact that Pakistan is only a cat's paw in China's nuclear posture. At another level India also needs to take note of the fact that whatever information on Indian nuclear installations India passes on to Pakistan is readily available to China as well as other allies of Pakistan.

The ongoing interlude of nuclear debates at the international level, gained mainly through the NMD debate and the unprecedented attention of the USA on the terrorism issue can be utilised to India's tactical advantage. In this interregnum India must finish its agenda of improving required strategic improvements in its nuclear arsenal. It must store adequate fissile material, improve its weapons and delivery systems.

CONCLUSION

Since the genie of NMD is out of the bottle, it is far better to be prepared to deal with it rather than wish it away. Even within the USA's scientific community, there is no agreement on the efficacy of this system. There are consistent doubters like Ted Postol and others. However, the defence establishment is bent upon putting together a missile defence system for USA and its allies. Among the Pentagon establishment and its linked lobbies in military industrial complex as well as at the congressional level also there are many advocates of this system. If one looks at it objectively, this proposal by itself is not jeopardising India's national interests directly. Under these circumstances it is better for India to deal with it as it comes and articulate reactions on the basis of a well-thought out strategic perspective.

Having stated this, India's long-term strategic interest remains dependent on whatever is happening in its periphery. The Chinese approach to NMD is not at all giving any comfort to the Indian security. China has already built enough missiles and nuclear warheads to deter India for the present. Therefore, India's efforts to make a counterforce to those weapons have already become that much more complicated. This calls for India to make a credible deterrence capability against any possible future threat from China. It should not be in a position to subject India to nuclear blackmail in the future. India has to adopt a more aggressive diplomatic posture in its dealings regarding nuclear deterrence and the entire issue of non-proliferation mechanisms.

China's efforts in the short term will be to project India as the villain in the world: "...if India further arms its troops with nuclear weapons, Pakistan will be certainly able to adopt corresponding measures and the South Asian region will once again get into the mess of nuclear arms race." To counter this it will try to appeal to the international community to cap India's nuclear capabilities at the current levels. The same article exhorts, "If India insists on preparing to establish nuclear armoured troops in an effort to act as the overlord of the region with its nuclear arms, such efforts will undoubtedly give a head-on blow to the international community's arms control and disarmament efforts." These matters need the urgent attention of Indian policy-makers. One main lacunae in the Chinese logic is that they are not taking into consideration the fact that India is already living in a highly nuclearised environment. It is neither a party to any nuclear non-proliferation mechanism, nor does it enjoy the nuclear umbrella of a big power. Therefore, it has to protect its own interests all alone.

Due to the ongoing conflict in Afghanistan, the peripheral situation has already undergone a sea-change in the last few weeks, wherein Pakistan has once again become a frontline state for the USA. During the 1980's when Pakistan enjoyed the same position, the USA conveniently looked the other way when Islamabad acquired its nuclear capability clandestinely. Even after that the US has not done anything substantial to dissuade China from giving nuclear and missile technology to Pakistan. The history has taken a full circle and we are yet again in for a long haul in the Afghanistan quagmire. China is still a partner of the USA in this struggle against terrorism. Therefore, the chances are that Pakistan will continue to get required supplies for its nuclear and missile manufacturing facilities without any hindrance.

This has further complicated the job of Indian policy-makers and diplomats. India has later "volunteered" to be a partner of the USA this time. Therefore, its effort must be to complete successfully the remaining work on developing a robust nuclear capability during this interregnum. At the diplomatic level, India has to understand that all the non-proliferation regimes are frayed at their edges and if they are collapsing under their own weight let it be so. Not only that India's effort should be to position itself at a level where it can take advantage of the situation when these teetering old structures give way on their own. Meanwhile India must be ready to take part in a new round of global disarmament measures, where it has a better stake and say.

At the same time it will be in India's interest to pursue a policy of good neighbourliness with China to be in a position to deal with it in an equitable manner at bilateral and multilateral levels. Meanwhile India must guard against US and China forming any mechanism to work against the genuine interests of the nuclear deterrence capability of India.

END NOTES

1. David Shambaugh, "Facing Reality in China Policy", *Foreign Affairs* vol. 80, no. 1 (January-February 2001), pp. 50-64.

5

Developments in the PLA Navy: Implications for India

VIJAY SAKHUJA

In the 21st Century, China's strategic vision envisages building credible naval power to build an impregnable security perimeter that had once led to China's domination by colonial powers during the 15th to the 19th Century. Significantly, for China, the colonial supremacy came from the sea and therefore the foremost strategic objective of China is to possess maritime military capability to preclude intrusive dominance of the littorals by any external power.

The Chinese navy is developing significant power projection capabilities and the current force structure and future acquisitions indicate that it can exercise considerable regional influence. The navy is building platforms capable of long range sustained operations by surface, subsurface and air units that are supported by space based assets. Also, the threat of a nuclear intervention impacts on the Chinese strategic thinking and necessitates appropriate response from the sea.

At the strategy level, the PLA Navy is focused on developing capabilities for its 'offshore active defence strategy' to serve as a strategic-tactical force and affirm China's image of a regional maritime power with a robust naval capability. The strategy is also meant to safeguard China's burgeoning coastal economic regions and defend its maritime interests on the high seas. The strategy also takes advantage of the navy's strategic and tactical capabilities and integrates these into national defence planning.

Multinational naval exercises are also gaining importance in Chinese naval thinking. These engagements help China to remain abreast of global trends in naval weaponry, operating procedures, and better understanding of the changing nature of naval warfare. The exercises also help China showcase to the international naval community its military industrial prowess and the Chinese navy's technological sophistication. At another level, China is also developing capabilities to project its soft power by engaging in humanitarian missions.

In the above context, this paper attempts to showcase recent advancements in PLA Navy that can impact on India's maritime security. The paper examines developments in China's naval force structure, acquisition of new weapon systems, expanding geography of the PLA Navy and trends in multinational operations. In recent months, China's strategic geography has expanded to include Gulf of Aden where it has deployed its navy for sustained anti piracy roles for more than a year. The Arctic is fast emerging as a strategic sea space in Chinese strategic calculations given that the impact of climate change has resulted in melting of the permafrost and facilitated movement of shipping albeit for a short period in the summers.

Aircraft Carrier

There is no other naval platform that attracts greater attention in China than the aircraft carrier. That China is building an aircraft carrier has been a subject of intense debate and discussion among the Chinese leadership and international strategic and security community. There have been articulations such as 'I'll die with an everlasting regret if China does not build an aircraft carrier"[1] and "since the Second World War, aircraft carriers as the symbol of a country's important deterrent power have been accorded more attention. For some historical reasons, China has not yet built aircraft carriers". As the building process is long, we simply cannot afford to dig wells after being thirsty"[2] and these symbolize the criticality of aircraft carriers in Chinese strategic thinking.

The strategic literature originating in the United States, India, Japan, Russia, South Korea and Southeast Asian countries has closely followed the development relating to Chinese plans either to acquire or build an aircraft carrier. The US Pentagon's 'Annual Report on Military and Security Developments Involving the People's Republic of China' has for many years included the developments in China's aircraft carrier acquisition plans. In recent times, Admiral Gary Roughead, US Chief of Naval Operations observed "There has been no doubt in my mind that the acquisition of an aircraft carrier and carrier aviation was something that was clearly an ambition and an objective of the PLA Navy…The advent of an aircraft carrier on the part of the PLA Navy, to me, really doesn't change the nature of our operations at all."[3]

It has also been noted that there is likely to be a shift in the balance of power in Asia after China deploys its aircraft carrier. Apparently, Admiral Gary Roughead had asked Chinese naval Chief Admiral Wu Shengli "So we're hearing you're going to announce an aircraft carrier." And he said, "We're not there."…But I know and I shared with him, we know the development is going on. They've had an ambition for an aircraft carrier since the '90s. They have a very methodical approach. And they are working down that timeline. The [Chinese] navy is going to have an aircraft carrier some day. That's just my assessment of it. How they elect to use it and where they operate it is the big question".[4]

The Chinese have been very careful in not raising regional tensions and the 2009 Defence White Paper made a passing reference to 'improving strategic capabilities in distant waters' but it does not mention about aircraft carriers. However, the trends during the last two decades suggest that China has been aggressively engaged in acquiring an aircraft carrier from foreign sources (the 67,000 ton, 307 meters long vessel Varyag renamed as renamed *Shi Lang* after Admiral Shi Lang, the Chinese Commander-in-Chief of the Manchu fleets that conquered Taiwan in 1681) or to build it indigenously.

There has also been some discussion on China building a nuclear powered aircraft carrier. In 2007, there were reports to indicate that China had drawn plans to construct a 93,000-ton nuclear propelled carrier under Project 085. This was in addition to the development of a 48,000-ton non-nuclear carrier under Project 089.[5] There is no doubt about China's ability to install nuclear reactor for propulsion on such large platforms given its ability to develop miniaturized reactors for its nuclear submarines. Meanwhile, reports suggest that a large shipyard has been built to facilitate construction of large vessels such as aircraft carriers and the Chinese ship building officials in Shanghai have noted that "it's a matter of time now" that the shipyard could commence building an aircraft carrier.[6] According to Japanese media reports, 'Chinese military plans to build two diesel powered carriers before 2015 and as many nuclear powered ones by 2020'.[7]

Submarines

The PLA Navy submarine force is currently estimated to be about 60. Over the years it has become more sophisticated both in terms of stealth and firepower. The nuclear submarines are high on agenda and the Chinese are building a credible sea based deterrent. Satellite pictures have revealed that two Type 094 Jin class SSBN may have been launched.[8] These are fitted with twelve three stage, solid fuel, JL-2 SLBM, a modification of the Dong Feng 31 ballistic missile. China may build four to five such units. Similarly, two Type 093 Shang class SSNs are under construction[9] and are reported to host Russian technology and would represent a major technological improvement.

Two important developments during the last decade have been the acquisition of the Kilo class submarines from Russia and the development of the Song and Yuan class submarines built indigenously. Some of these vessels are fitted with subsurface missile capability to engage targets at sea as also on land.

The 2010 US 'Annual Report on Military and Security Developments Involving the People's Republic of China' notes that "in more traditional domains, China's anti access/area-denial focus appears oriented toward restricting or controlling access to China's periphery, including the western Pacific.'[10] The Report also notes that if the PLA Navy continues to improve its surface, sub surface and air capabilities, it can 'engage adversary surface ships up to 1,000 nautical miles from the PRC coast.'

In the past, China has very effectively deployed its submarines in the classic role of anti access. In 1994, Chinese Han class nuclear submarine was sighted some 450 nautical miles from the US aircraft carrier USS Kitty Hawk which launched S3 antisubmarine aircraft. The Chinese too dispatched fighter aircraft to intercept the US planes. The cat-and-mouse game continued till the submarine came to within twenty-one nautical miles from the carrier. It then returned to base. Nearly twelve years later, in the second incident in 2006, a Chinese Song class diesel submarine surfaced within weapons range of the USS Kitty Hawk. According to US Navy sources, the aircraft carrier was surprised. These incidents clearly showcase that China is keen to develop strong anti access capabilities.

Expeditionary Platforms

The PLA Navy has watched with great interest the acquisition of expeditionary platforms by several navies in the Asia Pacific. It has added new classes of amphibious and troop transport ships and these have enhanced PLA Navy's capability to undertaking expeditionary-amphibious operation in China's immediate and adjacent waters as well as distant territories in the South China Sea.

However, its ability to undertake humanitarian assistance and disaster relief (HADR) operations such the Tsunami has invited international attention due to its 'no show' during the 2004 Indian Ocean Tsunami. The Chinese leadership has acknowledged the fact that China must develop expeditionary platforms which can also serve to respond to HADR missions.

In May 2009, China issued a white paper entitled, "China's Actions for Disaster Prevention and Reduction'[11] that called for developing capability to respond to natural disasters and to engage in rescue and relief operations both at home and overseas. In order to effectively address HADR missions, China must also develop a coordinated and efficient disaster management system.

Since the early 1980s, China has also conceptualised hospital ships. For instance, a Qiongsha-class attack transport ships was converted into a Nankang-class hospital ship. In the Chinese context, hospital ship is classified as 'national defense mobilisation ship' (guofang dongyuan jian)[12] and such platforms have the ability to mobilize civilian assets for military use.

In August 2010, China deployed the 10,000-ton Type 920 Daishandao/ Peace Ark hospital ship to the Gulf of Aden on its first overseas medical mission.[13] According to Chinese sources, the vessel is expected to be on deployment in the Indian Ocean for about three months and will call at ports in Djibouti, Kenya, Tanzania, the Seychelles and Bangladesh to provide medical treatment.

Anti-ship Ballistic Missile (ASBM) and Ballistic Missile Defence (BMD)

In 2007, China shot down a satellite and this action had invited international attention. In 2009, the report that China had developed capability to attack US aircraft carriers further added to the debate on the fast pace of China's military-space modernisation. The US Congressional Research Service Report titled *China Naval Modernisation: Implications for U.S. Navy Capabilities—Background and Issues for Congress* has noted that China is fast developing anti-ship ballistic missiles (ASBMs) with maneuverable reentry vehicles (MaRVs) capable of hitting moving ships at sea including aircraft carriers.[14] The report observes that "China is developing an ASBM based on a variant of the CSS-5 MRBM [medium-range ballistic missile] as a part of its anti-access strategy. The missile has a range in excess of 1,500 km, is armed with a maneuverable warhead, and when incorporated into a sophisticated command and control system, is intended to provide the PLA the capability to attack ships at sea, including aircraft carriers in the western Pacific Ocean."

Further, it would be useful to keep in mind that among the Asian navies, it is only China which has a nuclear triad. This prompted several Asia Pacific countries to start developing a robust Ballistic Missile Defence (BMD) at sea. Japan, Korea and Australia are engaged in fitting out Aegis type BMD system onboard their naval vessels. China is concerned about the proliferation of BMD in the region and in 2007, Lieutenant General Zhang Qinsheng, deputy chief of the general staff of the PLA had expressed his concerns about the extension of the regional BMD to Taiwan and noted that "We are worried that this kind of deployment will destabilise the Asia-Pacific region and will create uncertainty in terms of regional stability and peace."[15] The US had dismissed Chinese concerns and Defence Secretary Robert Gates observed that "The missile defence systems we are planning both at home and abroad are intended to deal with the acquisition of ballistic missiles and weapons of mass destruction by either rogue countries or rogue governments or terrorists groups,"[16]

Mini Submarine

In August 2010, the Chinese State Oceanic Administration and Ministry of Science and Technology jointly announced that a mini submarine had successfully positioned the national flag at 3,700 meters under the sea in South China Sea.[17] Although the stated aim of the event was to conduct underwater resource survey and also to demonstrate China's undersea technological capability, the statement by one of the engineers of the China Ship Scientific Research Centre, who designed the hull of the submarine, is of concern. It was noted "It might provoke some countries, but we'll be all right. The South China Sea belongs to China. Let's see who dares to challenge that."[18] The Chinese engineer further stated that "The closer to Philippines, the deeper the sea. We will put down national flags all the way until we reach their border,... And then we will go beyond and aim for the Mariana Trench."[19] It should be pointed out that the Mariana Trench is 11,034 meters and is located to the northeast of the Philippines.

The event can be discerned as an attempt by China to establish sovereignty over the South China Sea. It has been noted that "We [China] were inspired by the Russians, who put a flag on the floor of the North Pole with their MIR [deep sea submarine]."[20] In 2007 Russia placed national flag on the seabed in the Arctic to demonstrate to the other Arctic claimants over its sovereignty in the Arctic. At that time, the Canadian Foreign Minister had remarked "This isn't the 15th Century...You can't go around the world and just plant flags and say 'We're claiming this territory'."[21]

Bases

The Sanya Naval base has sophisticated infrastructure to host both nuclear and conventional submarine and is a perfect launching point for nuclear submarines into the Pacific Ocean. Some of the recent pictures taken by satellites provide a detailed layout of the submarine related infrastructure at an island off Hainan and what perhaps merits attention is that a network of tunnels across the island serves as submarine pens.

China has built significant military infrastructure on some of the islands in South China Sea. In particular, the infrastructure at Woody Island is impressive. It hosts a range of military related infrastructure including a well developed runway for military aircraft, a mobile missile battery, naval facilities for ships and a network of intelligence and communication infrastructure.

The Chinese military has deployed a variety of modern military aircraft like the Su27, Su30, and the JF 10 that can be staged from either Hainan or the Woody Islands thus facilitating quick response to any military contingency in the South China Sea. With mid-air refueling, these aircraft have enhanced loiter time and their standoff weapon capability makes them formidable.

Responding to Asymmetric Threats

China has been concerned over the growing menace of piracy in the Straits of Malacca. Nearly 60 percent of Chinese crude is sourced from the Middle East and given the growing demands this figure is sure to rise beyond 70 % in the near future and bulk of which would naturally transit through the Straits of Malacca.

In 2000, it offered financial and technological assistance to improve the safety and security of merchant traffic transiting the Strait of Malacca. In 2005, during the International Maritime Organisation (IMO) meeting in Jakarta, China reiterated its position of supporting the littoral states in enhancing safety and security in the Strait. Ju Chengzi, Director General of China's Ministry of Transportation, stated that China could provide technical support, navigation aids, training programs, capacity building and hydrographical surveys.[22] In 2005, China offered to finance the project for the replacement of navigational aids damaged during the 2004 Indian Ocean Tsunami and the estimated cost for the project was $276,000. Perhaps what merits attention is the fact that China only announced financial and technological support to keep the Straits of Malacca safe and secure and did not support naval deployment. In fact in 2000, it had strongly objected to Japanese attempts to deploy vessels to patrol the Straits of Malacca where shipping had been threatened by piracy.[23]

The Chinese reaction to Somali piracy is quite different from its response to piracy in the Straits of Malacca. The Chinese leadership announced their intention to deploy a naval task force to the Indian Ocean in the Gulf of Aden off Somalia. The announcement came in the wake of the rising number of pirate attacks on Chinese flagged vessels, including ships carrying Chinese cargo or manned by Chinese crew.

To dispel any fears among the countries of Southeast Asia and Indian Ocean littorals on the intended naval deployment, Beijing noted that it is acting in response to the United Nations resolutions that calls all nations to fight piracy in the Gulf of Aden as also to protect shipping. The Chinese government also noted that the PLA naval task force could work with other navies engaged in escorting vessels transporting humanitarian relief material for Somalia.

Accordingly, since 2009, PLA Navy has kept a sustained presence off Somalia and the Chinese flotilla comprises of at least two destroyers and a supply ship and their deployment lasts for up to three months during which the ships engage in escort and patrol duties in the area. The task force is quite strong and is well supported by a logistic support vessel. Interestingly, the composition of the force follows the earlier pattern of distant deployments in the Indian and the Pacific Oceans.

The PLA naval deployment has invited reaction from some countries have likened the deployment to the historical voyages under Zheng He, the famous mariner who was responsible for seven expeditions from 1405 to 1433 visiting Southeast Asia, India Persian Gulf and East Africa engaging in diplomacy, projecting China's glory, and quelling piracy.

Multinational Naval Exercises

China's forays in the Indian Ocean date back to mid 1980s when the PLA Navy made port calls to ports in Pakistan, Bangladesh and Sri Lanka. The first ever Sino-Pak joint naval exercise was held off the coast of Shanghai in 2003 and the second bilateral exercise was held in the Arabian Sea in November 2005. In 2007, the PLA Navy was invited by Pakistan to join the multinational naval exercise, Aman 2007 (Peace 2007) held off Karachi. During the exercises, warships from Bangladesh, China, France, Italy,

Malaysia, United Kingdom, and the United States engaged in maneuvers in the Arabian Sea[24] giving the Chinese navy an exposure to multinational naval exercises. Interestingly, the Commander of the Chinese flotilla Luo Xianlin was designated as the tactical commander for the joint maritime rescue exercise and the Chinese missile frigate 'Lianyungang' was entrusted with the coordination of the exercise.[25] The naval maneuver was observed by representatives from over 21 countries who were onboard different ships. The exercises were significant since it provided the PLA Navy with the opportunity to test the interoperability of its navy and coordinating complex maneuver with other naval forces. In 2009, the PLAN once again participated in Aman 2009, which was held in the Arabian Sea and this time it carried out exercises along with 19 foreign naval ships.[26]

Developments in South China Sea

In the past, South China has witnessed show of force, saber rattling and clashes at sea between China and the other claimants. In 1974, the Chinese were in occupation of some of the islands in the Western Paracel. Between 1979 and 1982, the Vietnamese made several attempts to regain control of the islands but failed. The second clash between China and Vietnam took place in 1988 over the Western Spratly. In 1992, China enacted the Territorial Waters Law and accounced claim to the entire South China Sea. The third encounter in February 1995 was between China and the Philippines over Mischief Reef.

A non-binding multilateral agreement '2002 Declaration on the Conduct of Parties in the South China Sea' (DoC) with focus on the Spratly Islands has been in place since 2002. In order to uphold the spirit of the 2002 DoC and abide by the 1982 UN Convention of the Law of the Sea, China, Vietnam and the Philippines agreed to jointly undertake oil exploration in the Spratly Islands.

The recent standoff between United States and China was in response to China declaring the South China Sea as the "core interest" similar to Tibet and Taiwan and the United States declaring the region as of 'national interest'. The US Secretary of State Hillary Clinton noted that "The United States has a 'national interest' in freedom of navigation, open access to Asia's maritime commons and respect for international law in the South China Sea.[27] Further, "We [US] oppose the use or threat of force by any claimant."

These articulations by the US and China sent out some very discomfort signals to the ASEAN countries. Interestingly, Beijing also sent out a veiled warning that "Few Southeast Asian countries would like to get in the middle of Sino-US tensions, but like many other regions, they are caught in a dilemma: economically close to China yet militarily guarded against China...Southeast Asian countries need to understand any attempt to maximise gains by playing a balancing game between China and the US is risky. China's long-term strategic plan should never be taken as a weak stand. It is clear that military clashes would bring bad results to all countries in the region involved, but China will never waive its right to protect its core interest with military means."[28]

Arctic: The Chinese Geography

Geographically, Arctic is far from China but with its increasing importance as a source of energy and minerals, it is finding an important place in Chinese thinking. China sees several scientific, commercial and strategic opportunities in the evolving dynamics in the Arctic region and the Chinese government has allocated significant resources for conducting Arctic research, assess untapped energy resources, explore the possibility of transit through the Northern Sea Route (NSR).[29]

China established its Arctic research facility at Yellow River Station located on the Norwegian island of Spitsbergen in 2004[30] and in 2007 it joined the Arctic Council as an observer. The Chinese scholars have urged the government to play a proactive role in Arctic affairs, but the official viewpoint is that "active overtures would cause alarm in other countries due to China's size and status as a rising global power."[31]

In 1993, China acquired *Xuelong* (Snow Dragon, 163 meters long with displacement of 21,000 tonnes) a non-nuclear polar expedition vessel from Ukraine. To further augment polar research expeditions, a new high-tech 8000 tonnes polar expedition research ice-breaker is under construction in China which is expected to be operational in 2013. The vessel is being developed with foreign technical assistance and expected to cost about US $300 million.[32]

It has been argued that the 'climatic and environmental process in the Arctic' have a direct bearing on China's national economy thus it is natural for China to study the Arctic. Further, Chinese believe that "Natural resources in the region belong to all peoples of the world. China has the responsibility, duty and the ability to take part in the peaceful exploration and protection of natural resources there. China's economic and social development already has a demand for the natural resources."[33] In is in this context, the Arctic energy resources for China offer yet another frontier for sourcing its energy needs. On the other hand, Chinese military officers are concerned about the evolving military dimensions of the Arctic region particularly in the context of the decision by five Arctic littoral states to strengthen their military capabilities. Senior Colonel Han Xudong has warned that 'the possibility of use of force cannot be ruled out in the Arctic due to complex sovereignty disputes'.[34]

Chinese Strategic Initiatives in South Asia

There are several geo-economic and geo-strategic causal factors that shape China's interest in Indian Ocean. In spatial terms, Indian Ocean is a seamless sea space and offers connectivity to the sources of energy, resources and markets in the region. As part of its resource access strategy, Beijing has relentlessly tried to develop politico-economic relations with several countries in the Indian Ocean particularly in South Asia. These have matured into military relations with generous supply of arms, equipment including missiles.

These Chinese initiatives, particularly in South Asia, have caused considerable discomfort in India. Indian strategists have often argued that China supported maritime infrastructure being built in Pakistan, Sri Lanka, Bangladesh and Myanmar would be capable of conducting sustained operations in the Indian Ocean.

India has characterised Chinese initiatives in South Asia as 'strategic encirclement'. This is based on the understanding that China has developed naval infrastructure, which reportedly includes berthing facilities, shipbuilding yards and electronic monitoring stations in Myanmar (Hianggyi, Kyaukpyu, Zadetkyi, Mergui, and Great Coco Island) and these could serve the PLA Navy as and when it is deployed in the Bay of Bengal/Indian Ocean.

Similarly, China has been the primary supplier of naval hardware to Bangladesh thus boosting its naval capability. China has also offered assistance to launch a satellite for Bangladesh to develop its 'telecommunications services, map natural resources, broadcast television programs and obtain meteorological data for disaster warnings'. Likewise, Sino-Pak relationship has been termed as 'strategic partnership' and China is developing strategic infrastructure to seek access into the Arabian Sea through the 'Karakoram Corridor' that can link Xinjiang-Pakistan onward to the Persian Gulf with access to energy sources in the Persian Gulf. In spatial and strategic terms, access and basing arrangements particularly in Gwadar in the Arabian Sea and Chittagong, Hambantota in Sri Lnaka and Burmese ports in the Bay of Bengal ensure a strategic initiative of China to check Indian advances in South Asia.

Indian fears are accentuated by the suggestion by a Chinese admiral to

Admiral Timothy J. Keating, then-chief of the U.S. Pacific Command (PACOM) of dividing the Indo-Pacific region into two areas of responsibility between the United States and China.[35] Reportedly, the Chinese Admiral had stated, "You, the United States, take Hawaii East and we, China, will take Hawaii West and the Indian Ocean. Then you will not need to come to the western Pacific and the Indian Ocean and we will not need to go to the Eastern Pacific. If anything happens there, you can let us know and if something happens here, we will let you know" [36]

At the tactical level, the Chinese ASBM programme has caused unease in the Indian security establishment. The Indian Navy does not possess a sea based anti ballistic missile system and this capability gap can make the Indian aircraft carriers highly vulnerable. The Indian Navy may have integrated the anti ship missile threat from surface , sub surface and air platforms of the Pakistan Navy, the Chinese ballistic missiles poses an 'existential threat'.

India's Response

Nearly fifty percent of India's sea borne trade is east bound for countries in Southeast Asia, East Asia, east coast of US and Canada and transits through the Straits of Malcca-South China Sea. In 2009, India and ASEAN signed the FTA that came into force in July 2010.[37] This FTA is believed to be quite extensive covering a market of approximately 1.8 billion people and the plans envisage gradually cutting down tariffs over 4,000 product lines by 2016.[38]

Further, India has been engaged in offshore energy development projects in the South China Sea. The state owned ONGC Videsh Limited (OVL) in partnership with PetroVietnam and British Petroleum began exploration in South China Sea in 1992-93 which resulted in the discovery of the Lan Do and Lan Tay gas fields that estimated to contain reserves of around 58 billion cubic metres that would result in three billion cubic metres of gas a year.[39] In 2010, due to Gulf of Mexico oil spill liability, BP announced plans to sell its energy assets in Vietnam and OVL along with Vietnam's PetroVietnam have joined hands to bid for the BP's stake in Nam Con Son gas fields spread over 955-square kilometre include two offshore gas fields, a pipeline and power project.[40]

Given the above economic realities, India is an important stakeholder in the evolving security dynamics in South China Sea and any insecurity in the region could adversely impact on India's trade and economy. New Delhi's economic vitality pivots on assured supply of energy and safe and secure trading routes in the region including the Straits of Malacca. It has high stakes in keeping the sea-lanes open in the region.

India's Military Maritime Strategy defines area of interest and operations for the Indian Navy. It is quite natural that the Indian Ocean region gains primacy in its formulation and encompasses the sea space around the Strait of Bab-el-Mandeb—Strait of Hormuz- Straits of Malacca and Cape of Good Hope.[41] The strategy also envisions South China Sea and the East Pacific Region as the secondary area of interest to the Indian Navy. According to the Military Maritime Strategy, these sea spaces would gain primacy in case of events and incidents that impinges on Indian interests.

In the past, the Indian Navy has conducted exercises in South China Sea much to the discomfort of China. India is keen to obtain berthing arrangements for Indian Navy at Vietnamese ports and keen to supply military hardware including missiles. India also has Strategic Partnership with Japan (2007) and Vietnam (2008). New Delhi appears to be responding to the Chinese 'string of pearls' by developing pressure points around China in the Asia Pacific region.

Finally, as Indian and the Chinese navies grow in size, capability and sophistication, their maritime ambitions would undergo change keeping in mind the changing security environment. A new appreciation of the evolving maritime environment, as also the changing strategic and tactical vision of naval planners, is already visible in the region. Given the limitation of the sea space (Bay of Bengal-Malacca Strait—South China Sea), Chinese and Indian naval forces would meet more often than before when engaged in surveillance, reconnaissance or during exercises. Their submarines are likely to encounter each other more frequently, be it for shadowing or snooping.

End Notes

1. Men Jing, "Changes of Security Thinking and Its Application to Military Construction in China", Jean Monnet Working Papers in Comparative and International Politics, *JMWP* no. 37, May 2001.
2. You Xu and You Ji, "In Search of Blue Water Power: The PLA Navy's Maritime Strategy in the 1990's and Beyond", Working Paper no. 222, The Strategic and Defence Studies Center, Australia: Canberra, Australian National University, 1990, p. 12.
3. Wang Linyan, "U.S. Admiral: China Naval Strength No Surprise", *China Daily*, April 20, 2009.
4. Andrew Scutro, "From the top: CNO on China, InSurvs, pirates", available at http://www.navytimes.com/news/2009/05/navy_roughead_050409w/ accessed on May 5, 2010.

5. "China to build 93,000-ton atomic-powered aircraft carrier: source", available at http://www.hani.co.kr/arti/english_edition/e_international/199284.html accessed on October 7, 2010. Also see "China building aircraft carrier: Mao's grandson" http://www.deccanherald.com/content/96367/china-building-aircraft-carrier-maos.html accessed on October 7, 2010. Apparently, Major General Mao Xinyu, the grandson of Mao Zedong has noted that," As a General, I was very interested in the development of the Second Artillery Corps and our Marine forces. I am glad to know that the marines are constructing the first aircraft carrier," The US intelligence agencies too have noted that 'China is building two 50,000-60,000 ton aircraft carriers to be equipped with Russian SU-22 fighters and these are expected to be ready by 2015.'
6. "China to build nuclear carrier", available at http://english.ruvr.ru/2010/08/22/16767452.html accessed on October 7, 2010.
7. Ibid.
8. Andrew S Erickson and Michael S Chase , "China's SSBN Forces: Transitioning to the Next Generation", China Brief Volume: 9 Issue: 12, June 12, 2009.
9. Ibid.
10. 'Military and Security Developments Involving the People's Republic of China', Office of Secretary of Defence, 2010, p.29.
11. 'China's Actions for Disaster Prevention and Reduction' Information Office of the State Council of the People's Republic of China , March 11, 2009.
12. Leah Averott, "China's Growing Maritime HA/DR Capabilities", *China Brief*, Vol. 10, Issue 12, June 11, 2010.
13. "Chinese Hospital Ship "Peace Ark" Sets Sail For Africa", available at http://defensetech.org/2010/08/31/chinese-hospital-ship-peace-ark-sets-sail-for-africa/ accessed on October 13,2010.
14. Ronald O'Rourke, "China Naval Modernization: Implications for U.S. Navy Capabilities—Background and Issues for Congress ", CRS Report for Congress, August 5,2010.
15. Shefali Rekhi, "US offers to discuss missile defence plans with China", *StraitsTimes* 4 June 2007.
16. Press Conference at Shangri-La International Security Conference, US Department of Defense Press Transcript, June 3,2007.
17. Stephen Chen, "Submarine Plants Flag on the Ocean Floor", *South China Morning Post*, August 27, 2010.
18. Michael Sainsbury, "China makes waves over deep-sea energy sources", *The Australian*, September 25, 2010.
19. Stephen Chen, *op cit*, n. 17.
20. Ibid.
21. "Russia Plants Flag Under N Pole", available at http://news.bbc.co.uk/2/hi/europe/6927395.stm accessed on September 8, 2010.
22. Cited Ian Storey, "China's "Malacca Dilemma"", China Brief , Volume: 6 Issue: 8, April 12, 2006.
23. Gaye Christoffersen, "Japan and the East Asian Maritime Security Order: Prospects for Trilateral and multilateral Cooperation", *Asian Perspective*, Vol. 33, No. 3, 2009, p. 117.

24. "Chinese Navy Ship Arrives at Pakistani Port for Multinational Exercises", *Xinhua*, March 5, 2009.
25. "Multinational Feet Ends Rescue Drill Led by Chinese Navy", *Xinhua*, March 10, 2007.
26. "Pakistan Naval Exercise 'Aman 2009'", available at http://www.riazhaq.com/2009/03/pakistan-naval-exercises-aman-2009.html accessed on October 15,2010.
27. Mark Landler, "Offering to Aid Talks, U.S. Challenges China on Disputed Islands", *The New York Times*, July 23, 2010.
28. John Chan, "S-China Tensions over South China Sea" available at *http://www.wsws.org/articles/2010/aug2010/usch-a04.shtml* accessed on September 8, 2010.
29. Linda Jakobson, "China Prepares For An Ice-Free Arctic", SIPRI Insights on Peace and Security No. 2010/2 March 2010 Stockholm International Peace Research Institute (SIPRI).
30. "China Opens First Research Station in Arctic", *Xinhua,* July 28, 2004.
31. Ibid. p.2.
32. Linda Jakobson, *op.cit.*
33. "Significance of Arctic Research Expedition", available at http://www.china.org.cn/english/features/40961.htm accessed on March 11, 2010.
34. Linda Jakobson, *op.cit.*
35. Manu Pubby, "China proposed division of Pacific, Indian Ocean regions, we declined: US Admiral", *Indian Express*, May 15, 2009.
36. Ibid.
37. "FTA with ASEAN to Eliminate Duties on 80% of Traded Goods", *Times of India*, August 14, 2009.
38. "ASEAN-India Dialogue Relations", available at http://www.aseansec.org/5738.htm accessed on May 12, 2010.
39. T.S. Subramanian, "The Vietnam connection", *Frontline*, Vol. 20, Issue 01, January 18-31, 2003.
40. "BP's Vietnam project: Deora to support ONGC bid", available at http://business.rediff.com/report/2010/oct/01/bps-vietnam-project-deora-to-support-ongc-bid.htm accessed on October 2, 2010.
41. "Freedom to Use the Seas: India's Maritime Military Strategy" (New Delhi: Integrated Headquarters Ministry of Defence (Navy), 2007), pp.59-60.

6

PEOPLES LIBERATION ARMY AIR FORCE: AN INCOMPLETE JOURNEY

VISHAL NIGAM

"We must have some of our people learn aviation, for we can use them whenever we are in need."

—Dr Sun Yat-sen (1909)

It was in the early part of the twentieth century just a few years after Oliver took the 'Flyer' on a twelve second sustained powered flight, Dr Sun Yat-sen, leader of Guangzhou revolutionary government proclaimed the vast potential of airpower to be the only coercive instrument of the state in future conflict. Sun Yat-sen was well ahead of time, because the much acclaimed pronouncement by Sir Winston Churchill *"for good or ill, air mastery is today the supreme expression of military power....."* was in fact made many years after his brilliant articulation. Sun Yat-sen, a visionary established an aviation bureau at Whampoa in 1920 and named Chiang Kai-shek as its first commandant. Whampoa Military Academy was the most renowned military school in Republic of China which trained graduates, who later fought gallantly in the second Sino-Japanese War. The Chinese Air Force during the Kuomintang (KMT) regime was called the Republic of China Air Force (ROCAF) and its origin along with People's Liberation Army Air Force (PLAAF) can be traced back to the establishment of the Guangdong Flying School at the Whampoa Academy in 1924. Eight graduates from the academy were selected to fly Curtis (Jenny) JN4. Subsequently in 1925, fifty flight cadets were comprehensively trained for a year at the academy, out of which eighteen cadets belonging to KMT (Kuomintang) and CCP (Chinese Communist Party) were handpicked to undergo advanced flying training in

Soviet Union. Chang Qiankun and Wang Bi both from the CCP were also amongst the selected few to travel to Russia.[1] Although the other cadets returned to China in 1927, Chang and Wang continued to work with the Soviet air force before being sent to the communist headquarters at Yanan (Shaanxi) to set up the aviation infrastructure for CCP in 1940.

ROCAF: 1930-40

During this period, number of Nationalist leaders including Chiang Kai Shek visited the Soviet Union for professional military education as well as building a rapport with the Russians. Although Soviets were first to assist the Chinese in setting up an air force; Nationalists were simultaneously developing an informal alliance with the Americans. Claire L Chennault, a former US Army Air Corps officer, who had earlier worked as a military advisor to Chiang Kai Shek; established an American Volunteer Group (AVG) to help Chinese fight the Japanese. The AVG, popularly branded as the *'flying tigers'* had frontline fighter aircraft which subsequently replaced the obsolete Russian fighter aircraft in ROCAF. AVG undertook clandestine missions assisting Chinese to fight the Japanese forces and these operations had *'a wink and a nod'* approval of President Franklin D Roosevelt.

At the peak of the crisis, Chennault visited America in the winter months of 1940-41 to personally supervise the purchase of 100 Curtis P-40 which were diverted from the Royal Air Force (RAF) order. He set up the 1st AVG in China with P-40 aircraft and 200 ground staff personnel.[2] These personnel were volunteers, discharged from the armed services and employed by Central Aircraft Manufacturing Company on a monthly salary of $600 along with an earmarked stipend for every kill of an enemy aircraft. The Chinese along with the AVG's carried out air attacks on Japanese warships on the eastern front of the Yangtze River and flew a number of interdiction and close air support missions. *The war for the first time witnessed aerial dog fights and kills between all metal monoplane aircraft in aviation history.* During this period the front line fighters mainly comprised of Curtis Hawk II &III and the Boeing P-26 which engaged the Japanese Mitsubishi A-5M and the A-6M 'Zero' fighters. The ROCAF along with the AVG flew a number of unique missions and one amongst them was on Martin B-10 bombers to drop anti-war leaflets over the Japanese cities of Nagasaki and Saga. This was done to generate a public opinion in Japan and stop the Japanese forces from committing carnage against the Chinese.

AVG not only had fewer aircraft but also inexperienced pilots compared to the Japanese. Chennault carefully studied the Japanese tactics and equipments and developed air combat strategy taking advantage of the shortcomings of the enemy. He ordered all his pilots to take on the enemy aircraft in teams from an altitude of advantage and not get into a turning fight with the agile Japanese fighters. He thus coined '*Dive and Zoom*' strategy where the pilots executed a diving or slashing attack, to dive away and set up for another attack. The '*flying tigers*' fought their first combat on December 20, 1941, where P-40 intercepted ten unescorted Kawasaki Ki-48 "Lily" bombers raiding Kunming. They shot down three Japanese bombers near Kunming and severely damaged the fourth without suffering any loss on their side and thereafter the Japanese were never to be seen over Kunming during the remaining part of the war. ROCAF also carried out over flight '*morale missions*' to boost the morale of the hard-pressed Chinese soldiers. Finally, the '*flying tigers*' performed reasonably well, operating in lesser numbers than the enemy and attaining a kill ratio better than the other allied groups operating elsewhere. By the middle of 1940, Nationalist had gathered a level of expertise on the effective utilisation of air assets however the same cannot be said of the communists, who during the entire period operated from the sidelines!

PLAAF in the Early Years

The Central Military Commission (CMC) established an aviation section at Yanan in 1944 under the 18th Group Army's General Staff Department without any aircraft or airfield under its control. This aviation section was headed by Wang and Chang, who were both instrumental in the early formation of PLAAF. In 1945, the aviation section at Yanan sent a 30-member team to Northeast China to explore the possibility of setting up an aviation school. In May 1946, the Northeast Old Aviation School was established in Mudanjiang (Heilongjiang province) with four basic trainers and a few Japanese Tachikawa Ki.55 type-99 advanced trainers. In three years, the school was able to train 560 personnel, which included 126 pilots and 434 ground support personnel.[3] The instructors mainly comprised members from the Japanese Imperial Air Force, who had continued to stay in China after the surrender in 1945.

At the end of the civil war, strength of the communist lay concentrated in the five Field Areas (FA) located in the north and northeast (Fig 1). PLAAF was formally established by transferring 2500 members of PLA from Wuhan to Beijing (Map 1). Liu Yalou, commander of the Wuhan army unit, took over as the first commander of PLAAF on November 11, 1949. By the end of 1950, PLAAF was reorganised into six military region air force (MRAF) within the existing five FA's. The early MRAF headquarters were not

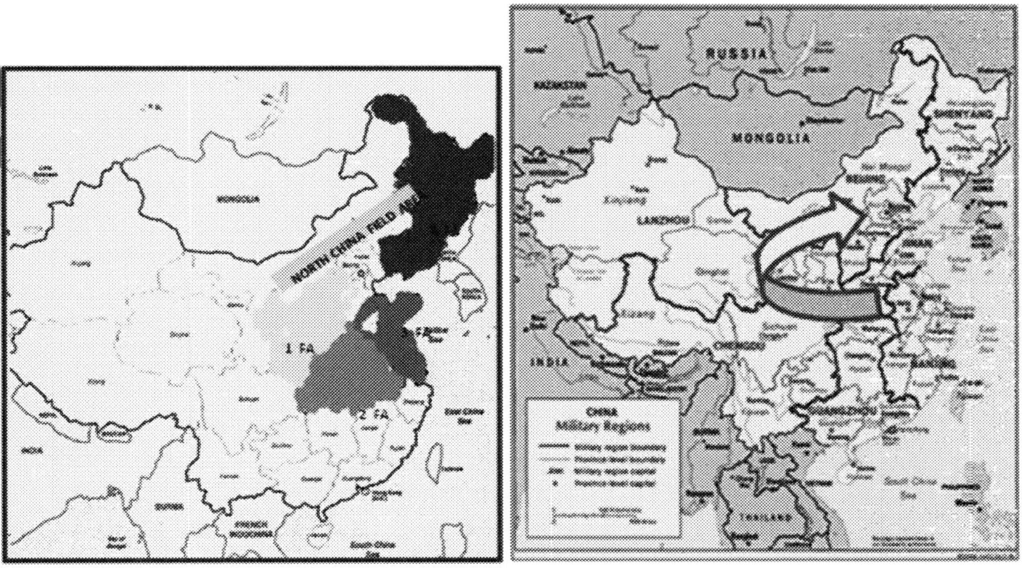

Map 1: PLA's Field Areas

operational commands, but groups formed to consolidate assets left behind by the Nationalists.

Liu Yalou, was earmarked to take over as the PLAAF commander, visited Moscow in early August of 1949 looking for Soviet assistance in setting up an air force for PRC (Peoples Republic of China). Stalin agreed to assist China with 435 aircraft, training schools along with Yak 18(CJ-5) produced by Yakovlev. The agreement to deliver four hundred and more aircraft consisting of 185 different types arrived in batches by end of 1949.[4] CJ-5 was a tandem trainer aircraft powered by a single 160 hp Shvetsov-M 11FR-1 radial piston engine which was later produced in China at the Nanchang factory[5] and Mao described it as a *"world-shaking event"*. The birth of this trainer (CJ-5) had marked a new high in the Chinese aviation industry and probably the beginning of a larger urge to produce a combat aircraft in the future.

PLAAF was finally born out of the PLA and the first flying squadron was established at Beijing, Nanyuan flying group in 1949 with four flights of two fighters, one bomber and one transport aircraft.[6] The aircraft consisted of six P-51 Mustang, two DH-98 Mosquito bombers, two Fairchild PT-19 trainers and probably C-46 and C-47 transport aircraft most of which were left behind by the *nationalist* and the *flying tigers*. The 4th Division was however established at Nanjing in 1950, consisting of two fighters, one bomber and one attack regiment.

The communist had inherited three thousand trained aviation personnel consisting of a few hundred pilots, handful of engineers and two and a half thousand technicians along with a cocktail of a few hundred foreign made aircraft, which had posed a nightmare for the maintenance and logistics. The initial lot of instructors came from the three aviation schools at Xinjiang, Guangdong and the PLAAF aviation school at Mudanjiang. The Japanese pilots who stayed back in Manchuria after 1945 were also utilised in the initial phase of the formation of PLAAF. Mao was well aware of the limitation of new PLAAF, which not only lacked professional leadership but also the requisite combat experience. He therefore, in the first plenary session of the Communist People's Political Consultative Conference (CPPCC) on September 21, 1949 mentioned that "*we will not only have a powerful army but also a powerful air force and a navy*". However the leadership in the late 1940's did not have a clear cut vision and what was evident was the absence of a well defined organisation structure and doctrine to guide PLAAF in its early and nascent state of formation. The organisation structure underwent a number of changes, however it was in 1980s that the transition from the old to the new became conspicuous and the world was witnessing the evolution of PLAAF; as an adjunct of the PLA to becoming an independent service.

Soft and Hard Transition

PLAAF in 1980s was in transition from an obsolete to a more advanced force structure. This transition involved upgrade of not only its hardware consisting of aircraft, missiles and weapon system but also refurbishing its systems like organisation, personnel, training, doctrine, logistics and maintenance which is referred to as 'software'. Both hardware and software aspects are inter-related and therefore play a vital role however at times there is a tendency to overstate the importance of hardware while looking at modernisation of the armed forces. During the course of this transition software as well as hardware aspect need to be analysed to understand the process of transition.

Organisational Transition

PLAAF has been traditionally divided into five branches which are Aviation, Anti Aircraft Artillery (AAA) and Surface to Air Missiles (SAM), Radar and Airborne Troops, listed in the order of protocol. There is a clear distinction between '***aviation***' which consists of aircraft and '***air defence***' which includes AAA, SAM and radar.

PLAAF's chain of command flows from Headquarters Air Force down to Military Region Air Force (MRAF), Air Corps, Command Posts, bases and operational units (Fig 1). MRAFs were organised to control large geographic areas, aligned with the ground forces military region (MR) to provide air defence to strategic areas and support to ground and naval forces. They were also responsible to provide logistics and maintenance support to lower formation. Realignment of MRAFs had taken place on a number of occasions since the formation of PLAAF, but the reduction from eleven to seven took place in 1985 and since then has been more or less static.

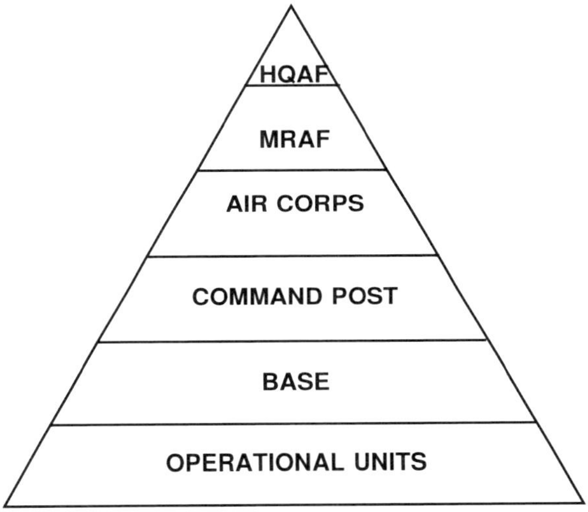

Fig. 1: PLAAF Command Pyramid

Air corps was established to control more than one division within the MRAF and command posts were established to control aircraft and air defence asset deployed to or operating in a special area. As PLAAF reorganised itself, eight of the thirteen air corps[7] were either abolished or downgraded to command posts. This was done with the intention of making the organisation operational by eliminating the unnecessary administrative functions. Finally, by 1993, all command posts[8] with the exception of Lhasa were further reorganised as bases in response to PLA's overall plan of reduction in forces in the 1980's.[9]

Air Defence Forces (ADF) command post was merged with PLAAF in 1957. Out of the seven deputy commanders in the hierarchy of PLAAF, two were nominated from the erstwhile ADF. PLAAFs organisation structure changed from three core first level department consisting of Headquarter, Political and Logistics in 1970s to four first level departments, by adding aeronautical engineering in 1976 to its structure. This was later changed to equipment–technical department in 1992 and once again in 1998 to General

Armament Dept (GAD). Since then the structure has by and large remained the same.

Training

Cultural Revolution crippled all institutions across the board but the worst affected of them all was training which took a back seat. Pilot training was reduced from 30 to 12 months, theory classes stopped, literally stunting the growth of PLAAF. The entire training system had to be revamped however the operational pilot training was the biggest challenge due to the ageing fleet, limited flying and rudimentary simulator systems. PLAAF started recruiting high school and graduate students to undergo pilot training which was now spread over three phases consisting of twenty months at the basic flight school, followed by twenty eight months at the flying academy and finally four to five years of operational flying in a unit. However, by middle of 1980s, PLAAF began to experiment with an additional fourth phase, wherein the third phase for fighter and ground attack pilots was restricted to one year conversion at a transition training base followed by, fourth phase of a slightly truncated version of old operational flying training at units. The programme was finalised in July of 1988, when CMC authorised each MRAF to establish a transition training base.[10]

PLAAF during this period of transition placed great emphasis on training at several levels for officers as well as for the soldiers. In case for officers, basic training at the academy was followed by a stint at the Command College for mid-level/senior level commanders followed by training at the National Defence University. Operationally, however, they were being continuously trained towards understanding the importance of intra service and joint service exercises, which continue even to date. These exercises not only help in increasing the training value but also showcasing their capabilities to the world.

Much has also been said about PLAAF training, quality of pilots and awareness of air combat strategy. Since the late 1980's, PLAAF started making concerted efforts to focus on realistic training. In 1987, PLAAF established a Flight Test and Training Center at Cangzhou airfield near Tianjin (Hebei province), to test new aircraft under development, train pilots on new types of aircraft and devise new air combat tactics. Since then it has been carrying out interesting studies on combat, such as maneuverable combat, air attack, fighting for air supremacy as well as night attack and defence. PLAAF was thus training hard to adapt to combat situations in future high tech conflicts. These tactics were tested and thereafter disseminated to units, where they were incorporated in live exercises. However, PLAAF's inhibition to employ multi mission tasking because of its orientation towards single mission, irrespective of the capability of the aircraft has been a challenge. PLAAF's tactical training and simulator flying has helped make up for the limitations and effectively conducts more than ninety percent of its tactical training on simulators.

In 1958, PLAAF constructed a large center for testing its AAM's and SAM's in Gobi desert near Dingxin in the Gansu province. In late eighties and early nineties, PLAAF upgraded the facilities at Dingxin, created a separate range and set up a tactical training center in association with the one set up at Cangzhou. The Jiuquan space center was established with sophisticated command and control center, air and ground tactical training ranges, simulated runways built to scale, radar, simulated enemy command posts, ammunition and oil depots, along with a large number of simulated tanks deployed in combat position as well as a mock Taiwanese air base, Ching Chuan Kang. PLAAF units could converge at the Gobi desert and practice tactics developed at Cangzhou in close to a real combat environment.[11]

As a result of these changes in training, PLAAF pilots have been noted flying in more sophisticated simulated air-to-air combat with the aggressor units, training in an ECM environment, flying over the Taiwan Strait and East China Sea, conducting live missile firings beyond the coast, dropping live bombs at ranges, and flying at low altitudes at day and night under different weather conditions. They have also practiced emergency mobility deployments to permanent and auxiliary airfields within and outside their assigned military regions. All these changes in the training pattern will positively show up, when PLAAF pilots have to engage in future combat.

Wang Hai Effect

Although PLAAF has been described as "an independent service", it continues to work in the shadow of the army. The fundamental question remains whether PLAAF will free itself from the clutches of PLA and also exercise the necessary clout, responsibilities and autonomy in the future. One reason for PLAAF to be kept subservient to PLA, could have been a result of the Lin Biao and Wu Faxian nexus towards an abortive coup against Mao in 1971. Deng too was sceptical, after he gained control of the Chinese Communist Party (CCP) in 1978, wanted to go slow, assert some kind of authority over the so called 'metaphorically' dangerous service and hence planted a number of political weights into PLAAF.

All PLAAF commanders until 1985 were army officers, transferred into air force command positions. Wang Hai, became the first aviator to take over as Commander of PLAAF. His experience in the Korean War, having shot down nine US aircraft and being awarded a *'war hero'* title helped him understand air power better than his earlier non aviator commanders. He had risen from the ranks, and worked at various levels as a flight commander, deputy division commander, division commander and deputy commander before being appointed as the commander of Guangzhou MRAF in 1975. He saw the 1979 Sino- Vietnam conflict from close quarters, which helped him draw a road map for future PLAAF. In 1985, Wang Hai was appointed as the PLAAF commander and deputy party secretary in the Chinese People's Political Consultative Conference (CPPCC).[12] This was also the first time that a PLAAF commander was appointed as a member of CPPCC. Earlier, Liu Yalou, Wu Faxian, Zhang Tingfa and Gao Houliang were PLAAF commanders or political commissars, who were appointed as members of the politburo or the Central Military Commission (CMC), but none prior to Wang Hai became members of the CPPCC.

Wang Hai defined the road map for PLAAF's transition and demonstrated how modern technology could change the role of air power and revolutionise the concept of future wars. He identified three parameters in air power: maneuverability, fire power and use of electronic warfare. He also emphasised the tremendous impact airlift capability could have on quick mobility of troops which in turn would have an adverse impact on the enemy. Use of aerial platforms for information, intelligence gathering and electronic warfare too would be important tools to expose enemy's strategic intention along with its deployment and movement of troops. Hence, PLA without effective use of airpower and its applications would become deaf and mute.[13] The importance of contact with the foreign air force was also overtly emphasised and a number of delegations were sent and received during this period. Zhu Guang became the first political commissar to ever travel abroad when he visited America in 1988, thus setting a trend for the later political commissars, who visited Cuba, Portugal and Turkey. The exposure to the world air forces influenced the thinking of not only the present leaders but also exposed the future leadership in their thought process which would show effect in years to come.

It was Wang Hai, who formally laid out a plan in 1987 that PLAAF could simultaneously have both offensive and defensive capability. He emphasised that the combined arms combat environment required a force that could move quickly over long distance, fight in an electronic environment, possess capability to attack an enemy and at the same time secure PLAAF from sustaining damage from an enemy air attack. However it was in 1996 that CMC along with PLAAF leadership started re-emphasising publicly about PLAAF's capability to fight an offensive air battle.

PLAAF in Transition

The defensive nature of the people's war doctrine over so many years did rub off on PLAAF, which in a way dampened its resolve to redefine the role of air power. Critically analysing the role of the air force through 1950's to later part of 1970's; PLAAF lacked proficiency in air combat missions like offensive counter air operations, close air support, battlefield interdiction and any kind of command and control systems, never a part of PLAAF's calculus and conspicuously absent from the Korean and the Sino Vietnam war. However, post Sino Vietnam conflict, there appeared to be an apparent shift from the traditional defensive posture to the extent that such mission statements were now being incorporated in their combat strategy. Whether this was an after effect of the recently reviewed US air land battle doctrine post US-Vietnam war or a realisation that close interaction between all air and ground capabilities was quintessential in future conflicts. Whatever be the case, there was definitely a shift in the air power strategy and concepts in 1980s and PLAAF's role was now expanded to include the dual role of not only defending the Chinese airspace but also supporting the ground forces.

The other objective of PLAAF during this period of transition was to improve its deterrent capability by strengthening airborne forces, increasing strategic reach and enhancing its quick mobility capabilities. It saw itself more likely to be engaged in local wars, hence possess capability to end the war quickly and also at the same time attain the political objectives. Therefore, PLAAF established a rapid reaction force within each theatre of operation, to include at least one fighter division in every battle area. Each division would then have a force package of three fighter regiment, one ground attack, one AEW, one ECM regiment, one reconnaissance aircraft along with reliable intelligence network comprising of one EW aircraft.

In terms of air power, PLAAF's main focus was on modernising six core combat capabilities; air superiority, ground attack, transporting troops, reconnaissance, AEW and logistics and maintenance. It started to believe that air superiority, development of technology, firepower, maneuverability and control of electronic means were all critical without which, strategic objective could not be achieved. Hence, PLAAF in its combat strategy initiated considerable reforms in force structure, training, and weapon systems. It defined its role with greater clarity, listing out areas of responsibility in terms of its offensive capability, control of air, air strike as well as air defence. Use of specific weapon system to accomplish special missions was also adequately discussed. Concepts like air deterrence and beyond visual range (BVR) weapons are examples of some concepts which influenced the strategic thinkers in PLAAF.[14] Also the realisation that any future war would have to be multidimensional involving land, sea, air and space; had an overbearing influence on the Chinese psyche. The period of transition witnessed PLAAF breaking away from the shackles of being subservient and evolving as an independent force with laid down objectives.

Transition from Defensive to Offensive Air Campaign

'Offensive campaign' has been articulately explained by R McCabe of the USAF; as one which seeks to maximise enemy's weaknesses by "moving the battlefield as far as possible towards the enemy's side" and forcing the enemy to fight on the defensive at 'China's' initiative. It intends to exploit air and space power's advantages of initiative, versatility, and suddenness. The air campaign should either have the capability to stand independently or become a part of an integrated joint campaign of surface-to-surface missiles, special operations forces, electronic and information strikes, and attacks by aircraft.[15]

Historically, PLAAF had never been an offensive air force, probably because of its own limitation in terms of its capability. PLAAF's inventory of its frontline aircraft in 1980s was obsolete with limited capability to operate at night, in bad weather or in an electronic-countermeasures environment. The strategic bombers like the H-5/H-6 were far inferior to the bomber force possessed by its adversaries and neighbours; as they were incapable to launch air to air campaign, airfield attacks and suppression of enemy air defence. PLAAF's participation in close air support, battlefield air interdiction and interdiction had also been limited. Its force of attack aircraft was ill-equipped and the crews not adequately trained to provide direct support to ground units. Hence, PLAAF over the years had been a defensive force, merely supporting the role in any offensive campaign, with the major burden carried by the missiles.

It took PLA thirty years to realise; '*that the largest obstacle for any ground force or a united campaign came from the air*'. The impact of airpower was evident from multiple payloads, pinpoint targeting, strategic bombing and troop mobilisation, which could frustrate any adversary. Given the condition of antiquated PLAAF; ground forces started acknowledging that air attack by a potential enemy would be the greatest challenge in future high tech wars. This could have been one major reason for PLAAF's transition to an offensive force and eventually develop capabilities of carrying out air strike and if required be able to participate in joint operations.

The transition from a 'defensive air force' to an 'offensive air force also coincided with the process of modernisation, which included restructuring, enhanced training and hardware upgrades. The Chinese had noticed and absorbed these changes taking place in other air forces around the world. In late 1980s, Chinese carefully studied the American air land doctrine, analysed the rationalisation of force structure in USAF and the Russian Air Force and observed that USSR had reduced its fighter jets by fifty five percent and the Americans by twenty four percent. Both countries were of the opinion that in high tech conditions simple function fighters could not establish air superiority or a level of deterrence and hence had to be replaced by multi role aircraft.[16] In late 1980s, PLAAF tabled a proposal to reduce the fighter jets from seventy to fifty five percent and strengthen it with specialised function aircraft like AWACS, aerial refueling, large transport aircraft, electronic warfare and reconnaissance aircraft.[17]

PLAAF was transforming to conduct major air battles far away from home, thereby enhancing the size of its air war zone so that the distinction between air defence front line and in depth strike zone becomes fuzzy. As an offensive force, PLAAF required to prepare itself not only for strategic targets in enemy's rear but also for defence against opponent's aircraft and long distance missile strike. Future wars would be a product of information and high technology, weaponry and air power. Acceptance of air power being a part of the decision making apparatus, independent instrument for application of state interest and integration of a joint campaign can be seen in the context of transition from a historically defensive force air force to an offensive one.[18]

Hard Transition

It has been a haughty journey for PLAAF since 1949, borne out of a cocktail of a few hundred obsolescent aircraft. The Chinese brilliantly consolidated and by 1954 set up 28 divisions consisting of more than three thousand aircraft. It was further expanded to fifty divisions, which remained pretty static until mid 1980's; thereafter they were reduced to thirty two divisions. PLAAF inventory for considerable time consisted of the aircraft of 1950s and 1960s technology, like the J-5, J-6, Yakovlev, Lavochkin and the IL 10. Though these aircraft were world class in their times, but now were nothing more than ***'junkyard'***.

The workhorses of PLAAF during this period were the J-6, second generation fighter and Q-5 ground attack aircraft, both variants of MiG 19s. J-6 made up for the bulk in the PLAAF inventory through 1960's to the turn of the century, with more than three thousand aircraft. Q-5 was a close air support aircraft with ground attack and air-to-air combat capabilities. Although, Q-5's was capable of carrying nuclear payload, it was limited by its relatively short range (about 600 km radius of action) and primitive avionics. H-5 was the Chinese version of the Soviet IL-28, medium bomber which served as PLAAF's primary dedicated bomber. The H-5's effectiveness in a traditional bombing role was once again limited by its range and slow speed, which made it highly vulnerable to modern air defence systems.[19] These aircraft were far inferior in technology, avionics and radar systems to many aircraft possessed by countries in the neighbourhood[20] as is evident from the capability tabulated in Table 1.

Table 1: Role and Capability of PLAAF Aircraft in 1980's

Type	Derivative	Role	Combat radius	Payload
J-6	MiG 19	Fighter	600 KM	PL2/PL5 AAM, 250 KG BOMB
Q-5	MiG 19	Ground Attack	600KM	PL2, PL5,PL7 AAM, BL 755 Cluster Bombs, Durandal Anti Runway Bombs
J-7	MiG 21	3RD GEN Fighter	800KM	PL2,PL5,PL7, PL8,PL9 AAM, R 550 Magic,[21] 500 KG Bomb,
J-8	-	3rd GEN Fighter	800KM	PL2, PL5, PL8, PL12 AAM,1500 KG Bombs
H-5	IL 28	MED Bomber	1000 KM	3000 KG Internal Bombs
H-6	TU 16	Bomber	2000 KM	9000 KG

Source: Compiled from Wikipedia, FAS and Janes

The J-5 and J-6, which had reached the end of their service life, were being gradually phased out. Dr You Ji mentions that PLAAF scrapped over 6000 old aircraft in 1980s, out of which J-5 and J-6 constituted a large chunk, profoundly affecting PLAAF's overall size in the later part of 1980.[22] The force structure of PLAAF increased linearly until mid 1980s except for a brief period during the Cultural Revolution. It peaked in mid 1980s and thereafter showed signs of decline as bulk of the aircraft had reached the end of their service life. Fig 3 illustrates that J-6, which had been a work horse for PLAAF, was being gradually replaced with variants of J-7, J-8 and future fourth generation aircraft. Since the replacement of the combat aircraft was not on one-to-one basis as was evident from the production line in 1980s (Table2), the force structure of the fighters in PLAAF declined in 1990s, though still majority of its fighter aircraft consisted of J-6. Analysis of Graph. 1 and Table 2 gives a fairly good picture of the dynamics of the force structure from 1954-93 and also draws out an excellent sketch of the combat capability of PLAAF. Induction of J-7 and J-8 was a logical step to augment the depleting force structure of PLAAF in 1980s and 1990s.

Table 2: China's Annual Combat Aircraft Production for Domestic use, 1980-92

	1980	1981	1982	1983	1984	1985	1986	1987	1988	1989	1990	1991	1992
J-6	150	-	-	-	-	-	-	-	-	-	-	-	-
J-7 I	-	40	50	50	50	50	50	50	50	50	50		
J-7 III												24	24
J-8		10	18	18	18	18	18	18					
J-8 II												12	12
H-5	20	20	20										
H-6	6	6	6	6	6	66	6	6	6	6	6		

• Q 5 production stopped in 1975.
Source: China's Military, Srikanth Kondapalli.

To fill the void created by the existing technological gap and the force structure, Chinese produced variants of J-7 and J-8 in 1980's as a replacement for the obsolete second generation J-6. Ironically, both J-7 and J-8 were aircraft of 1960 vintage and nothing more than marginally 'advanced' obsolete aircraft in 1980s,[23] far behind the capabilities of the fourth generation aircraft deployed by Russia, America and its neighbours.

Transition to J-7

J-7, a derivative of MiG 21F, was assembled and built on incomplete data received from the Russians. The programme commenced in 1960,s at the Shenyang Aircraft Factory and the static test on the aircraft was carried out in November, 1965 followed by the first flight test in January, 1966 with WP-7(WoPen),[24] Chinese copy of Soviet Tumansky R 11F -300 turbo jet engine. The fighter was certified for production in 1967.

The J-7 production was reassigned to a newly built Chengdu Aircraft Industry Corporation (CAC) in Sichuan province. The production of WP-

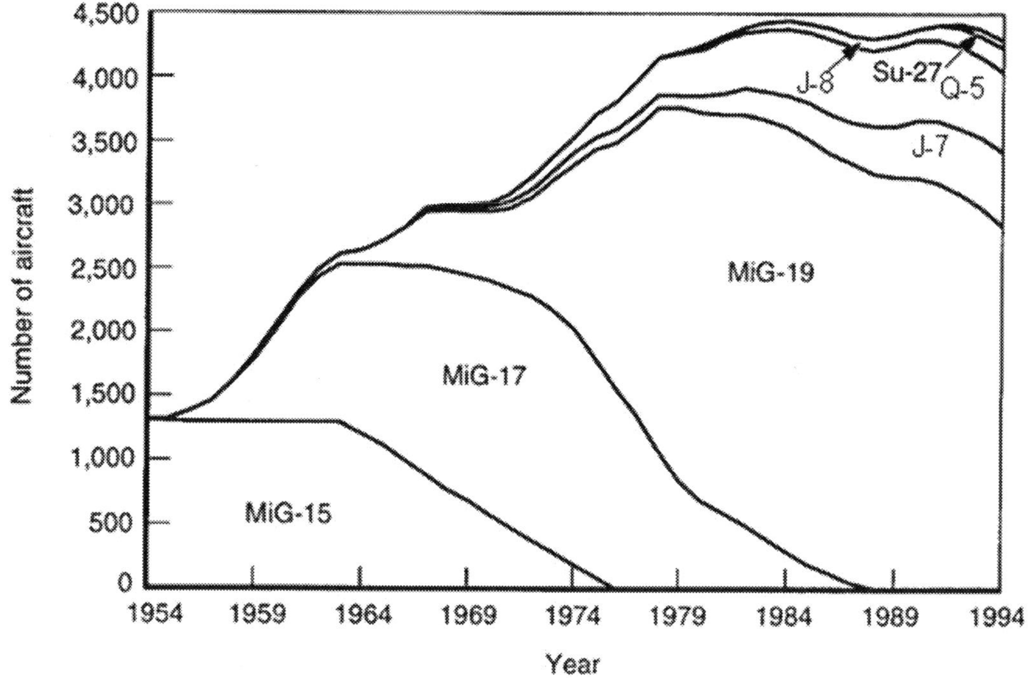

Chinese Jet Fighter Inventory, 1954–1994

Source: Allen, Krumel and Pollack 1995.

Fig. 3: China's Combat Aircraft

7 was also handed over to Liyang Aero Engine Company at Guizhou province in 1968. From 1969-75, Chengdu modified the J-7 design to roll out the J-7-I version in 1976. The programme was severely hampered by the 'Cultural Revolution, and when the first aircraft rolled out in 1976, it had already become obsolete. The J-7-I modernisation continued with upgrades in the avionics suite, airframe, weapon system and engine. The result was an upgraded version with WP-7B engine, certified for production in 1979 and called the J-7II.

The J-7II upgrade was assisted by British GEC-Marconi. It included the 956 HUDWAC (head up display and weapon aiming computer), Skyranger air to air ranging radar with anti jamming capability, air data computer(ADC), radar altimeter, IFF(identification of friend or foe), and a secured radio communication. After 1989 Tiananmen incident, GEC-Marconi Skyranger radar was replaced by Italian Grifo 7 fire control radar with a range of more than 55 Km. Indigenous modifications of the weapon system, airframe structure through computer aided design continued on J-7-II. Rearview mirror, more number of fuel tanks under the dorsal fairing and an enlarged vertical fin were incorporated to improve the performance of the platform. The aircraft was fitted with pylons capable of carrying the PL7 AAM, Magic R 550, PL-2, PL-5 short range AAM. J-7 EB version was used for the aerobatic team fitted with smoke canisters.

However, J-7-II lacked the capability to combat in all weather day/night conditions. Chinese were eyeing the multi role capability of MiG 21 MF; which they were able to acquire from the Egyptians in 1979. CAC reverse engineered MiG 21 MF with help of computer aided design to roll out the first version of J-7-III in 1984. The aircraft was fitted with JL-7(J band) multipurpose pulse Doppler fire control radar, target tracking using optical gun sight, IFF, HUD(head up display), autopilot, ADC, radio altimeter, HF/VHF communication system, RWR along with chaff and flare dispensers. It was powered by WP 13 turbojet engine, developed by Guizhou Liyang Aero Engine Company. The J-7-III lacked the 'punch' as its JL-7 fire control radar was unreliable, without BVR and 'look down shoot down' capabilities, which by now was available on all major western aircraft. The J-7D's, incorporated minor improvements over the J-7-III; upgraded the avionics suite, fire control radar and replaced the engine with a slightly more powerful WP-13 F1. The weapon capabilities were marginally enhanced to carry PL-7 and PL-8, however it was still lacking in the BVR capabilities. Chengdu's attempt to reverse engineer MiG 21 MF was not entirely successful and hence it reverted back to the J-7-II design to develop an improved version; J-7 E for PLA. This aircraft was first flown in 1992 and inducted in PLAAF in 1995.

Improvements on the J-7E mainly focused on aerodynamic performance and avionics. The original delta wing plan-form was replaced by the new "double-delta" design similar to that of the Russian Su-15 and Swedish Saab J-35 Draken and the engine changed with WP7F. Avionics included JT-1 HUD, KW8602 RWR, 8430 ADC, JD-3 tactical aircraft navigation (TACAN), KG-8605 internal radar noise jammer, and 941-4AC chaff/flare dispenser.

The J-7MG was an export variant developed by CAC based on the J-7E, with WP 13F engine. The fighter was fitted with X-band British Marconi Electronic Systems and Super Sky Ranger pulse-Doppler fire-control radar. It had the 'look-down/shoot-down' capability and five working modes that could track up to 8 targets simultaneously. Marconi HUD along with and fire-control computer and a HOTAS (hands on throttle-and-stick) improved the cockpit design and ergonomics to allow the pilot to fly the aircraft without taking his eyes off the horizon and HUD and thus improving his situational awareness. The system could also be integrated with the helmet-mounted display (HMS). It also featured a coloured electronic flight control system (EFCS), Automatic Direction Finder (ADF), VHF Omni-directional Range (VOR), TACAN and Instrument Landing System (ILS).

The J-7 PG had been in service with the Pakistani Air Force (PAF) and was almost similar in configuration to the J-7MG. The J-7MG/PG series export fighter had been the most successful amongst the J-7 and hence Chengdu developed its domestic equivalent, the J-7G. The J-7G was equipped with an I/J-band KLJ-6E pulse-Doppler fire-control radar based on Israeli EL/M2001, helmet mounted sighted AAM, new one-piece front windscreen for better cockpit visibility, Type III IFF, indigenous zero-height, zero-speed ejection seat and an improved ECM suite. The J-7G aircraft first flew in June 2002, and finally entered PLAAF in 2004.

CAC was also developing an updated version of J-7 M under the Super-7 program. The programme was a trilateral agreement between US, China and Pakistan, to replace the WP 7B/WP 13 engines with GE F 404. The project had to be shelved because of the sanctions imposed on China in 1989. CAC however continued with the wind tunnel experiments of a completely configured Super 7 and rebranded the design as FC-1(JF-17), a future fourth generation aircraft.

Peace Pearl

J-8 was the first indigenously designed aircraft in PLAAF. The aircraft was built at Shenyang Aircraft Corporation (SAC) and designed at the 601

Aircraft design Institute. It was an enlarged version of the J-7, with two WP-7 engines. The work on theoretical evaluation commenced in May, 1964 at the Research Academy of the Chinese Military of Defence to produce a Mach 2 aircraft capable of intercepting the US B-58 and F-105. Within a year, J-8 entered the engineering development phase with the first mock up ready for inspection in December, 1965 and the prototype production commenced in 1966. The first two prototypes rolled out in July, 1968 and were flown on July 5, 1969. This programme was also interrupted because of the Cultural Revolution, and the test flights could not be completed until 1979. The J-8, mounted with delta shaped wings and two Liyang WP-7 aero engines finally entered service in 1981.

Though, the aircraft achieved more or less all the design targets, lack of modern avionics and armament capabilities did not give J-8 any distinctive advantage over the J-7. Slow progress in developing fire control radar and the unsuccessful trial of the PL-4, left the aircraft capable of carrying only a PL-2 IR homing short range AAM for air combat. Around fifty such aircraft were produced, and remained in service until 1990. J-8-I was an improvement over the J-8; which included JL-7 monopulse fire control radar, SM-8A aeronautical gun sight, on board computer, improvised cockpit panel along with a new ejection seat and an oxygen system. This aircraft went through its midlife modernisation upgrade in 1990s, with an ECM suite and RWR, and was called the J-8 E.

The J-8-II was a redesigned J-8 developed once again by SAC. Thereafter various versions of upgraded J-8-II were alphabetically classified. The original nose air inlet of J-8 was moved to the sides to provide space for larger size radar. The two under powered WP-7B were replaced by more powerful WP-13 A II engines. J-8B was the first variant of the upgraded J-8-I which flew its first flight in 1989. The upgrade included a Type 208A mono-pulse fire control radar with extended range coupled with an interception fire control computer, HK 13 E HUD, JD-3II TACAN. The later version of J-8B was upgraded with KLJ-1 pulse Doppler fire control radar and KJ-8602A RWR. Capability to carry semi active radar homing MRAAM and air to ground rockets along with an auto pilot were added to J-8, however J-8B still lacked the BVR combat capability, mainly because of its ineffective fire control radar.

To address various limitations in J-8-II, China decided to get into a military alliance with US. This was the largest $550 million foreign military sales (FMS) agreement between US and China to upgrade the J-8-II interceptor aircraft by Grumman under the 'Peace Pearl' project. There were forty two Chinese military officers who were working on the joint arms project with the United States at Grumman Corp in Bethage, NY and Wright–Patterson AFB near Dayton, Ohio.[25] The upgrade package for the fifty aircraft included the Westinghouse APG-66V radar (also fitted on F 16), 1553B MIL-STD data bus, fire control computer, HUD, cockpit multi functional display (MFD), navigation system and ejection seat. Grumman in its urgency to grab the deal coupled with PLAAF's obsession with secrecy prevented Grumman understanding the cockpit of each of the fifty Chinese aircraft, which were unique and hence required individual adjustment leading to cost over runs.[26] However the project was only short lived and cancelled post 1989 Tiananmen Square incident, as part of sanction imposed by America and the west on China.

Following the cancellation of the 'Peace Pearl' project, the SAC continued to upgrade the J-8II, possibly under the assistance of Israel or Russia. In the early 1990s, Shenyang proposed a radically upgraded variant, J-8C (also known as J-8III) featuring new avionics and power plant, which would eventually bring the fighter into the same league as modern Russian and Western combat aircraft like the MiG-29 and Mirage 2000-V. The J-8C programme entered full scale development around 1991 and the aircraft first flew successfully in 1993.

J-8C was an upgraded J-8-II, which included a new multi-mode pulse Doppler radar based on the Israeli Elta EL/M 2035 radar technology. It was also equipped with a digital fire-control system and a new glass cockpit with multifunctional displays (MFD). The aircraft's original WP-13 A II turbojet engine was replaced by the more powerful WP-14 turbojet then being developed by Shenyang Liming Aero-Engine Company. The J-8C project in late 1990s had to be shelved in favour of the SU 27/J11, however the same technology was later used in developing the J-8F.

J-8D was a modified J-8, with a fixed refueling probe on the starboard side of the cockpit. The first hook-on with the H-6 tanker took place in early 1990s; however PLAAF demonstrated its capability of air to air refueling to the world on October 01, 1999. The air to air refueling was a big boost, as it increased the combat radius of J-8 from 800 km to 1200 km.

The J-8F was an improved variant of J-8C with a stiffened nose and two wing fences on each wing. It was also regarded as the first true 'multirole' fighter, hence the most capable variant in the J-8II family. New features in the J-8F included a glass cockpit, more powerful WP-13 B II engine, new fire-control radar (JL-10) with the capability of a radio command transmitter to provide mid course correction to its PL 12 MRAAM during BVR attack. It was also capable of guiding R 27, R 77 along with an enhanced air to air and air to sea modes of firing precision guided armaments including laser or satellite guided bombs. The J-8F could also be fitted with a fixed in-flight refueling probe.

SAC was now able to upgrade the J-8II with Russian technology because of the turnaround in the Sino-Russian relations in early 1990s. The J-8IIM intended primarily for the export market, featured with the Russian Phazotron Zhuk-8II pulse-Doppler fire-control radar specially tailored for the J-8II fighter, coupled with the Vympel R-27R1(NATO code named AA10), semi-active radar-homing MRAAM. The package provided the J-8IIM with 'real' BVR combat capability and the aircraft was flown successfully on 31 March 1996.

The J-8II ACT (Active Control Technology) was a technology demonstrator, designed for studying and testing the 'fly-by-wire' (FBW) technology. The aircraft based on the J-8II airframe, with a shorter fuselage and a pair of front canards just behind the air inlets. The J-8II ACT was introduced in 1990s to replace the older FBW demonstrators based on the J-6(J-6 ACT) and J-8 (J-8 ACT). The J-8II ACT played an important role in the future development of PRC's third-generation fighter programme.

Transport and Helicopter

Other than combat operations and aggressively modernising its fighter fleet, PLAAF's other mission was also to provide airlift in support of its ground forces. Its capacity to augment PLA's airlift requirement was restricted because of its antiquated aircraft. PLAAF's transport fleet mainly consisted of Y-5(An2), Y-7(An24), Y-8(An 12), IL 18, indigenously manufactured Y-11 and Y-12 along with a few old Lisunov (Li 2) and IL 14. The 15th Airborne Corp was also a part of PLAAF and utilised An 2, IL 14, IL 18 and Y-7's for its missions. The transport element of the PLAAF had participated in a few combat operations in past campaigns, which included airborne assault landing and attack on enemy's line of communication. Hence, 15th Airborne Corp was envisaged to play an important role and was thus elevated to a strategic force, directly controlled by the Central Military Commission (CMC). During crisis, PLAAF was empowered to utilise civil aircraft to transport troops; as was demonstrated in the 1989 Tiananmen incident. Until mid 1990s, due to limited airlift capabilities, PLAAF could deploy only three divisions consisting of around 11,000 troops along with light tanks and self propelled artillery within 48 hours. The airlift capability was however later enhanced in 1993, with the induction of 10 IL-76 heavy lift aircraft.

The transport aircraft were also utilised in maintaining the signals intelligence in the Asia Pacific region. The principle Chinese airborne ELINT platform was the EY 8, indigenously developed as a derivative of the An 12. The system was designed to detect, identify, analyse and locate land-based or shipborne radar emitters with a high probability of intercept. It was more than established that Israel was actively involved in assisting the development of China's airborne ELINT/EW capability.

China also produced the French Super Frelons (SA 321); anti submarine warfare (ASW) and search and rescue (SAR) variants for the navy. The Super Frelons were called the Z-8; first helicopter in PLA capable of operating from the deck of surface vessels.[27] It also developed the JH-7, primarily for the navy at the Xian Aircraft Company (XAC); the test programme commenced in 1988 and the prototype flew in 1993. The aircraft was powered by the Rolls Royce Spey Mk 202. As we look at the development programmes in the aviation industry through 1980s and 1990s, it is evident that the 'geopolitics' of the region had influenced the process of modernisation in PLAAF. China in the 1980s was in alliance with America and after Tiananmen and end of cold war aligned with the Russians. The inter changeability of actors and them guiding the process of military modernisation was quite evident during this period.

Capabilities of the New PLAAF

China by the turn of the century was heading towards a level of self sufficiency in building advanced weaponry following decades of importing aircraft, missile technology, ships and submarines mainly from Russia, Israel as well as from a few European countries. In Mid 1990s, Beijing was on a defence spending spree on wide range of high-tech weaponry, which included fighter jets like the Su-27, attack helicopters and missile systems. Also unveiling of J-10 in early part of this century has been a culmination of a long time aspiration of the Chinese Aviation Industry to launch its first domestically designed fighter jet. This aircraft was produced amidst controversy, ending saga of international-military hardware wheeling and dealing that has seen US designed or funded high tech weaponry fall into the hands of potential military rivals. Nevertheless, unleashing this aircraft to the world was indeed a path breaking event for the Chinese. It is true that J-10 could not have happened without assistance from Israel and Pakistan, who apparently provided a single F-16 and with assistance from Israel engineers associated with Israel's US–financed Lavi fighter programme, the Chinese were able to develop the J-10.

Although George Schultz, then the Secretary of State in the

administration of the US president Ronald Reagan later admitted his advocacy and assistance of US $1.3 billion aid to Israel for the Lavi project as a "costly mistake". David Lari, Director General of Israel's Ministry of defence acknowledged that "some technology on aircraft" (Lavi) had been sold to China and that some Israeli companies may not have "clean hands". Whether it was by hook or by crook, the Chinese were able to successfully roll out a fighter jet with almost the same capabilities to that of Su 27, MiG 29 and F-16 at a price tag of less than US$ 10 billion. PLAAF at the same time was aware that air power was not just about fancy aero planes but more about being able to manage these toys. It was also aware of its own limitation plagued by a relatively underdeveloped aviation establishment. Hence its strategy was based on the premise that even a 'strong enemy with absolute superiority is certainly not without a weakness ... and therefore their military preparation needs to be aimed at finding tactics to exploit the weakness of their adversary rather than exposing their own limitations. They also realised that air superiority in pure Chinese context was not just about doing seductve stuff like dog fights between fancy aircraft or the 'Yo–Yo' but to focus on their strength to ensure their ability to attain air superiority either by what could be an anti access strategy, which is prevent access to an area of operation or area denial strategy, which is prevent freedom of action. They therefore envisaged an aerospace campaign which could be a joint campaign between the air force assets, electronic counter measures and second artillery as integral component of firepower warfare or in the future even a joint air sea battle concept by expanding their long range strike capability alongside subsurface operation as part of their anti denial strategy. At the same time they were heavily investing in computer network operations (CNO) and it is now estimated that there are over 3,00,000 organised as well as unorganised manpower involved in cyber warfare. They are also investing in connectivity for data transmissions and what this means is laying down huge network of fibre optic cables. This is indeed a fascinating stuff as every Chinese ground exercise has part of its tasking to lay new fibre optic cables, hence whenever you exercise in mainland China, your job is to lay new fibre optic cable and sooner than later China would head towards an integration capability across MR. Their vision for the future being that at any point in time all censors must be able to replicate two common air situation picture simultaneously, one in the MR headquarter and the other in sector headquarter. This cannot be simplistically done through internet and therefore investments are made in buying processors that allow them to collate data coming in from different sources and be able to fuse all of it in a way to be able to see a common air situation at two different locations simultaneously. Thus what we see is that PLAAF modernisation is not just about accumulating beautiful flying machines but building an air force to do things when operating in joint context and this is indeed an important aspect.

There is still some time before China would be able to use PLAAF as a complete force package. China is in the process of building an advanced fifth generation multi role stealth fighter that would rub shoulders with the 'Raptor' by the end of this decade.[28] Their ambition is to have a long range precision strike capability along with a full spectrum of air and missile defence capability. The Chinese would need to augment their force structure with AWACS, AAR as well as a brand new fleet of strategic bombers and until that happens, they would have to concentrate on other facets of air power to achieve air superiority. Their aim being to carry out advanced strategic strike mission at ranges in excess of 3000kms and finally to be seen as a force to reckon, but this would have to wait for a while.

Challenges for the Indian Air Force

IAF's strength by itself would be its greatest challenge as PLAAF's approach to dealing with India will be asymmetric. What this means is that if IAF's combat proficiency is its strong point then PLAAF will not be dealing with IAF through air combat in future wars until unless it achieves at least the same level of proficiency if not more. Moreover, PLAAF like a hawk has been monitoring IAF and its performance in all its international exercises like the Red Flag, Sindex, Indradhanush and Garuda. Their main concern rests on the fact that the performance of the Indian Air Force in all these exercises has been outstanding and therefore, they would in all possibilities resort to a strategy embedded with an element of surprise. They would not for all tea in China like to get into an air combat situation with the IAF for at least some more time to come until they are themselves convinced about their professional competence. During this period of vacuum, they would want to do a few things to enhance their capability in case of a conflict and be able to operate from a position of strength. Therefore in all likelihood, their strategy would be to attack command, control and communication centres, impede sortie generation, focus on electronic warfare so that incase an aircraft does get airborne he does not get a clean fire control solution and disrupt data transfer through a concerted computer network operations (CNO).

They will also try to maintain a high end component of PLAAF that will exceed our total force and this for our planners is going to be a nightmare. Though the present structure of PLAAF has been rationalised, it still has a large component of high end aircraft that will exceed our total force and that is the change when comparing PLAAF of yester years to the PLAAF of today! By 2015, it is estimated that they would have almost 1,500 high end state of art fighters consisting of SU 30, J-11, J-10, J-8 and upgrades of J-7 including a whole lot of JF- 17. Routine deployment in India relevant MR will become a fashion and PLAAF would at any given time maintain upward of 200 aircraft, however their limitation would remain operating from the plateau, where the terrain does not permit to load the aircraft optimally. From the Indian standpoint, the main threat would continue to be from ballistic and cruise missile attack on command and control centers, use of MiG 19 drones or UAVs to bring down early warning and GCI network and jamming the AWACS radar. In other words, China's focus would therefore be to carry out '**Operational Paralysis of India**' which is defeating its enemy through its weakness and this would probably be China's short term philosophy to contain India.

Clausewitz had said that in International Security action elicits a reaction; India must act or react whichever way; to build its force. It therefore has to enhance its capability by improving AD network, missile systems,C4ISR and airfield repair and more importantly construction of new airfields. The logistics network also needs to be improved as the Chinese on the other side have over the years built an excellent network of road and railway line with high speed trains which would help them in augmenting their capability. Also the earlier perception that India would be able to achieve command of the air in 48 to 96 hrs, a study carried out by RAND; in today's context would be fallacy and should be quickly dispensed with!

China is indeed a great challenge; it has built relations both in its neighborhood as well as far flung regions rich in resources, which are essential for its economic growth. China seeks to lead a unipolar Asia under the concept of multipolarity as a smokescreen, while India on the contrary is looking at a multi polar Asia and a multi polar world. This is where the difference lies and to bridge the gap India should work towards playing a balancing role in Asia and be accepted as a preferable strategic partner by strengthening relations with some key countries in Asia- Japan, Vietnam, Taiwan, Singapore and Iran without compromising on its military buildup. India and China have historically enjoyed good relations for over two thousand years. Even today, though both countries have different cultures, polity and model of growth, but still there is tremendous potential as well as space for the two 'Superpowers' to coexist and grow; however the relationship should be premised on mutual self respect.

The Journey....

In terms of airpower, India is doing its bit and appears to be on the correct track maybe we can work on expediting the process and reducing the time gap between conception, proposal and acquisition of a project. However when it comes to aerospace power we need to do a little more in terms C4ISR, CNO, missiles and missile defence. And by the way missile defence today is like a **'beamer'**, a must have 'military fashion accessory' for any country having a military posture! China over the years has been working hard towards building an air force not just as an adjunct of the PLA but an independent service capable of carrying out strategic strike missions by moving the battle field as far away towards the enemy's side. The transition from the obsolete J-6 class of aircraft to the J-7 and J-8 was in fact the foundation being laid for future modernisation. China has been pursuing these goals with an ultimate aim to achieve sustained military modernisation, which has also been brilliantly articulated in the 2006 white paper on national defence to state that:

> 'The first step is to lay a solid foundation by 2010; the second is to make major progress around 2020; and the third is to basically reach the strategic goal of building informatised armed forces and being capable of winning informatised war by mid-21st century.'

China is aware that it has no other option but to forge ahead with the development of its defence sector or it will "slip behind the rest of the world. It also realises the importance to modernise the country's defense system as it draws the conclusion from history and reality that power is an important condition and guarantee for peace. China is rising and shaping the world as never before and if we remember what Napoleon said two hundred years back, "*let her sleep, for when she wakes, she will shake the world*". The sleeping giant has awakened, the world frightfully looks on but the journey towards modernisation continues.

End Notes

1. Kenneth. W. Allen, Glenn Krumel, Jonathan, D. Pollack, *China's Air Force enters 21st century* (RAND), p. 35.
2. "Flying Tigers", Wikipedia, http://en.wikipedia.org/wiki/Flying_Tigers
3. Kenneth. W. Allen, Glenn Krumel, Jonathan. D. Pollack, n.1, p. 36
4. Chen Jian, "Sino-Soviet Alliance and China's entry into the Korean war", *Woodrow Wilson International Center for Scholars Washington*, Working Paper No 1,June 1992, p. 17.
5. "Yakovlev Yak 18", Wikipedia, http://en.wikipedia.org/wiki/Yakovlev_Yak-18
6. Kenneth. W. Allen, Glenn Krumel, Jonathan. D. Pollack, n. 1, p. 38.
7. The five active Air corps were 1st/Changchun, 7th/Nanning, 8th/Fuzhou, 9th/Wulumuqi and 10th/Datong

8. The seven existing command post were Dalian, Tangshan, Xian, Shanghai, Wuhan, Kunming and Lhasa.
9. This section on Organisational transition is adapted from the writings of Kenneth Allen, senior analyst at the CNA Corporation, who has descriptively analysed the organisation structure of PLAAF during this period.
10. Kenneth W Allen, Glenn Krumel, Jonathan D Pollack, *China's Air Force Enters the 21st Century* (RAND) Ch 7, p.130.
11. "PLA Air Force Organisation and Modernisation", http/www.china-defense.com/aviation/plaaf-ops/plaaf-ops_10.html
12. http://www.sd.xinhuanet.com/sdsq/2006-03/02/content_6366248.htm
13. You Ji, *The Armed Forces of China* (IB Taurus Publishers), Ch 5, p.126.
14. n. 13, Ch 5, p.125.
15. Lt Col R McCabe, USAF, "*Chinese Air Force and Air and Space Power*", Air and Space Power Journal, Fall Sep 2003.
16. n.13, Ch 5, p. 133.
17. n. 13, Ch 5, p.137.
18. Ashley J Tellis, Senior Associate, Carnegie Endowment for International Peace, Washington, *Talk at CAPS on PLAAF on April 28, 2010*
19. The Chinese use standard designators for their military aircraft. "J" (Jian) is a designator for fighters, "Q" (Qiang) for ground attack, "H"(Hongzha) for bombers, "Y" (Yun) for transport and "Z" (Zhi) for helicopters.
20. Roy Kamphausen and Andrew Scobell "*Right-Sizing the People's Liberation Army: Exploring the Contours of China's Military*", Future Force Structure of Chinese Air Force, Philip C. Saunders and Erik Quam, Ch 8, p. 387.
21. Janes: All World's Aircraft 2006-07, Edited By Paul Jackson, *J-7B version with R550 capability was supplied to Egypt and Iraq in 1982-83.*
22. n. 13, Ch 5, p.134.
23. Lt Col Patricia M Fornes, *"Modernising China's Air Force: It's Strategy, Budget and capabilities*", Research report Submitted at the Air War College.
24. Chinese nomenclature for engines: HS (HuoSai: Piston engine), WJ (WoJiang: Turboprop),WP (Wopen: Turbojet),WS (WoShan: Turbofan),WZ (WoZhou: Turboshaft)
25. The Washington Post, October 29, 1989, *US Allows Chinese Military back into Joint Arms Project*
26. Thomas L Wilborn, "*Security Cooperation With China: Analysis and a Proposal*", 25 Nov 1994,Strategic Studies Institute
27. "Super Frelons, Sinodefence," http://www.sinodefence.com/airforce/helicopters / sa321.asp
28. Jim Wolf, "New Chinese Fighter Jet expected by 2018: US Intelligence", Reuters May 21, 2010.

7

Chinese Space Programme and Implications for India

AJEY LELE

Context

The early years of space exploration in the late 1950s and 1960s provided the world a simple narrative: the competition amongst the erstwhile Soviet Union and the United States (US). However, the first decade of the 21st century provides a more complex narrative for space exploration[1] particularly in the context of Asia. The questions like: 'Is there a space race brewing in Asia?' is been raised from various platforms for last few years. This is happening because of the phenomenal success achieved by Japan, China and India.

Space exploration involves learning more about the planets and the stars. This entails putting artificial satellites in the outer space at different heights in different orbits. Also, these satellites tell us more about the earth and manage our communication and national requirements. To put satellites in space is a technologically and financially challenging task. Till date very few states (less than ten) in the world have achieved this feat. Naturally, the space activities require significant state support, budget provisions, meticulous planning, a vibrant research and development organisation and in many cases international collaborations too. Today, the space programmes of Japan, China and India have reached various levels of achievements mainly depending on how and when these states have prioritized their requirements and level of technical expertise available with them.

In the post Cold War era particularly after opening of their economy, states like China and India have made significant progress in various fields. The period post-1990s has started showing a substantial growth in China's Global power status. This has essentially happened because of the current and 'projected' economic transformation of China. The economic growth in China has accelerated along with increased integration with the global economy.[2] Since the establishment of its economy in 1978, China has averaged around 9.4 per cent annual GDP growth, one of the top growth rates in the world. The last three decades of economic liberalisation have revealed the magnitude of China's labour force, creativity and purchasing power to the world; its commitment to development and its degree of national cohesion has also come to the fore.[3] As per the International Monetary Fund (IMF) projection China is expected to grow at a rate of 10.5 per cent in 2010 and 9.6 per cent in 2011.[4] Today, "Rise of China" (the term coined in 2003 by China's political establishment is Peaceful Rise of China[5]) has become a part of the lexicon.

China's prominence in world science is growing very rapidly. China understands the importance of the role science and technology play towards development of the any nation-state. Chinese Premier Wen Jiabao articulates that for China "scientific innovation is an important process of shifting from *made in China* to *created in China*. Also, transforming the economic growth made through developing Chinese creation and service was a key issue if the Chinese economy was to keep a balanced, coordinated and sustainable growth."[6] The recent analysis indicates that China's output of peer-reviewed scientific papers has been growing more than five times faster than that of the US.[7] Apart from economy and growth of technology there is one more area where China has made significant investments such as in the military. The rise of China has become a reality because of the vision and the hard work of the party. At the same time the prevailing geopolitical situation could also be held responsible for China's evolution. End of the Cold War and the declining influence of Russia over the region and the total pre-occupation of the US in the war against terrorism post-9/11 have also indirectly helped China to become more relevant.

China understands that for any state the primary importance of technology is for the purposes of industrial growth and also as a tool to enhance the socio-economic development. At the same time military being an important element to display the nation's might it is important to derive major advantages for the military from the developments in technology. In the 21st century, the military planning is undergoing rapid transformation. The defence leadership in the region is involved in developing efficient and effective armed forces. The various recent military campaigns like the 1991 and 2003 Gulf Wars and the war in Afghanistan demonstrate the importance of military technology. This success of technology with various war waging mechanisms has dictated a Revolution in Military Affairs (RMA). China is also witnessing a RMA and is investing into various modern military technologies. The Iraq campaigns in 1991 and 2003, NATO's intervention in Kosovo, the war against terrorism in Afghanistan, and the determination of the US to pursue ballistic and theater missile defence systems has demonstrated the value of space assets in controlling modern warfare to the world. On the other hand, universally technology (more so strategic technologies) is usually viewed as a policy instrument for a state and the prevailing geopolitical milieu of the region confirms that China understands this fully and is intelligently using it to achieve its political aims.

For space technologies the Chinese polity appears to have attached a greater importance probably believing that such investments would positively impact economic, social and technological progress. Technology has always stretched the uses of 'space' frontier beyond science, enabling systems that can exploit its economic potential as well as potential for militaries. To appreciate the meaning of Chinese investments in space technologies it is important to set a context. It is important to visualize at macro level about actually what China wants to achieve by pitching from one initiative to another in space that fits into the broader context of its national ambitions. This is important because China has not articulated any specific space vision that allows the world at large to see its accomplishments in a larger context. In view of this it is crucial to understand the overall growth of the state which directly or indirectly may have played a role towards developing its vision for investing in space technologies.

From a researcher's perspective and secrecy notwithstanding, China's size and complexity has meant that evidence can be found to support just about any hypothesis anyone sets out to prove. While analysts usually agree on what China is doing and what it plans to do, views diverge on the question to "what end."[8] The basic problem with understanding Chinese space programme arises mainly because the entire programme is generally shrouded in secrecy.[9] This lack of transparency about China's intentions mainly raises concerns about their intentions. The backdrop set in the preceding paragraphs is important at least partially to begin the analysis of what is, and probably what could be, China's mission in space and its vision for the future. This chapter attempts such analysis. The chapter also attempts to understand the significance of China's programme to the Indian state.

China in Space

China celebrated its 50th anniversary of space progress in the year 2006. Their space programme is a sweeping plan for lofting earth orbiting satellites for a large number of duties, expanding its human spaceflight abilities, and carrying out a multi-step programme of lunar exploration and mission to explore mars. Currently, five of their different operational systems are in service namely telecommunications, meteorological, earth remote sensing, as well as recoverable satellites and technology demonstration spacecraft.[10] China also has plans to establish a space-based laboratory and to set up a permanent space station. All these efforts are guided towards promoting the diplomatic interests of the state and its national security concerns, all in an effort to garner greater prestige.[11] China is aware that the role of satellites and overall space applications has evolved considerably over the years and the dual use nature of this technology is fast influencing also the development of their military thinking.

China's space programme began in the late 1950s when the State Council implemented the "12 year development plan of science and technology", which included rocket programming, radio electronics, automatic control, and computer and semiconductor technology.[12] Over last five decades China has established a well-balanced and coordinated infrastructure of space related institutions, including research and development centers, launching sites, tracking, telemetry and command stations and centers, and manufacturing plants. For last decade or so China is on a fast track into space. The achievements and announcements about launch timetables, space laboratories, shuttles, space stations, lunar bases and Mars mission has swiftly transformed the Chinese space programme.[13]

Mechanics for Space Agenda

The PRC's space programme initially began with an agenda to promote its Maoist ideology. It has transcended that ideology's decline to become a major political symbol of Chinese nationalism, an important economic sector, and an effective dual-use technology collaborator with the Chinese military. In 21st century the programme has become more important than ever before to China's Communist regime.[14]

China's civilian and military space programmes are tightly interwoven. The China National Space Administration (CNSA—established in June 1993) carries out the management and operation of China's space activities.[15] The organisational structure and evolution of China's space programme is complicated and constantly undergoing change may be the dual use potential of the Chinese space programme dictates such changes.

China Aerospace Corporation (CASC), a subordinate to CNSA, is a state-owned corporation directing five primary divisions responsible for building military missiles and civilian rockets: the Academy of Launch Vehicles (ALV), which designs and manufactures the Long March rocket series; the Academy of space technology, which designs and manufactures satellites; the Academy of Solid-Fuel Rockets (ASFR); the Academy of Tactical Missile Technology; and the Academy of Cruise Missile Technology.[16]

In the recent past China has made considerable investments in the manned space flight programme. The programme has its roots in an ambitious project that was formulated in early 1992 and initially known under code name 921.[17] CASC has general authority over manned space flight and Long March series rockets. Ultimately, however, the military (specifically the Second Artillery Corps) controls the Chinese space programme. Although specific efforts have been made towards separating the military aspects from civil/commercial aspects, China like Russia, did not initially bifurcate its programme as did the US.[18] CNSA is specifically designated as Chinese counterpart to work with other international space agencies. In reality, CNSA personnel have been dual-hatted with the China Aerospace & Technology Corporation.[19]

A Brief Review of Chinese Space Capabilities[20]

Broadly speaking China is self-sufficient in most of space technology areas. Currently, China is capable of launching various military satellites as per its own requirement. China has developed an impressive range of launch rockets to support its military and commercial space assets. Launch vehicle technology is one of the foundations of China's ambitions space programme. With its Long March (LM) series of launchers and has achieved a great deal of launcher autonomy. Long March series includes 14 kinds of launch vehicles and 12 types of carrier rockets. The first launch (LM-1) vehicle had successfully launched the first Chinese satellite 173 kg Dongfanghong 1 into orbit in 1970.[21] As of August 2010, 128 launches have being carried out with the help of various versions of this vehicle. China is developing one of its most powerful rockets to date—Long March-5—that would sport engines with the thrust of 120 tonnes and is expected to be operational by 2014. When operational, Long March-5 is expected to deliver up to 25 tonnes of payload, in to the low earth orbit, and up to 14 tonnes into the geostationary transfer orbit, where most communications satellites are released after launch.[22]

Communication satellites are a high priority for China because of its commercial utility. The development of China's communications satellites started at the beginning of the 1970s. China's first experimental geostationary orbit communications satellite was launched successfully in 1984.[23] China is successfully using such satellites for the purposes of TV transmission, education, long-range telephone and telegraph, data transfer in finance and air and railway traffic. A variety of communication satellites have been launched by China and include Apstar Series, AsiaSat Series, Sino Sat Series and Zhonxing Series. One of their most useful programmes in recent times is the Sino Sat series satellite. The first satellite in this series is SinoSat-1 which was launched in 1998. The SinoSat-2 satellite was launched in 2006 but malfunctioned because it failed to deploy its solar panels and communication antennae. Sino Sat-6 satellite which was launched successfully on September 5, 2010 now serves as a substitute for SinoSat-3 launched on 1 June 2007.[24] Next generation communication satellites are expected to carry C, Ku, Ka and L band transponders.

Chinese leadership understands the importance of dual use nature of space technology. Jiang Zemin on 7 June 1991 issued the instructions that it is not necessary to use separate military systems for civil use and military use. Presently China has got various national and commercial communication satellites in space. Chinese space white paper (2000) mentions that efforts are on to distribute very small aperture terminal (VSAT) communication services. China launched its first military communication satellite in January 2000. This is supposed to be China's first advanced technology spy satellite.

China uses space technologies for gathering Electronics Intelligence (ELINT), Communications Intelligence (COMINT) and Imagery Intelligence (IMINT). Chinese military is exploiting the importance of remote sensing technologies towards building information superiority. In these areas of intelligence gathering and reconnaissance China is depending both on indigenous space capabilities as well as on commercially available international space satellite constellations.

Integration of imagery and signals intelligence from space based assets to an overall intelligence network and simultaneously making the information available in the real time basis to the solder on the ground is a complex task. It requires more flexible command structure and a greater emphasis on communications and the use of information at all levels of command. China lags behind in this area. China has a ground based SIGINT network that has been described as 'the most extensive signals intelligence capabilities of all countries in Asia. This capacity is based on ground stations, ships, and mobile platforms. China has mainly acquired modern aircraft platforms, not satellites, to carry out its SIGINT missions.

It is interesting to note that China started with FSW (Fanhui Shei Weixing, Recoverable Test Satellite) satellite series initially more from the point of view of using for military reconnaissance purposes. But, in the late 1980s, the design was employed for earth resources photography and experiments in crystal and protein growth, cell cultivation and crop breeding. It may be noted that China is the third country in the world to master the technology of satellite recovery. Currently, China is working towards developing new generation photo-reconnaissance satellite FSW Series (1 m or less resolution). They also have Yaogan series satellites which was started in 2006 used for the purposes of remote sensing. Latest in this series Yaogan X was launched on 12 August 2010.

Navigational satellite system is another area where China has major plans for the future both commercial and military purposes. In early 1980s China began to utilize other countries' navigational satellites and developed application technology of satellite navigation and positioning, which is now used for land survey and ship and aircraft navigation. Now China has its Beidon Navigation Satellites (BNTS) programme. This three/four-satellite system is all weather and a round the clock operation system. All these satellites are in geo-stationary orbit. It is expected that this technology must be of great use for 2.5 million strong People's Liberation Army. This system is a regional positioning system mainly covering the country and its neighbouring areas, thus making vertical positioning impossible while limiting the number of users. A global positioning system is a space infrastructure that it is essential for China to possess if it is to be a space power in the 21st century.[25] China has plans to develop its own global positioning systems on the lines of the US GPS constellation. Compass (Beidou 2)-Global system is expected the offer China a global reach. This system would have 35 satellites to cover China and the entire Asia-Pacific region by 2012. Currently, the project is in the second stage and the 5th satellite in this constellation was launched on 2 August 2010.

The Chinese quest for a global navigation system does not end here. Europe is developing its own satellite navigation and positioning system called Galileo. This system comprises 30 satellites orbiting at a height of 15,000 miles and promises accuracy within one meter. China is one of the major partners of this project. However, China does not have 'right to entry' to Galileo's military applications. China will not have access to Galileo's public regulated service (PRS), which is an encrypted signal to be used only by European security and emergency forces.[26]

Launch vehicles and communication, remote sensingand navigation satellites could be conserved as the basic tenets for the successful developing any modern day space programme. In regards to China all these basic tenets are in place. Few other dedicated or multipurpose satellites are also launched by them which could take care of meteorological, space research and educational needs.

SPACE TECHNOLOGIES FOR NEW MILLENNIUM

China's space programme has gone through phases of tough beginning, reform and revival, and not so dependable international cooperation. Over the years the Chinese space industry has been developed almost from a non-existent industrial infrastructure and scientific and technological level to a modern business. After 50 years of struggle China today is ranked among the fastest advancing countries in fields such as communication, remote sending, reconnaissance and navigation. They have made considerable progress in arenas like manned spacecraft, satellite recovery, multi-satellite launch by a single rocket, cryogenic propulsion, strap-on boosters, geostationary satellites, satellite tracking and control, remote-sensing, communications, and navigation satellites, and micro-gravity experiments.[27] Following paragraphs discusses few of the important ongoing programme which currently at various levels of development.

Micro Satellites

Cost effectiveness has attracted China to invest in arena of micro satellites. For last one decade China is giving lot of emphasis to microsatellite technology. A Russian Booster launched the first satellite in this category, Tsinghua 1, on 28 June 2000.[28] It was a joint project of Tsinghua University of Beijing and Surrey Satellite Technology Limited. It is a 50 kg bird and its launch put China into the selected bracket of countries, which can design and operate micro and nano-sized satellites. This success has implications for both China's scientific programmes as well as for enhanced military satellite capabilities. It is equipped with CCD camera that can image objects up to 39m in three spectral bands.

Small satellites can avoid detection; they also have the potential to be used as ASAT (anti-satellite) space mines. In April 2004, China had launched two new indigenously developed research satellites, including a nanosatellite (Experiment Satellite I and Nanosatellite I) weighing 25 kg. What are the capabilities of these satellites and how much are they constrained by size, however, are questions that remain to be answered.[29]

It has been reported that Experiment Satellite I transmits remote sensing data for mapping and Nanosatellite was designed to perform unidentified technology experiments. Such small, cheap satellites could provide China with an easier path to attaining some space capabilities and provide the potential for asymmetric warfare in space. The cost advantage of micro-satellites could, if properly handled, allow China to compete at some levels with larger and more expensive US systems without having to match the US dollar for dollar.[30]

China has developed a new generation of small satellite launch vehicles, Explorer I, which uses solid fuel. It has been designed to take small or micro satellites into space, and compliment Long March group, the country's large-scale liquid fuel space launchers. Explorer I will be able to carry loads weighing less than 100 kilograms. The low costs and high thrusts of solid fuel rockets make them an important factor in the commercialisation of the space industry.[31]

In the wake of China's successful spacewalk which was conducted during the Shenzhou-7 (SH-7) mission launched on 25 September 2008 (it was China's third human space flight mission). A micro satellite was released during the mission called the BX-1. This Companion Sat was a very small cube approximately 40 centimeters on a side and weighing around 40 kilograms. Technically, this satellite was to provide images of the Shenzhou-7 capsule and demonstrate the ability to inspect the orbital module and conduct some limited proximity operations. It also carried out a data relay experiment. However, some observers have concluded that this satellite was meant to test some of the capabilities required for a co-orbital ASAT attack.[32]

Human Space Mission

China started preliminary work on advanced manned spaceflight in July 1985. The decision came against a background of vigorous international space activity the then US President Regan's pet project 'Strategic Defense Initiative'. The erstwhile USSR had programmes like Buran shuttle system, Mir and Mir-2 space station. Europe was developing the Hermes space plane. Hence for China it was necessary to take action in regards to its space activities to remain as a center of attraction.

In early spring 1986, a proposal for seven projects under Project 863 plans to accelerate Chinese technical development was made. Astronautics plan 863-2 included section 863-204 space transportation system, which would service the 863-205 space station. It was estimated that two years would be needed for concept studies. An expert group was established for the 863-204 shuttle.

The final 863-204 Expert Commission report in July 1989 advocated building the manned capsule, with a first flight date of 2000. However, the report failed to impress the Chinese government. Chinese leader Deng Xiaoping rejected this plan. Deng stepped down as Chairman of the Central Military Commission in 1989. In his absence the Chinese military decided it could safely lend its critical support to a manned space program. In January 1991 the Air Ministry established a manned space programme office. The final plan was approved on 21 September 1992, and Project 921 to create a Chinese manned space capability began in earnest.[33]

It took a decade's preparation for China to realize its dream of Chinese visiting the space. By October 2003 China successfully launched and recovered its first manned space mission. This Shenzhou 5 mission was preceded by four successful unmanned Shenzhou launches. Reports about these missions suggest that China used the Shenzhou missions for electronic and imaging intelligence gathering. In October 2003, *SpaceDaily* reported that the Shenzhou 1 - Shenzhou 4 test flights likely carried military payloads in the form of electronic intelligence or imaging reconnaissance equipment.[34] It is also inferred that the primary mission of China's first manned spaceflight might have been imaging reconnaissance. However, it is important to note that carrying out operations like imaging reconnaissance either by manned or unmanned space vehicle is not is a good option. Even a simple satellite could do this job in a better option. Hence it would be incorrect to assume that such missions are carried out only for the purpose of imaging reconnaissance.

Today China is the third country in the world to send man into the space. In its report on China's military power, the US department of Defence has stated, 'While one of the strongest immediate motivations for China's manned space programme appears to be political prestige, China's efforts will contribute to improve military space systems in [the] 2010-20 timeframe'.[35]

China's Shenzhou design is a replica of Russian design (Soyouz) but has some more additional features, which has more military relevance. Chinese craft consists of an orbital module, a reentry vehicle that carries crew back to earth, and a service module for propulsion and for performing retro fire sequence. But unlike Soyuz, the Chinese module could detach from the re-entry capsule and remain in orbit for several months, acting as robotic mini space station, using its solar panels to power instruments and experiments. However, the unit is not a re-entry vehicle and burns up while entering the atmosphere.[36]

PLA strictly controls the Shenzhou programme. One indication of

Shenzhou military operations was likely electronics carried on nose of the Shenzhou 3 orbital module that functioned autonomously in space for six months following the return to earth of the decent module after seven days aloft in March 2002. As per few analysts Shenzhou III mission could also have carried a significant electronic intelligence eavesdropping payload. The system could have recorded UHF and radar emissions applicable to a variety of military uses including ocean surveillance.[37] Shenzhou 5 had also left its orbital module aloft, unmanned, likely again carrying military relevant equipment.

From 12-17 October 2005 China launched its spacecraft-Shenzhou 6 carrying two astronauts, and secured its smooth return to the earth after 115-hour and 32-minute flight in orbit. This event has reaffirmed China's raising stature in the space arena.[38] The establishment of a landing system for manned space flights implies that China has succeeded in building a complete and matured spacecraft tracking and control network. Such networks are capable of carrying out accurate tracking and control of satellites and missiles. With this breakthrough, China is in a position to fly into space, return to the earth, manage synchronisation with a fixed point, operate one network with multiple satellites, manufacture internationally compatible space systems and successfully manage spacecraft recovery.[39] China successfully undertook the spacewalk which was conducted during the Shenzhou 7 mission launched on 25 September 2008.

The extent to which this manned activity will translate into a military advantage for China remains debatable. Most benefits to the military from the manned programme will be indirect or a function of improved Chinese technical abilities, generally in an area such as computational analysis, systems integration, and miniaturisation.[40] It also could be argued that notwithstanding that both the US and Soviet militaries have been unable to identify important advantages of a man in space over unmanned systems, the Chinese seem determined to explore that premise for themselves, likely through the use of orbital module at some later date.

Deep Space Missions

Any activity conducted in space about 100,000 km and beyond about earth's surface is generally known as deep space activity. China's long-term goals in space exploration include sending a satellite into lunar orbit, followed by a robotic explorer and an eventual moonwalk. China also has plans to build a space station on the Moon. In addition, in August 2003 China concluded an agreement with Russia to pursue future joint space exploration efforts.[41]

Subsequently, on 26 March2007—China and Russia signed an agreement for joint exploration of Mars. Further details about their plans are not known. However, it is likely at that first attempt they would send a satellite towards Mars to study its surface and collect information for future programmes.

China has drafted a multi-step program for lunar exploration. By 2013, China space planners will be landing a rover on the Moon surface. In 2017, China's lunar exploration plans call for robotic lunar sample return missions.[42] It is also expected that by 2020 to 2025 China could plan a manned moon mission.

China has successfully completed its first lunar mission. Under this mission it had sent a satellite in close vicinity of the moon's surface to record observations of its surface. This satellite was launched on 24 October 2007 (Chang'e-1)[43] and the mission was scheduled to continue for a year. The mission was extended for some more time. China has successfully completed stage one of its moon mission. Cheng'e-1 fully completed its mission on 1 March 2009. This spacecraft was de-orbited and it impacted the moon. During this mission China has explored the space environment between the earth and the moon. This understanding would help planning their further missions. They have also done the three-dimensional survey of the moon's surface and have carried out the analysis of the distribution of elements on lunar surface. Their aim was to know more about the availability of the Helium-3 on the moon's surface. It has been predicted that the Helium-3 on the moon can significantly meet the energy needs for human kind.

China has launched of its second lunar probe Chang'e-2 on 1 October 2010. This probe would monitor the moon's surface within 15 kilometres of the moon. This unmanned probe will conduct various tests over a six-month period in preparation for the expected launch in 2013 of the Chang'e-3, which China hopes will be its first unmanned landing on the moon.[44]

Anti-Satellite System

For many years various speculations were carried out regarding China's interest in space weaponisation. All these interests were put to the rest when on 11 January 2007 China destroyed its own aging weather satellite (FY-1C) by firing a rocket towards it. This satellite had a mass of 750 kg and was orbiting at an altitude of 850 km. To kill this satellite China has used the anti-satellite weapon a non-explosive called "kinetic kill vehicle (KKV)". This weapon was nothing but a metal piece mounted on the top of the missile KT-2 which destroyed its target simply by colliding with it. This Chinese act has created significant amount of concerns globally about the likely weaponsation of space.

For the last couple of years the Chinese's interest in developing and testing various methodologies for carrying out anti-satellite operations are being debated. There are reports that China has completed ground tests of advanced anti-satellite weapon called 'Parasitic satellite'. It is likely to be deployed on an experimental basis and enter the phase of space test in the near future. These satellite systems are probably already ground tested. This ASAT system can be used against various types of satellites such as communication satellites, navigational satellites and early warning satellites in different orbits. The cost of building this satellite system is 0.1 to 1 per cent of typical satellite.[45]

According to Pentagon report, "PLA is building lasers to destroy satellites and already has beam weapons capable of damaging sensors on space based reconnaissance and intelligence systems. Consequently, China could blind the US intelligence and military space equipment systems vital for deploying US military forces in current and future warfare."[46]

Implications for India

The process of economic liberation started in India during early 1990s. Over the years India has made considerable economic progress over last few years. The growth rate has averaged around 7 per cent since 1997 and India was able to keep its economy growing at a healthy rate even during the 2007-09 recessions, managing a 5.355 per cent rate in 2009.[47] As per the IMF projections India's economy is likely to grow by 9.7 per cent in 2010 and 8.4 per cent in the next fiscal, driven by robust industrial production and macro-economic performance.[48] India's investments in the field of science and technology and particularly the growth of Information Technology (IT) industry in the country have played a major role towards achieving this economic growth.

Over the years India has made considerable technological progress. Its achievements in the space field are particularly noteworthy. It all started with a humble beginning during 1963 in a small church building in South India with the launching of sounding rockets in 1963.[49] By 2010 India has already completed its first moon mission successfully. India also has a significant space agenda for the future which includes having own navigational system, playing a major role into the global space commerce, human space mission and a mission to mars.

India which has fought a war with China during 1962 and still have few unresolved border issues have slowing managed to develop a harmonious relationship with China over the years. However, it could be seen more as a functional relationship than a striking comradeship. Naturally, various activities undertaken by China at times are viewed with different perceptions and with inherent biases. Some international observers viewing the progress made both by China and India in the space arena express a concern that greater Chinese presence in space activities and India's attempt to match them is an indication of the start of another space race. However, it may not be correct to draw a direct relation between capability and intent. But, at the same time it is important to do an assessment about the likely implications of China's space programme to India.

Space supremacy and information warfare are the key components of China's 'battlefield supremacy' theory. China is developing a multi-dimensional space programme to improve its capabilities to limit or prevent the use of space-based assets by potential adversaries.[50] Naturally, India has to factor in this Chinese notion of utilisation of space assets for battlefield supremacy in its security calculus.

Interestingly, most of the global discourse on China's interests in military space technologies is more leaning towards analyzing its impact for the US. To an extent this is understandable because of the uneasiness in their relations. Under the backdrop of the Sino-US relations and the Chinese ambition of reaching a major power status in the near future, the possible rationales for Chinese military space programmes could be categorised as: (a) catch-up (b) leap-frog (c) conspicuous consumption. The first involves China trying to bring its space forces up to par with US capabilities. The second scenario has China taking advantage of new technologies and adopting an information oriented approach to warfare to surpass US capabilities in unexpected ways. This approach could mean that military space architecture for China could look very different from that used by the US. A 'conspicuous consumption' rational would involve activities in space done primarily to affirm or enhance China's prestige and influence rather than build a continuous operational presence. While there are elements of all three in China's military space efforts, judging from expenditure and payloads, the latter two motives seem to predominate.[51]

The analysis of the impact of Chinese space technologies on India's security preparedness should be done by giving due consideration to above realities. The discussion so far in this paper essentially provides a macro view of Chinese space capabilities. What is important is to analyze how these capabilities could impact India. The likely impact over India could be viewed at different levels ranging from geopolitics to technology. The positive impact could be that the Chinese achievements demonstrate that how a state can achieve wonderful results in a short period of time without much of external help. China's work in the space field should offer an inspiration for other states including India.

At geopolitical level it could be said that China's space programme offers it prestige and influence both at regional as well as global level. It is a symbol of its global stature and demonstration of growing technical expertise. Within the state the achievements in space help the party to raise the level of nationalism. China has also succeeded in constrictively engaging few states for collaboration in space like. Particularly, their relationship with the European space agency (ESA) is noteworthy. After their investments in the Galileo navigational programme the ESA is keen to induct them as a partner in the ongoing programme on international space station (ISS).[52] If this becomes a reality then China could be a partner in the US-Russia-ESA-Japan programme. At regional level Chinese attempts towards formation of a multilateral grouping are noteworthy. Asia Pacific Space Cooperation Organisation (APSCO) multilateral grouping headed by China has evolved in 2005 from Asia Pacific Multilateral Cooperation in Space Technology and Applications (AP-MCSTA), which came into being when a MoU was signed between China, Pakistan and Thailand in 1992.[53] The objectives of APSCO are to focus on space science, technology and to promote peaceful uses of outer space in the region. Interestingly, the 14 states which form the group do not include India.

China is playing the disarmament and arms control politics brilliantly. In spite of doing the ASAT officially China is vocal about demilitarisation of outer space. They are strong proponent of multilateral treaty banning space weapons. They have suggested new space architecture against space weapons in association with Russia.[54] The hidden motive behind this idea appears to be to stall the US plan of development and deployment of missile defence shield. The restrictions put by any such treaty mechanism could make the US missile-defense interceptors redundant and in turn would enhance the capability of Chinese/Russian ICBM arsenal. For India, it is important to note that it is only a matter of time that the UN will start developing disarmament and arms control structures to address the issues related to arms race in space.. When the actual deliberations on formulating the treaty regime start, we could expect significant negotiating and procedural hurdles. China has already started taking proactive measures in the field and may dictate from a position of strength when such deliberations happen.

Achievements in space arena offer an opportunity to China to display the 'soft power' status of the state. Also, space could be used as a tool for international diplomacy. States like China are doing sustained investments in Africa including development of space infrastructure for countries like Nigeria. China is gaining more friends in this fashion particularly in the region which have some answers for energy security.

Actual technology comparison on ground could broadly argue that China is ahead of India in space arena. However, India being a late starter lagging behind China is obvious. It also needs to be appreciated that technology development in both the states is requirement and vision dependent. India has one of the fastest growing telecommunications industries in the world. It is projected that India will have 1.159 billion mobile subscribers by 2013. Furthermore, projections by several leading global consultancies indicate that the total number of subscribers in India will exceed the total subscriber count in the China by 2013.[55] DTH and video/audio transmissions are witnessing a boom in both the states. Satellites play a major role in communication industry. Apart from indigenously developed satellites, also the services of few other commercially available satellites are being hired in both the countries. There is an ever increasing requirement of transponders in both the states. The investments by both the states in communication essentially are driven by commercial interests. China is using satellites in the series ChinaSat (the versions 22A and 20 are dedicated military communication satellites), Sino Sat, Apstar and AsiaSat also for military communication purposes.[56] India has much to learn over here. India is still in the process of launching the satellites for military communication purposes. It is also important to note that Pakistan could benefit from Chinese space technology. For example, precision guidance and control of Pakistani missiles would increase their accuracy further.[57] In navigational arena China's ambitions are global while India's are regional. China has plans to develop an independent space station while India has no such plans. In deep space missions it appears that both the states have similar programmes.

ASAT technology is available only with China. If China decides to use ASAT against India's space assets then it is important to identify the probable targets of China. These weapons cannot be used for geostationary satellites (INSAT Series), which actually is the heart of India's space programme. So, China can use such weapons only against India's LEO (low earth orbit-satellites positioned at around 300 to 400km about the earth's surface) series of satellites. This means Indian Remote Sensing satellites (IRS), a series of earth observation satellites could be the possible target. China could eye India's Cartosat series of satellites, which with sub-meter resolution could provide valuable information for terrain visualisation, updating of topographic maps, generation of national topographic data base and other utilities. Such satellites being dual in purpose, any attack (physical or electronic) on them could harm India's military interests too. This is not to say that other types of remote sensing satellites may not the targeted. An attack on them could help China to make a 'statement' about their intentions in space.

There are reports that China is procuring state-of-the-art technology to improve its intercept, direction finding, and jamming capabilities. A possible target for the jammers could be the receivers utilised in the Global Positioning System (GPS) satellite constellation.[58] However, in case of conflict with India, China would find it politically difficult either to jam GPS or Glonass (A Russian navigational system, various Russian equipments on Indian inventory are Glonass friendly.) However, China may undertake temporary jamming depending upon the immediate demands of battlefield. More importantly India's own navigational satellites could be jammed. India has already started developing the Indian Regional Navigation Satellite System (IRNSS). This system will have a constellation of 7 satellites and complementary ground infrastructure. The IRNSS system is planned to be made operational by end of 2014. However, it is important for China to note that this system would not be in the medium earth orbit (MEO) like all other navigational systems but in the geostationary orbit (GEO).

China's preeminent position in the region in space arena has been now an established fact. In the space launch industry, it will continue to provide strong competition for India. Currently Antrix Corporation is involved in the global marketing of Indian Remote Sensing (IRS) Satellite data products. Also, ISRO provides launch facilities for satellites and already few countries have used these facilities to launch their satellites. This is one area where India may compete with China to an extent.

Both India and China have their indigenous space technology programmes. However, Chinese philosophy in acquiring space knowledge appears to be different! China starts with basics developed by others and then make the design of their own, often improving it, to suit their own needs. A specific example could be the Chinese manned space mission which is based on the Russia technology. Also, China makes use of international collaborations to enhance own technology level. Galileo is another example of how China must be using foreign partnerships to speed its indigenous space effort by participating in and learning from the experience of other programmes. On part of India its increasing bonhomie with the US (post-2005 Indo-US nuclear deal) may give them access to some technology to match with China in future. However, it is important to note that still few of the Indian scientific laboratories are under the US sanctions list.

Overall the international and regional posturing by China in space arena indicates that China is taking a two-track approach to space matters: discouraging international activity in space weapons while actively pursuing countermeasures and options of their own.[59] Hence India needs to be watchful.

CONCLUSION

China is rapidly developing both economically and militarily. China understands the need of investments in the field of space technologies to satisfy the need of both civilian and military requirements. It also understands the importance of dual-use space technologies in serving its own national interests. China is silently building its space industry and also making important developing countries dependent on them in space field.

From Indian point of view China is capable of gathering wartime as well as peacetime intelligence over the Indian subcontinent. China's policy in regards to ASAT technology probably has multiple objectives. By conducting an ASAT China is sitting at the high pedestal and could play a major role in designing of any likely new space regime. To an extent China has succeeded in establishing a strategic balance amongst the space faring states by conducting ASAT. It has succeeded in giving a signal to states like India and the US about its capabilities.

From Indian point of view the growth in China's space capabilities is both a motivator as well as a cause of concern but definitely not a reason to panic. India needs to continue with its existing road map which is India specific and not get bogged down by developments in China. However, India needs to evolve a separate approach to address its military requirements in space. India needs to participate in the disarmament debate more proactively and at the same time keep its options open for the conduct of ASAT.

END NOTES

1. Brian Harvey et al., *Emerging Space Powers*, Springer, Chichester, 2010, p. xi.
2. Ronaldo Munck, *Globalisation and Contestation*, Routledge, New York, 2007.
3. Zheng Bijian, "China's "Peaceful Rise" to Great-Power Status", *Foreign Affairs*, September/October 2005, pp. 18-19.
4. "IMF projects India's economic growth at 9.7% in 2010", 6 October 2010, http://timesofindia.indiatimes.com/business/india-business/IMF-projects-Indias-economic-growth-at-97-in-2010/articleshow/6699063.cms, accessed on 8 October 2010.
5. Zheng Bijian developed his influential thesis of China's "peaceful rise" in 2003.

For details please refer **to** Zheng Bijian, *China's Peaceful Rise Speeches of Zheng Bijian 1997-2005*, Brookings Institution Press, Washington, DC, 2005.

6. Wen Jiabao on the sidelines of the World Economic Forum (WEF) Annual Meeting of the New Champions 2010, or the Summer Davos, held in north China's port city of Tianjin. Sept 13, 2010. http://news.xinhuanet.com/english2010/china/2010-09/13/c_13493083.htm, accessed on 10 October 2010.
7. Science-Metrix, a data-analysis company in Montreal, Canada's report titled "geopolitical shifts in knowledge creation" since 1980 available at http://www.newscientist.com/article/dn18546-iran-showing-fastest-scientific-growth-of-any-country.html, accessed on 12 September 2010.
8. Joan Johnson-Freese, "Scorpions in a Bottle," *The Nonproliferation Review*, Summer 2004, pp. 170-171.
9. Joan Johnson-Freese, *The Chinese Space Program: A Mystery Within a Maze*, Kreiger Publishing, Melbourne, 1998.
10. http://www.space.com/news/060405_nss_china.html, accessed on 22 December 2009.
11. John J. Klein, *Space Warfare* , Routledge, New York, 2006, p. 37.
12. Win Rui Hu, *Space Science in China*, Gorden and Breach Science Publishers, Australia, 1997, p. 15.
13. Joan Johnson-Freese, "China's Manned Space Program," *Naval War College Review*, Summer, 2003, Vol. LVI, No. 3, p. 51.
14. William S. Murray III and Robert Antonellis, "China's Space Program: The Dragon Eyes the Moon (and Us)," *Orbis*, Fall 2003, p. 645.
15. Jon Sigurdson, *Technological Superpower China*, Edward Elgar Publishing, Massachusetts, 2005, pp. 194-195.
16. William S. Murray III and Robert Antonellis, "China's Space Program: The Dragon Eyes the Moon (and Us)," *Orbis*, Fall 2003, p. 648.
17. Jon Sigurdson, *Technological Superpower China*, Edward Elgar Publishing, Massachusetts, 2005, p. 191.
18. Joan Johnson-Freese, "China's Manned Space Program," *Naval War College Review*, Summer 2003, Vol. LVI, No. 3, p. 60.
19. Joan Johnson-Freese, "Scorpions in a Bottle", *The Nonproliferation Review*, Summer 2004, p. 173.
20. Main sources for certain information in this section and subsequent sections are: K.K. Nair, "China's Space Programme: An Overview", *Air Power*, Vol. 1, No. 1, Monsoon 2004 and Ajey Lele, "China as a Space Power", *Strategic Analysis*, April-June 2002.
21. http://www.wsichina.org/space/program.cfm?programid=5&charid=1, accessed on 22 September 2010.
22. Anatoly Zak, "China considers big rocket power", 26 July 2010, http://www.bbc.co.uk/news/science-environment-10762634
23. http://www.globalsecurity.org/space/world/china/comm.htm, accessed on 5 Sep 2010.
24. http://www.indiasummary.com/2010/09/06/china-sinosat-6-communication-satellite-launched-successfully-by-chinese/, accessed on 9 October 2010.

25. Jon Sigurdson, *Technological Superpower China*, Edward Elgar Publishing, Massachusetts, 2005, p. 208.
26. Ajey Lele, "China's Posture in Space and its Implications," *Strategic Analysis*, Vol. 32, No. 4, July 2008, pp. 605-620.
27. www.astronautix.com/articles/china.htm, accessed on 23 August 2009.
28. http://www.eoportal.org/directory/pres_Tsinghua1.html and http://www.spaceandtech.com/spacedata/logs/2000/2000-033c_tsinghua-1_sumpub.shtml, accessed on 12 October 2010.
29. Joan Johnson-Freese, "Scorpions in a Bottle," *The Nonproliferation Review*, Summer 2004, p. 178.
30. James A. Lewis, "China as a Military Space Competitor," *Center for Strategic and International Studies*, January 2004, p. 9.
31. "China to launch new solid-fuel rocket", *China Daily*, 30 January 2004.
32. Brian Weeden, "China's BX-1 microsatellite: a litmus test for space weaponization" 20 October 2008, http://www.thespacereview.com/article/1235/1, accessed on 24 July 2009.
33. www.astronautix.com/articles/china.htm, accessed on 23 July 2009.
34. Mark Wade, "Shenzhou—Divine Military Vessel," *SpaceDaily.com website*, 2 October 2003, http://www.spacedaily.com/news/china-03zd.html, accessed on 22 August 2008.
35. Joan Johnson-Freese, "China's Manned Space Program," *Naval War College Review*, Summer 2003, Vol. LVI, No. 3, p. 52.
36. Frank Sietzen Jr., "From Mercury to CEV," *Aerospace America*, Feb 2005, p. 29.
37. Craig Covault, "Chinese Milspace Ops," *Aviation Week and Space Technology*, 20 October 2003, p. 26.
38. Pan Zhenqiang, "Shenzhou VI and China's Spaceflight Programs", *Foreign Affairs Journal*, No. 78, December 2005, p. 52.
39. "Spacecraft Recovery Technology of China Matures Steadily," *PLA Daily*, 21 October 2003.
40. Joan Johnson-Freese, "Scorpions in a Bottle," *The Nonproliferation Review*, Summer 2004, p. 174.
41. http://cns.miis.edu/research/space/china/mil.htm, accessed on 12 September 2010
42. Leonard David, "China Unveils Ambitious Space Plans at National Space Symposium" April 5, 2006 accessed on 12 September 2010 at http://www.space.com/news/060405_nss_china.html
43. http://www.cctv.com/english/20071102/100731.shtml and Chris Bergin, "China enters the new moon race with Chang'e-1 launch", October 24, 2007, available at http://www.nasaspaceflight.com/2007/10/china-enters-the-new-moon-race-with-change-1-launch/ accessed on 14 January 2009.
44. "China launches second lunar probe", Oct 2, 2010, http://www.spacedaily.com/reports/China_launches_second_lunar_probe_999.html, accessed on 8 October 2010.
45. Desmond Ball, "Assessing China's ASAT program" Austral Special Report 07-14S, 14 June 2007, http://nautilus.rmit.edu.au/forum-reports/0714s-ball/ and http://www.spacedaily.com/news/china-01c.html , accessed on 15 October 2009.

46. Annual Report to Congress, *The Military Power of the People's Republic of China 2005*, (Washington, D.C.: Office of the Secretary of Defense, July 2005), p. 36, http://www.defenselink.mil/news/Jul2005/d20050719china.pdf.
47. http://www.economywatch.com/indianeconomy/, accessed on 9 October 2010.
48. "IMF projects India's economic growth at 9.7% in 2010", **6** October 2010, http://timesofindia.indiatimes.com/business/india-business/IMF-projects-Indias-economic-growth-at-97-in-2010/articleshow/6699063.cms, accessed on 9 October 2010.
49. S.K. Das, *Touching Lives*, Penguin Books, New Delhi, 2007, p. 1.
50. George Leopold, "Space Log: China and Space", 17 Aug 2010, http://www.eetimes.com/electronics-blogs/other/4206239/Space-China-Blog, accessed on 8 October 2010.
51. James A. Lewis, "China as a Military Space Competitor", http://csis.org/files/media/csis/pubs/040801_china_space_competitor.pdf
52. http://www.parabolicarc.com/2010/09/27/video-bolden-ponders-chinese-involvement-iss-preps-trip-middle-kingdom/
53. news.xinhuanet.com/...12/.../content_10514901.htm, accessed on 5 October 2010
54. To overcome the limitations of the 1967 Outer Space Treaty (OST) which bans only the stationing of weapons of mass destruction in space Russia and China have proposed a new international treaty to ban the use of weapons in outer space on 12 February 2008 in the Conference on Disarmament in Geneva. The basic lacunae with this draft treaty is it only to stop the weapons in space and not the ground based weapons like the one used by China in 2007 to conduct the ASAT.
55. http://en.wikipedia.org/wiki/Communications_in_India, accessed on 11 November 2009.
56. http://www.sinodefence.com/space/spacecraft/comsat.asp and http://en.wikipedia.org/wiki/AsiaSat
57. S.S. Deshpande, "Dragons in orbit: Implications of Chinese Manned Space Programme", *Trishul*, Vol. XVI, No. 2, p. 32.
58. http://www.space.com/news/china_dod_030801.html, accessed on 2 September 2010.
59. Joan Johnson-Freese, "China's Manned Space Program", *Naval War College Review*, Summer 2003, Vol. LVI, No. 3, p. 123.

ANNEXURES

ANNEXURE 1

Comparison between China's and India's Military Forces, 1963-2010

Year	Total Forces		Army		Air Force		Navy	
	China	India	China	India	China	India	China	India
1963	2,476,000	585,000	2,250,000	550,000	90,000	18,000	136,000	16,000
1965	2,486,000	869,000	2,250,000	825,000	100,000	28,000	136,000	16,000
1970	2,780,000	930,000	2,450,000	800,000	180,000	90,000	150,000	40,000
1975	3,250,000	956,000	2,800,000	826,000	220,000	100,000	230,000	30,000
1980	4,450,000	1,104,000	3,600,000	944,000	490,000	113,000	360,000	47,000
1985	3,900,000	1,260,000	2,973,000	1,100,000	490,000	113,000	350,000	47,000
1990	3,030,000	1,262,000	2,300,000	1,100,000	470,000	110,000	260,000	52,000
1998	2,820,000	1,175,000	2,090,000	980,000	470,000	140,000	260,000	55,000
2000	2,400,000	1,303,000	1,700,000	1,100,000	420,000	140,000	220,000	53,000
2005	2,250,000	1,325,000	1,600,000	1,100,000	400,000	170,000	215,000	55,000
2010	2,285,000	1,325,000	1,600,000	1,129,000	330,000	127,200	255,000	58,350

Year	Main Battle Tanks		Artillery Pieces		APCs	
	China	India	China	India	China	India
1963	NA	NA	NA	NA	NA	NA
1965	NA	NA	NA	NA	NA	NA
1970	NA	NA	NA	NA	NA	NA
1975	8,500	2,300	15,000	3,000	3,600	NA
1980	11,000	2,050	16,000	1,300	NA	2,000
1985	11450	2,500	12,800	NA	2,800	500
1990	7,500	3,150	14,500	3,860	2,800	400
1998	8,800	3,414	14,500	4,175	5,500	157
2000	7,060	3,414	12,000	4,175	4,800	157
2005	7,580	3,978	14,000	5,625	4,500	817
2010	7,050	4,117	12,462	4,010	2,700	331

Year	Infantry Divisions		Combat aircraft	
	China	India	China	India
1963	120	13 (incl 3 mt)	2,000	NA
1965	115	16 (+9 mt)	2,300	NA
1970	118	13 (+10mt)	2,800	625
1975	125	15 (+10 mt)	3,800	725
1980	118	17 (+10 mt)	5,200	630
1985	118	19 (+10 mt)	4,500	846
1990	80	19 (+9 mt)	5,070	833
1998	59	18 (+9 mt)	3,566	772
2000	61	18 (+9 mt)	3,000	774
2005	64	18 (+10mt)	2,643	852
2010	65	18 (+10 mt)	1,687	665

Year	Destroyers		Frigates		Tactical Submarines	
	China	India	China	India	China	India
1963	0	NA	31	0	0	NA
1965	8	3	30	0	12	8
1970	13	11	32	0	24	8
1975	16	3	51	8	15	26
1980	12	16	97	8	17	29
1985	16	3	107	8	28	23
1990	18	5	92	18	37	20
1998	18	6	62	19	35	18
2000	20	8	64	16	40	12
2005	21	8	68	19	42	17
2010	13	10	68	16	65	12

Year	Strategic Forces		ICBMs		IRBMs		SRBMs	
	China	India	China	India	China	India	China	India
1963	-	-						
1965	NA	-						
1970	NA	-						
1975	NA	-	0	0	20-30	0	50	0
1980	NA	-	4	0	65-85	0	50	0
1985	NA	-	6	0	60	0	50	NA
1990	90,000	-	8	0	60	0	NA	NA
1998	125,000	-	17	0	46		NA	
2000	100,000	-	20	0	100		240	
2005	100,000	-	46	0	35	24	725	45
2010	100,000	-	66	0	118	100	204	60

Notes: 1. The Seven White Papers released by China on defence since 1998 do not mention how many troops or equipment the PLA possesses. Hence the figures above are taken from the International Institute of Strategic Studies estimates.

2. Errors in the above tables due to the rounding of figures.

Source: The Military Balance (various years) and others.

ANNEXURE 2

Comparison of the Military Forces of China and India, 1963-2010

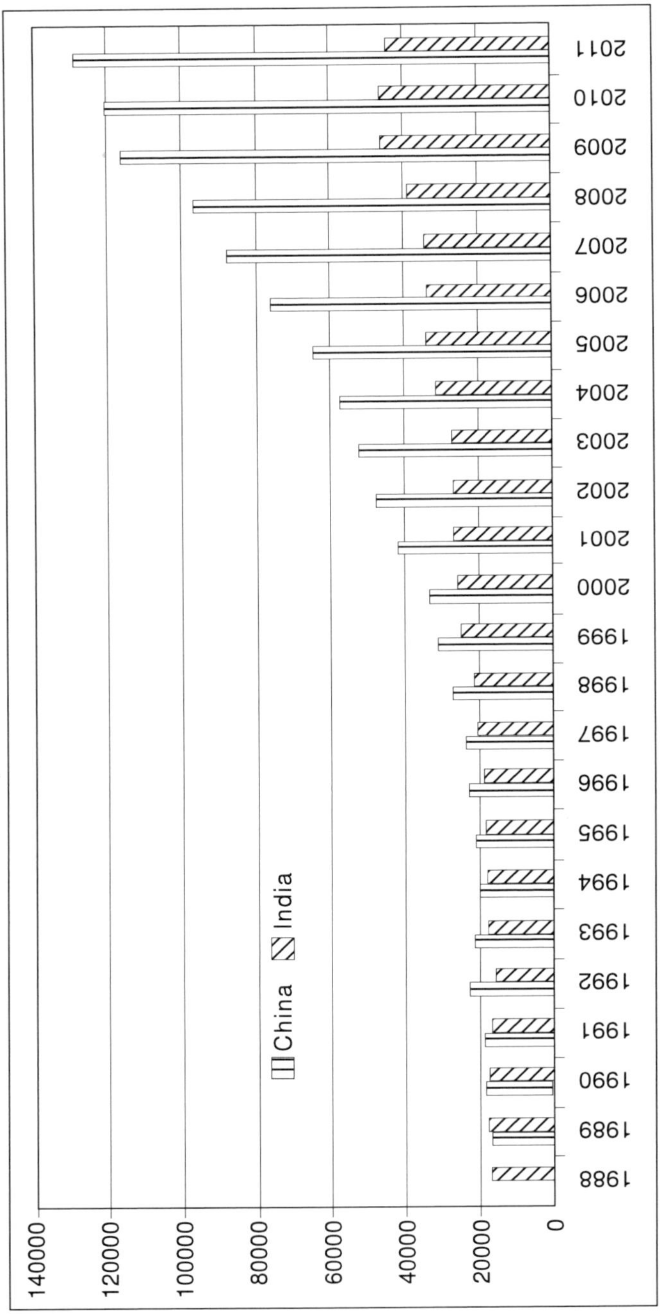

Source: This is based on SIPRI Database.

Annexure 3

China's Transfers of Major Conventional Weapons to Southern Asia, 1950 to 2011

Recipient/ supplier (S) or licenser (L)	No. ordered	Weapon designation	Weapon description	Year of order/ licence	Year(s) of deliveries	No. delivered/ produced	Comments
1	2	3	4	5	6	7	8
Afghanistan/Mujahideen							
S: China	(500)	Type-63 107mm	Towed MRL	(1983)	1984-89	(500)	Aid; Mujahideen designation BM-1
	(400)	HN-5A	Portable SAM	(1985)	1986-89	(400)	Aid; probably incl HN-5B version
Bangladesh							
S: China	4	MiG-15UTI/Midget	Trainer aircraft	(1974)	1975	4	Probably ex-Chinese
	(24)	F-6/Farmer	Fighter aircraft	(1975)	1976-78	(24)	Ex-Chinese; incl some FT-6 trainer version; no. delivered could be up to 36
	(38)	BT-6/CJ-6	Trainer aircraft	(1977)	1977-85	(38)	No. could be 46; BT-6A version
	(12)	F-6/Farmer	Fighter aircraft	(1980)	1983	(12)	Probably ex-Chinese; status uncertain
	8	Type-062/Shanghai	Patrol craft	(1980)	1980-82	8	Shanghai-2 version; Bangaleshi designation Shaheed
	(50)	Type-53 120mm	Mortar	(1980)	1981	(50)	Supplier uncertain
	36	WZ-120/Type-59	Tank	(1980)	1980-81	(36)	Aid
	2	Type-037/Hainan	Patrol craft	(1981)	1982-85	2	Bangaleshi designation Durjoy
	(20)	HY-2/SY-1A/CSS-N-2	Anti-ship missile	(1982)	1983	(20)	For Hegu (Durbar) FAC; SY-1A (CSS-N-2) version
	4	Project-123/P-4	FAC	(1982)	1983	4	Probably ex-Chinese
	4	Type-024/Hegu	FAC	(1982)	1983	4	Bangladeshi designation Durbar; option on more not used

(Contd.)

1	2	3	4	5	6	7	8
	(20)	M-30 122mm	Towed gun	(1983)	1984	(20)	Type-54-1 version
	(36)	Type-62	Light tank	(1984)	1985	(36)	
	(192)	Red Arrow-73	Anti-tank missile	(1985)	1985	(192)	
	(40)	HY-1/SY-1/CSS-N-1	Anti-ship missile	(1987)	1988-89	(40)	For Jianghu-1 (Osman) frigate and Huangfen (Durdharsha) FAC
	4	Type-021/Huangfen	FAC	(1987)	1988	4	Bangladeshi designation Durdharsha
	4	Type-025/Huchuan	FAC	(1987)	1988	4	
	1	Type-53/Jianghu	Frigate	(1988)	1989	1	Bangladeshi designation Osman; Jianghu-1 Version-4 version; plan for 1 more cancelled
	(12)	A-5C/Fantan	FGA aircraft	(1989)	1989-90	(12)	No. could be 20
	20	F-7M Airguard	Fighter aircraft	(1989)	1989-90	20	F-7MB version; incl 4 FT-7B
	(250)	PL-2	SRAAM	(1989)	1989-90	(250)	For A-5C and F-7M combat aircraft
	(50)	YW-531/Type-63	APC	(1989)	1989-90	(50)	Status uncertain
	(50)	HN-5A	Portable SAM	(1990)	1991-92	(50)	
	42	M-30 122mm	Towed gun	(1991)	1992	42	Designation uncertain; possibly Type-54-1 version
	(50)	WZ-121/Type-69	Tank	(1991)	1991	(50)	Type-69-I and Type-69-II version
	(10)	HY-1/SY-1/CSS-N-1	Anti-ship missile	(1992)	1992	(10)	For Huangfen (Durdharsha) FAC
	(5)	HY-2/SY-1A/CSS-N-2	Anti-ship missile	(1992)	1992	(5)	For Hegu (Durbar) FAC; SY-1A (CSS-N-2) version
	1	Type-021/Huangfen	FAC	1992	1992	1	Bangladeshi designation Durdharsha
	1	Type-024/Hegu	FAC	(1992)	1992	1	Bangladeshi designation Burbar
	1	Project-254/T-43	Minesweeper	1993	1994	1	Bangladeshi designation Sagar
	(5)	W-653/Type-653	ARV	(1993)	1993	(5)	
	1	Type-062-1/Haizhui	Patrol craft	(1995)	1995	1	Shanghai-3 version; Bangladeshi designation Barkat
	(18)	Type-59-1 130mm	Towed gun	(1995)	1996	18	Designation uncertain; possibly ex-Chinese
	4	F-7M Airguard	Fighter aircraft	(1996)	1999-2000	4	FT-7BG version

1	2	3	4	5	6	7	8
	(21)	HN-5A	Portable SAM	(2000)	2001	21	HN-5JA1 version
	(114)	Red Arrow-8	Anti-tank missile	(2000)	2001	114	
	20	Type-83 122mm	Towed gun	(2003)	2004	20	
	1	Crotale	SAM system	(2004)	2007	(1)	FM-90 version; for DW-2000 frigate
	(250)	QW-2	Portable SAM	2004	2007	(250)	
	(10)	C-802/CSS-N-8	Anti-ship missile	(2005)	2008	(10)	For 1 Jianghu (Type-053 or Type-510) frigate
	(54)	D-30 122mm	Towed gun	(2005)	2006-07	(54)	Type-96 version
	(100)	PL-7	SRAAM	(2005)	2005-07	(100)	For F-7MG combat aircraft
	(14)	PL-9	SRAAM	(2005)	2006-08	14	For F-7MG combat aircraft
	(20)	R-440 Crotale	SAM	(2005)	2007	(20)	FM-90 version; for DW-2000 (Bangabandhu) frigate
	16	F-7MG	Fighter aircraft	(2006)	2006	16	$44-118 m deal; F-7BG version
	(300)	Type-59G	Tank	(2009)	2010-11	(55)	Bangladeshi Type-59 and Type-69 tanks rebuilt to Type-59G in Bangladesh with kits from China
	(2)	FM-90	SAM system	(2010)	2011	(2)	
	(75)	FM-90	SAM	(2010)	2011	(75)	
	(60)	C-802/CSS-N-8	Anti-ship missile	(2011)			For 6 CSOC-46m FAC
	16	F-7MG	Fighter aircraft	2011			F-7BGI version; delivery 2012
	3	Type-654	ARV	2011			
	44	Type-96G	Tank	2011			BDT12 b ($160 m) deal; delivery 2012-13
L: China	7	CSOC-46m	FAC	(2011)			Incl 5 produced in Bangladesh; delivery possibly from 2012

(*Contd.*)

1	2	3	4	5	6	7	8
Myanmar							
S: China	(3)	JLG-43	Height-finding radar	(1988)	1989-91	(3)	Possibly ex-Chinese
	(3)	JLP-40	Air search radar	(1988)	1989-91	(3)	Possibly ex-Chinese
	(55)	Type-63	Light tank	1989	1989-90	(55)	
	(30)	WZ-121/Type-69	Tank	(1989)	1990	(30)	Type-69-II version
	(100)	YW-531H/Type-85	APC	(1989)	1990	(100)	
	(12)	F-6/Farmer	Fighter aircraft	1990	1991-92	(12)	
	12	F-7M Airguard	Fighter aircraft	1990	1990-91	(12)	Incl 2 FT-7 version
	(200)	HN-5A	Portable SAM	(1990)	1990-92	(200)	
	(75)	PL-2	SRAAM	1990	1990-91	(75)	For F-7M combat aircraft
	10	Type-037/Hainan	Patrol craft	1990	1991-93	10	Myanmarese designation Yan Sit Aung
	(5)	EFR-1	Fire control radar	(1991)	2002-03	(5)	For 5 Myanmar patrol craft produced in Myanmar
	(5)	Type-76 37mm	Naval gun	(1991)	1998-2002	(5)	For 5 Myanmar patrol craft produced in Myanmar
	4	Y-8	Transport aircraft	(1991)	1994	4	Y-8D version
	24	A-5C/Fantan	FGA aircraft	(1992)	1997-98	(24)	
	12	F-7M Airguard	Fighter aircraft	(1992)	1993	12	Incl 2 FT-7 version
	1	JY-8A	Fire control radar	1992	1993	1	For use with Type-59 57mm AA guns
	(225)	PL-2	SRAAM	(1992)	1993-98	(225)	For F-7M and A-5C combat aircraft
	12	F-7M Airguard	Fighter aircraft	(1993)	1998-99	(12)	Incl some FT-7 version
	(40)	PL-2	SRAAM	(1993)	1998-99	(40)	For F-7M combat aircraft; status uncertain
	(40)	PL-5B	SRAAM	(1993)	1998-99	(40)	For F-7M combat aircraft
	(4)	Type-311	Fire control radar	(1993)	1993	(4)	For use with 24 Type-74 37mm AA guns; could be Type-702
	(50)	Type-63	Light tank	(1993)	1993	(50)	
	(30)	Type-63 107mm	Towed MRL	(1993)	1993	(30)	
	24	Type-74 37mm	AA gun	(1993)	1993	(24)	

1	2	3	4	5	6	7	8
	(50)	WZ-121/Type-69	Tank	1993	1995	(50)	Type-69-II version
	150	YW-531H/Type-85	APC	1993	1993	(150)	
	(50)	C-801/CSS-N-4	Anti-ship missile	(1994)	1995-97	(50)	For Houxin (Maga) FAC
	6	Type-037-1G/Houxin	FAC	1994	1995-97	6	Myanmarese designation Maga
	(3)	Type-344	Fire control radar	(1996)	2004-05	(3)	For 3 Myanmar FAC produced in Myanmar
	12	K-8 Karakorum-8	Trainer/combat ac	(1997)	1999	(12)	
	(8)	AK-230 30mm	Naval gun	2001	2004-07	(8)	For 4 Myamnar FAC produced in Myanmar; supplier uncertain
	(30)	C-801/CSS-N-4	Anti-ship missile	(2001)	2004-05	(30)	For Myanmar FAC; designation uncertain (could be C-802)
	(50)	K-8 Karakorum-8	Trainer/combat ac	2009	2011	(20)	No. could be 60 or 72; assembled in Myanmar
L: China	(3)	Anawratha	Corvette	(1997)	2001-05	3	
Nepal							
S: China	(5)	WZ-551	APC	2005	2005	(5)	
Pakistan							
S: China	(25)	Type-501B	Fire control radar	(1964)	1964-67	(25)	
	72	F-6/Farmer	Fighter aircraft	1965	1965-66	(72)	Aid
	4	Il-28/Beagle	Bomber aircraft	(1965)	1966	4	H-5 (B-5) version; Pakistani designation B-56
	(400)	M-30 122mm	Towed gun	(1965)	1965-74	(400)	Type-54-1 version
	(4)	MiG-15UTI/Midget	Trainer aircraft	(1965)	1966-67	(4)	Ex-Chinese
	(200)	WZ-120/Type-59	Tank	(1965)	1965-66	(200)	
	(550)	WZ-120/Type-59	Tank	(1966)	1967-70	(550)	
	(50)	ML-20 152mm	Towed gun	(1968)	1968	(50)	Supplier uncertain; probably ex-Chinese
	(50)	Type-63	Light tank	(1969)	1970-71	(50)	
	12	Type-062/Shanghai	Patrol craft	(1970)	1972-73	(12)	

(*Contd.*)

1	2	3	4	5	6	7	8
	(50)	Type-60	Light tank	(1970)	1971-72	(50)	
	200	D-74 122mm	Towed gun	(1971)	1971-73	(200)	Type-60 version
	(103)	F-6/Farmer	Fighter aircraft	(1971)	1971-72	(103)	Deal incl complete F-6 overhaul factory and probably some FT-6 trainer version
	4	Type-025/Huchuan	FAC	1972	1973	4	
	159	WZ-120/Type-59	Tank	(1973)	1974	159	
	(50)	FT-5	Trainer aircraft	(1974)	1975-76	(50)	
	(2)	MiG-17PF/Fresco-D	Fighter aircraft	(1974)	1975	(2)	
	(173)	Type-59-1 130mm	Towed gun	1974	1976-80	(173)	
	2	Type-037/Hainan	Patrol craft	1975	1976	2	
	(825)	WZ-120/Type-59	Tank	(1975)	1978-88	(825)	
	60	F-6/Farmer	Fighter aircraft	1977	1978-80	(60)	
	20	MiG-17PF/Fresco-D	Fighter aircraft	1978	1978	(20)	
	(25)	FT-6	Trainer/combat ac	1979	1980-81	(25)	
	2	Type-037/Hainan	Patrol craft	1979	1980	2	
	(20)	HY-2/SY-1A/CSS-N-2	Anti-ship missile	1980	1981	(20)	For Hegu (Haibat) FAC; SY-1A (CSS-N-2) version
	4	Type-024/Hegu	FAC	(1980)	1981	4	
	52	A-5C/Fantan	FGA aircraft	1981	1983-84	(52)	A-5III version
	(40)	HQ-2/CSA-1	SAM	(1983)	1983	(40)	
	1	HQ-2/CSA-1	SAM system	(1983)	1983	(1)	
	(30)	HY-1/SY-1/CSS-N-1	Anti-ship missile	1983	1984	(30)	For Huangfen (Azmat) FAC
	4	Type-021/Huangfen	FAC	(1983)	1984	4	
	14	FT-5	Trainer aircraft	(1984)	1985	(14)	
	(100)	HN-5A	Portable SAM	(1984)	1987	(100)	
	1	Fuqing	Support ship	(1985)	1987	1	
	24	F-7M Airguard	Fighter aircraft	(1986)	1987-88	(24)	F-7P (F-7MP) version; incl 4 FT-7 version

1	2	3	4	5	6	7	8
	75	F-7M Airguard	Fighter aircraft	1988	1989-91	(75)	$225 m deal; F-7P (F-7MP) version; incl 15 FT-7P version
	4	P-58A	Patrol craft	(1988)	1989-90	4	Pakistani designation Barkat; for coast guard
	(250)	WZ-121/Type-69	Tank	(1990)	1993-99	(250)	Type-69-IIP or Type-69-IIMP version; incl assembly and probably production in Pakistan
	40	F-7M Airguard	Fighter aircraft	1992	1993	40	F-7P (F-7MP) version
	(87)	Type-59-1 130mm	Towed gun	(1992)	1998-2000	87	
	3	LL-1	Fire control radar	(1994)	1996-97	(3)	For modernization of 3 Tariq (Amazon or Type-21) Class frigates; for use with LY-60N SAMs
	(36)	LY-60	SAM	(1994)	1996-97	(36)	For 3 modernized Tariq (Amazon) Class frigates
	2	Type-76 37mm	Naval gun	(1995)	1997-99	2	For 2 Jalalat FAC produced in Pakistan
	(6)	Y-12	Light transport ac	1995	1996-97	(6)	
	2	Type-347G	Fire control radar	(1996)	1997-99	2	For 2 Jalalat FAC produced in Pakistan
	(20)	C-802/CSS-N-8	Anti-ship missile	1997	1997-99	(20)	For Jalalat FAC
	46	F-7MG	Fighter aircraft	(2001)	2001-03	(46)	F-7PG version; incl 6 or 9 FT-7PG version
	11	F-7MG	Fighter aircraft	(2002)	2003	11	F-7PG version
	(6)	A-5C/Fantan	FGA aircraft	(2003)	2003	6	
	(20)	C-802/CSS-N-8	Anti-ship missile	(2003)	2006	(20)	For Jalalat FAC
	(143)	D-30 122mm	Towed gun	(2003)	2003-04	143	
	2	Type-347G	Fire control radar	(2003)	2006	2	For 2 Jalalat FAC produced in Pakistan
	1	YLC-2	Air search radar	(2003)	2003	1	
	10	YLC-6	Air search radar	(2003)	2005-06	(10)	
	(6)	AS-565SA Panther	ASW helicopter	2005	2009-10	(6)	Z-9EC version
	(70)	C-802/CSS-N-8	Anti-ship missile	(2005)	2009-11	(50)	For Jiangwei (F-22P) frigates

(Contd.)

1	2	3	4	5	6	7	8
	(100)	R-440 Crotale	SAM	(2005)	2009-11	(60)	For Jiangwei (F-22P) frigates; HQ-7 (FM-80) version
	(600)	PL-12/SD-10	BVRAAM	(2006)	2010-11	(175)	For JF-17 and possibly modernized Mirage-3/5 combat aircraft
	(900)	PL-5E	SRAAM	(2006)	2009-11	(310)	For JF-17 combat aircraft; PL-5E-II version
	(12)	A-100 300mm	Self-propelled MRL	(2008)	2010	(12)	
	(50)	C-802/CSS-N-8	Anti-ship missile	(2008)	2010-11	(30)	For JF-17 combat aircraft
	(750)	LS-3	Guided bomb	(2008)	2010-11	(150)	For JF-17 combat aircraft
	(750)	LS-6	Guided bomb	(2008)	2010-11	(300)	For JF-17 combat aircraft
	(750)	LT-2	Guided bomb	(2008)	2010-11	(150)	For JF-17 combat aircraft
	(2)	SLC-2	Arty locating radar	(2008)	2010	(2)	For use with A-100 MRL
	(100)	WMD-7	Aircraft EO system	(2008)	2009-11	(45)	For JF-17 combat aircraft
	4	ZDK-03	AEW&C aircraft	2008	2011	(1)	USD278 m deal
	(30)	C-802/CSS-N-8	Anti-ship missile	(2010)			For Azmat FAC
L: China	(45)	Type-83 122mm	Self-propelled MRL	(1981)	1982-83	(45)	Pakistani designation Azar; designation and supplier uncertain; could be BM-11 from North Korea
	6	K-8 Karakorum-8	Trainer/combat ac	1987	1994	6	Incl some components produced in Pakistan and some assembled in Pakistan
	(1000)	HN-5A	Portable SAM	(1988)	1989-98	(1000)	Pakistani designation Anza-1
	(55)	M-11/CSS-7	SSM	(1988)	1992-94	(55)	Incl assembly in Pakistan
	..	Red Arrow-8	Anti-tank missile	1989	1990-2011	(20850)	Pakistani designation Baktar Shikan
	(268)	Type-85-IIM	Tank	1990	1992-96	268	Type-85-IIAP version; incl assembly from kits and production in Pakistan
	..	QW-1 Vanguard	Portable SAM	(1993)	1994-2011	(1550)	Pakistani designation Anza-2
	(65)	W-653/Type-653	ARV	(1994)	1995-2000	(65)	Incl assembly/production in Pakistan; Pakistani designation ARV-W653

1	2	3	4	5	6	7	8
	(300)	Type-90-2/MBT-2000	Tank	(1998)	2001-11	(248)	MBT-2000 (Al Khalid or P-90) version
	(150)	JF-17 Thunder/FC-1	FGA aircraft	1999	2007-11	(50)	Developed for Pakistan; incl production of components and assembly in Pakistan; incl 8 mainly for testing and first 42 production version ordered 2009 for $800 m
	6	K-8 Karakorum-8	Trainer/combat ac	(2001)	2003	6	Incl production of components and assembly in Pakistan
	27	K-8 Karakorum-8	Trainer/combat ac	2005	2007-10	27	K-8P version
	4	Type-053H/Jiangwei	Frigate	2005	2009-10	3	$500-750 m deal; F-22P version; incl 1 produced in Pakistan; Pakistani designation Zulfiquar, delivery 2009-2013
	2	Azmat	FAC	2010			Incl 1 produced in Pakistan; delivery 2012
	6	Type-041/Yuan	Submarine	(2011)			Designation uncertain; contract probably not yet signed
Sri Lanka							
S: China	5	Type-062/Shanghai	Patrol craft	(1971)	1972	5	Sri Lankan designation Sooraya; aid
	2	Type-062/Shanghai	Patrol craft	(1979)	1980	2	Shanghai-2 version; Sri Lankan designation Weeraya
	6	Y-12	Light transport ac	1986	1986-89	(6)	Possibly aid; incl for use as bomber aircraft against LTTE rebels
	2	Y-8	Transport aircraft	(1987)	1987	2	Incl for use as combat aircraft against LTTE rebels; possibly aid
	5	F-7A	Fighter aircraft	1990	1991	5	F-7B version; incl 1 FT-7; mainly for use against LTTE rebels
	2	FT-5	Trainer aircraft	1990	1991	2	
	(12)	Type-59-1 130mm	Towed gun	(1990)	1991	12	
	3	Y-12	Light transport ac	1990	1991	3	Incl for use as bomber aircraft against LTTE rebels

(*Contd.*)

1	2	3	4	5	6	7	8
	(35)	YW-531H/Type-85	APC	(1990)	1991-92	(35)	Designation uncertain (possibly YW-531/Type-63)
	3	Type-062/Shanghai	Patrol craft	1991	1991-92	3	Modified Shanghai-2 version; Sri Lankan designation Rana
	(10)	WZ-551	IFV	(1991)	1991	(10)	
	(10)	YW-309/Type-85	IFV	1991	1991	(10)	
	(1)	Y-8	Transport aircraft	1992	1994	1	Possibly second-hand; possibly incl for use as combat aircraft against LTTE rebels
	1	Type-037-1/Haiqing	Patrol craft	1994	1996	1	Sri Lankese designation Parakramabahu
	3	Type-062-1/Haizhui	Patrol craft	1994	1996	3	Sri Lankese designation Ranajaya
	1	Type-074/Yuhai	Landing ship	1994	1995	1	Sri Lankan designation Shakthi
	3	Type-062/Shanghai	Patrol craft	(1996)	2000	3	Shanghai-2 version; Sri Lankan designation Rana
	2	Type-062-1G/Lushun	Patrol craft	(1997)	1998	2	Sri Lankese designation Prathpa
	36	D-20 152mm	Towed gun	1998	1999	(36)	Type-66 version
	10	BT-6/CJ-6	Trainer aircraft	2000	2000	10	BT-6A version
	6	K-8 Karakorum-8	Trainer/combat ac	(2000)	2001	6	
	(10)	WZ-551	APC	(2001)	2002	(10)	
	(3)	CEIEC-408C	Air search radar	2004	2004-06	(3)	Designation uncertain; incl for civilian air traffic control
	3	K-8 Karakorum-8	Trainer/combat ac	(2004)	2005	3	
	(4)	F-7MG	Fighter aircraft	(2007)	2008	(4)	Possibly aid; F-7GS version
	1	JY-11	Air search radar	(2007)	2007	(1)	Mainly for use against LTTE rebels
	(25)	PL-5E	SRAAM	(2007)	2008	(25)	For F-7GS combat aircraft
	2	Y-12	Light transport ac	(2009)	2010	2	

Note: The 'No. delivered/produced' and the 'Year(s) of deliveries' columns refer to all deliveries since the beginning of the contract. Deals in which the recipient was involved in the production of the weapon system are listed separately. The 'Comments' column includes publicly reported information on the value of the deal.

Source: SIPRI Arms Transfers Database.

Annexure 4

India-China Defence Personnel Visits, 1956-2012

Period	Place	Remarks
1956	Different places in China	Indian Defence Services delegation of nine members from the three services led by Lt. Gen. JN Chowdhury
1958	Shanghai	INS Mysore headed by Adm. Srinivasan's port call.
April 1987	Beijing	Defence Minister KC Pant's stop over visit en route India from Pyongyang.
July 1992	Beijing	Defence Minister Sharad Pawar's visit.
November 1993	Bombay	Chinese Naval training ship Zheng He's visit.
December 1993	New Delhi	Deputy Chief of General Staff Lt. Gen. Xu Huizi's visit.
July 1994	Beijing	Chief of Army Staff General BC Joshi's visit.
September 1994	New Delhi	Minister for National Defence General Chi Haotian's visit
March 1996		Chief of Naval Staff Admiral VS Shekhawat's visit
May 1997	Beijing	5-membered delegation headed by Vice Chief of Army Staff Gen VP Malik
June 1997	New Delhi	Chengdu Military Region Commander Lt. Gen. Liao Xilong visited
April 1998	New Delhi	Chinese NDU delegation led by Lt.Gen. Dong Lisheng's visit to NDC
April-May 1998	New Delhi	Chief of General Staff Fu Quanyou's visit. The first ever visit by a Chinese Chief of General Staff.
November 21, 1999	Nathu La Pass	A telephone link was established in Sikkim sector between Yatung garrison in Tibet and the 17th Mountain Division of the Indian Army to keep each other informed of activities along the border and "defuse border tensions".
March 6-7, 2000	Beijing	As a result of EAM Jaswant Singh's visit to Beijing in June 1999, the first ever security dialogue between the two countries held by MEA Joint Secretary (Disarmament) Rakesh Sood and Director-General of the Asian Department of the MFA, Zhang Jiuhuan. PRC told India to abide by the Chinese-backed UN

Period	Place	Remarks
		Resolution 1172 of rolling back nuclear programme. The meeting comes two weeks before US President Clinton's visit to India.
April 1, 2000	Nathu La Pass	Commemorative border meeting of Nathu La Brigade of India and Yatung garrison of the Chinese army authorities on the occasion of the 50th anniversary of the establishment of diplomatic relations between the two countries.
May, 2000	Beijing	National Defence College's delegation to PRC.
August 2000	New Delhi	Chinese Academy of Military Science delegation's visit
September 2000	Shanghai	Indian naval port calls at Shanghai with INS Delhi and a frigate.
April 2001	Beijing	Lt.Gen Kalkat, GOC-in-C, Eastern Command
May 2001	Beijing	Air Chief Tipnis
May 2001	Mumbai	2 Chinese naval ships port call
September 2001		Deputy Commander of Chengdu MR Gen. Liu Baochen
December 2001		Deputy Chief of Staff Lt. Gen. Zhang Li
November 2002	Chengdu and other places	Indian Central Command delegation's visit
2002	Beijing	Indian Navy sent officers to attend China's National Defence University to attend courses
April 2003	Beijing	Defence Minister George Fernandes visit with 16-member delegation
July 2003	New Delhi and other places	60 member Chinese Air Force delegation's visit
August 11, 2003	Port Blair, India	Indian Coast Guard vessels MT CHM Piru Singh and MV Chieftain II rescued China's merchant ship MV Yujia with 28 crew members.
September 2003	India	PLA Training delegation's visit
November 14, 2003	Shanghai	India-China naval ships INS Ranjit and Kulish in search and rescue exercises with Jiaxing (Frigate with integral helicopter) and tanker Panyang Hu
October-November 2003	Lhasa	Indian military delegation's visit with GOC 4 Corps, Lt. Gen. Mohinder Singh, and an inter-services training delegation led by Air Marshal G.C.S Rajwar
December 2003	New Delhi	PLA Deputy Chief of General Staff Wu Guanxuvisited
March 2004	New Delhi	Defence Minister Cao Gangchuan visited

Period	Place	Remarks
September 2004	Henan	First time an Indian delegation participated in a PLA military exercise held in Henan province
December 2004	Beijing	Indian Chief of Army Staff visited
June 2005		Navy Vice Chief Adm. Raman Puri attended an international symposium in China on Non-traditional security challenges
August 2005	Qingdao	Indian Armed forces officers participated as observers in the second phase of Russia-China Joint Exercises
September 2005	Beijing	Indian Armed forces officers participated in "Northern Sword 2005" Exercise at Beijing Command
May 29, 2006	Beijing	Defence Minister Pranab Mukherjee visited. The Memorandum of Understanding signed envisages regular and institutional contacts between the armed forces and defence officials and experts of the two countries
October 2006	New Delhi	Gen Qiao Qingchen, Commander of PLA Air Force, was on a 'Good-Will Visit'
April 2007	Qingdao	Indian Naval ships visit
May 2007	Beijing	Chief of Army Staff General J.J. Singh visited
November 2007	Beijing	The first India-China annual Defence Dialogue was held
December 19-27, 2007	Kunming	The first ever joint Army training exercise was held with China
May 2008	Sichuan	Indian Air Force flew 9 relief sorties of Il-76 transports carrying materials worth 6.2 crores which included tents, blankets, sleeping bags, MREs, water purifying straw and medicines
November 2-6, 2008	Beijing	Chief of Air Staff, Air Chief Marshal F. H. Major visited
November 2008	New Delhi	The PLA Naval Chief Admiral Wu Shangli visited
December 2008	New Delhi	The second Annual Defence Dialogue with China was held
December 4-13, 2008	Belgaum	The second Joint Army Training Exercise 'Hand in Hand' on the theme of 'Counter-Terrorism' was held
April 18-25, 2009	Beijing	Admiral Sureesh Mehta, Chief of Naval Staff delegation
August 31 to September 3, 2009	Beijing	Lt Gen V.K. Singh, GoC-in-C Eastern Command
August 10-16, 2009	New Delhi	PLA Air Force Command College led by Maj Gen Wang Yisheng Deputy Chief of Staff, PLA Air Force visited

Period	Place	Remarks
December 1-6, 2009	New Delhi	Gen Ge Zhenfeng, Deputy Chief of General Staff visited
December 7-12, 2009	New Delhi	Lt.Gen Shu Yutai, Commander of Lhasa Military Area Command visited
January 6, 2010	Beijing	Third Annual Defence Dialogue with China held
June 19-23, 2011	Beijing, Urumqi and Shanghai	Major General Gurmit Singh of Northern Command visited
November 7-9, 2011	New Delhi	China's Border Troops delegation visited
December 9, 2011	New Delhi	The 4th Annual Defence Dialogue was held
December 25-31, 2011	New Delhi	A 27-member PLA Staff Officers delegation visited
January 10-13, 2012	Beijing	A 15-member Staff Officers delegation led by Air Vice Marshal P.S Mann visited

Sources: Govt of India, Ministry of Defence Annual Reports; Various Indian Parliament debates; *Zhongguo Waijiao* (various); and newspaper reports

INDEX